# THE PROGRAM

# THE
# PROGRAM

## INSIDE THE MIND OF
## KEITH RANIERE AND THE RISE AND
## FALL OF NXIVM

# TONI NATALIE

## with CHET HARDIN

**GRAND CENTRAL**
PUBLISHING

*New York Boston*

Grand Central Publishing
Hachette Book Group
1290 Avenue of the Americas, New York, NY 10104
grandcentralpublishing.com
twitter.com/grandcentralpub

First Edition: September 2019

Grand Central Publishing is a division of Hachette Book Group, Inc. The Grand Central Publishing name and logo is a trademark of Hachette Book Group, Inc.

The publisher is not responsible for websites (or their content) that are not owned by the publisher.

Library of Congress Control Number: 2019945475

ISBNs: 978-1-5387-0106-5 (hardcover), 978-1-5387-0103-4 (ebook)

Printed in the United States of America

LSC-C

10  9  8  7  6  5  4  3  2  1

*To my mother, Joan Schneier, and my brother,*
*John Natalie, the angels that watch over me,*
*sending me dimes and pennies from heaven so I*
*know I am never really alone.*
*I miss you both every day…*

*To those who have had no voice, I dedicate this*
*book to you.*
*You are not alone anymore.*

*We will never forget—Gina Hutchinson and*
*Kristin Marie Snyder.*

>              ...and perhaps
> I also erred, in overmuch admiring
> What seemed in thee so perfect, that I thought
> No evil durst attempt thee; but I rue
> The error now...
>
>                         —John Milton,
>                              *Paradise Lost*

# CONTENTS

CONTENTS

# FOREWORD

Keith Raniere, a narcissistic con man, was the self-styled philosopher king called "Vanguard" who ruled over a cult known as NXIVM. After more than thirty years of cult-watching, I have rarely seen a group more tightly wound around its leader. Raniere's disciples hung on his every word and there appeared to be no limit to their devotion.

Whatever Raniere said was right, was right, and whatever he said was wrong, was wrong. This was the distilled essence of the training that was drilled into the heads of every NXIVM student. Raniere called it "Rational Inquiry"; others insist that it was "brainwashing." That is, a synthesis of coercive persuasion and influence techniques used to gain undue influence.

I first began to look into him when, in 2002, a family hired me to deprogram their children. They also commissioned two doctors to analyze Keith Raniere's methods of training. In 2003 those expert reports were published online at the Cult Education Institute website. Their reports concluded that Keith Raniere's training seminars employed coercive persuasion and thought-reform techniques to gain undue influence over participants. These findings reflected the same dynamics that I have seen in many authoritarian groups called "cults" over my thirty-seven years working as an observer and researcher of organizations like these. The CEI reports were the first to publicly expose the inner workings of NXIVM, prompting a lawsuit filed by Raniere and the corporate entity which became NXIVM.

When Toni Natalie called me so many years ago, I was just beginning my journey concerning Keith Raniere. Toni Natalie was the first person to recognize the evil in Keith Raniere. She was ground zero, the epicenter of the havoc wreaked by Raniere. The first to fully recognize his twisted mind and predict the path of his destructiveness. For me, Toni was the lone voice explaining what I could expect because she knew.

When Toni Natalie left him, Keith Raniere, who could never accept either rejection or criticism, responded with endless harassment until he was locked up. Toni painfully came to realize that there was no limit to Keith Raniere's vindictiveness and that he was relentless. He wanted to crush his perceived enemies, no matter what it cost, until it cost him his freedom. With this same persistence, he sued me for fourteen years, in an effort to remove the doctor's reports described above from the Internet.

I believed I was an extreme example of Keith Raniere's punishment, but when I spoke with Toni, her story of abuse and harassment was beyond belief. As each of us shared our individual stories of years of being stalked, sued and violated by

Keith Reniere, I learned that Toni had suffered much more than me, and that whatever Toni said was always true.

My journey with Keith Raniere largely ended when his lawsuit against me was dismissed.

My last encounter with Raniere was in the courtroom when I testified against him as a "fact witness" in his initial federal prosecution. Subsequently, he was found guilty on all counts.

Toni Natalie would lose both her parents and her brother before her torment was over.

Toni inspired and offered solace to Keith Raniere's victims. She never thought twice about telling the truth even if it meant personal sacrifice. She shared herself and her story to help others.

It is an honor to know Toni Natalie.

Keith Raniere will now join a list of notorious cult leaders such as Charles Manson, Jim Jones, and David Koresh. Raniere horribly abused women, but it was brave women who exposed and finally stopped him. And the first woman to stand against Keith Raniere was Toni Natalie.

*By Rick Alan Ross*

# THE PROGRAM

# PROLOGUE:

# THE HEARING

Brooklyn, New York, February 28, 2019

---

When it was renovated in the early 2000s, the Theodore Roosevelt United States Courthouse was fortified to withstand a 9/11-style terrorist attack. This is apparent in every detail. The place—a mammoth 750,000-square-foot complex in downtown Brooklyn, a short walk from the Brooklyn Bridge—looks and feels like a fortress, and that's what I like most about it: this is the safest of safe spaces.

I arrive early, well before dawn, to make sure I secure my usual seat in the back of the courtroom. My house is in Rochester, five hours away, but I attend all the major hearings related to the NXIVM case. I have to see this thing through to the end.

A year ago, NXIVM was an obscure multilevel marketing company built around executive coaching programs, with little more than a cult following. Then, on March 26, 2018, the arrest happened, and the world learned that "cult following" was not just a clichéd expression. The lurid details from the federal indictment—*cult leader, sex trafficking, slave branding*—were front-page news, endlessly fascinating. The media had a field day. I spoke to any journalist who asked for an interview, calmly telling the truth, as I'd been doing for years. But it was different this time. In years past, whenever I spoke to the press, the NXIVM people would rebut: "She's crazy."

No one thinks I'm crazy anymore.

The same cannot be said for the six defendants in the case. The five women are gaunt, ghostly, gray. An impartial observer might conclude that these are prisoners on a hunger strike. The truth is that the man they call Vanguard *wants* them to look like anorexics, demands they consume the bare minimum of calories per day. Even now, almost a year after his arrest, they eagerly starve themselves to please their Master. Their hungry devotion led them here, to this courtroom, where they see themselves as martyrs for the cause.

There is the one they call Prefect, Vanguard's longtime business partner and first acolyte and NXIVM's president. More meat on her bones than the others, but just as broken. I've known her for more than two decades. In fact, I was the one who brought the two of them together, all those years ago. The psychological experiments they did on me back then were the foundation of NXIVM's Executive Success Programs, or ESP, its self-help curriculum. She was a different person then—brilliant, ambitious, full of life: the very embodiment of executive success. You would never know it to look at her now.

Prefect's daughter is also a defendant. She was still in college when Vanguard first met her, a capable, whip-smart girl with a life of promise ahead of her. In short order, he turned her against her mother and then strung her along for decades with broken promises of a child, a family, a life together. That future did not come to pass, and now she is forty-two, and it never will.

The bookkeeper, Defendant #3, is the picture of defeat. Rail thin, sad-faced, cried out. She is my age or thereabouts but looks much older. Bookkeepers are usually the first to flip in cases like this, to cooperate with prosecutors in exchange for leniency, but I don't think she has it in her.

Next, we come to the liquor heiress. Not so young anymore, but as naïve as ever. Vanguard bamboozled her and her only slightly less naïve sister, appropriating their renown, exploiting their old-money business contacts, emptying their vast coffers. Everything NXIVM did was underwritten by the heiress. Her family's vast wealth financed the legal harassment any detractor or defector was subjected to, just as it pays for the attorneys of all six defendants in the courtroom today. But that's not the half of it. No: Vanguard has drained more than *$100 million* from the heiresses' personal trust funds. Lost most of it on catastrophically awful commodities trades, spent the rest. His transgressions are impossible to ignore, writ in red in the family ledgers, the earnings reports, the bottom lines. But the heiress can't, or won't, see it. She remains faithful. She has not repudiated her Master. Instead, she's stood by him, proclaiming his innocence as she proclaims her own. Doubling down, she has retained a fancy new attorney for today's hearing, a celebrity lawyer from the city of celebrity lawyers, Los Angeles. He doesn't look particularly impressive to me. Probably he sees her as Vanguard does—with dollar signs in his eyes.

The last of the women, the television actress, is still too thin, but not starving-to-death thin like the others. Some color has returned to her cheeks. But then, she has not spent the winter shoveling snow in Clifton Park, or languishing behind bars at MDC Brooklyn, where the heat is forever on the fritz. She is under house arrest, living with her parents in sunny California, thirty-five miles but light-years away from Hollywood, her former base of operations. She gets to leave the family home to go to church, run errands, take classes. Maybe she's learned something at school. She seems changed somehow, like a magic spell has worn off. (Waking from a magic spell and asking, "What just happened?" was a weekly occurrence on the television show that made her C-list famous.) She appears awake, alert—and terrified. After all, she was Vanguard's "alpha slave." It was her idea to brand the other slave women, her underlings—or so she claimed to a reporter at *The New York Times Magazine*. She's not getting out of this unscathed, and it looks like she knows it.

The sixth defendant, the star attraction, is the last to enter the courtroom. He may not have looked like a cult leader at the time of his arrest, but he's certainly dressed for the part this morning. He has the Jesus hair down to his shoulders, messily parted down the middle, a tangle of split ends desperately in need of a brush. He's clean-shaven, but his complexion is red and blotchy. He's wearing his prison jumpsuit—puke green, not orange, is the new black—over one of those long-sleeve thermal shirts worn by lumberjacks. Perhaps this is to call attention to his complaint that all through what has been a particularly harsh winter, the heat has not been functioning in the prison. And, strangely, he is not wearing his glasses. Another inmate took them, probably, or else they got smashed. Glasses must be hard to keep track of in jail.

The NXIVM Svengali does not so much as glance at his quintet of emaciated Trilbys, his dutiful disciples. Never mind that two of them—the two prettiest—have his initials branded onto their skin, inches from their vaginas: the wraiths do not interest him. He doesn't make, or even seek, eye contact with any of them, nor they with him. Not Prefect and her daughter, not the book-keeper, not the heiress and her fancy celebrity lawyer—not even the television actress, one of his lovers du jour, whose capacity for sadism may well match his own. They are all invisible to him, as if they have already withered away to nothing.

Instead, he looks at me. It's hard without his glasses, but he makes me out, here in the back row, and he squints, and his piercing blue eyes home in hypnotically on mine. There is no remorse there; there is no love—not even the smolder of nostalgia. There is surprise; there is desperation; there is resentment; there is fury.

He wanted so badly for the roles to be reversed, for me to be in a prison jumpsuit and him to be watching quietly from the front of the courtroom. He even predicted it, the last time we were in the same room together, in April of 1999: "The next time I see you, you'll be dead or in jail." He spent almost twenty years, and God knows how much liquor-heiress money, working to achieve that outcome. But he failed.

He failed, justice prevailed, and now *he's* the one on trial. In the process, he's dragged down five of the women in his inner circle: his second-in-command, Nancy Salzman, and her dutiful daughter, Lauren; Kathy Russell, the bookkeeper; Clare Bronfman, the liquor heiress and NXIVM's primary source of funding; Allison Mack, the *Smallville* actress who allegedly procured other women for him. They are all martyrs to the cause, all expendable.

But not me. Not Toni Natalie.

I'm the one who got away.

# I:

# YOUNG GENIUS

# CHAPTER 1:

# THE SMARTEST MAN
# IN THE WORLD

## Rochester, New York, 1991

---

H e's the smartest man in the world," my husband said.

"The smartest man? In the world?"

"Well, one of the smartest. His IQ is over 200. One of the highest ever measured. And he's coming here, to Rochester." He showed me the news clipping. The man in the photo was young, boyishly handsome, with a nice head of hair and round John Lennon glasses. He did not look like the smartest man in the world. He looked like one of those overgrown kids in the comic book stores who play Dungeons & Dragons. "Plus, there's a foot of snow outside. What else are we going to do?"

"Keith Raniere," I read out loud, incorrectly pronouncing the name with two syllables instead of three. (It's *ren-EAR-ee*, not *ren-EAR.*) "I don't know."

"You really don't want to go? I thought this would be right up your alley."

He sounded disappointed, and I didn't want to disappoint him. I was thirty-two years old, and Rusty was my third husband. He owned a chain of tanning salons—a successful business that afforded him ample free time. We were friends before becoming romantically involved. After three years of marriage, we still loved each other, but there's no question the ardor had cooled. In 1988, we'd adopted a baby boy. I'd always wanted children, but it hadn't worked out. The dynamics of the marriage shifted when Michael came into our lives. As we gave most of our attention to our beautiful new baby, Rusty and I were drifting apart. After two failed marriages, I recognized the warning signs. And I didn't want that. If Rusty really wanted me to go with him to the Holiday Inn to see the Smartest Man in the World, if this small gesture would please him, I was happy to make the concession.

Besides, it's not like my interest wasn't piqued. I have always been insecure about my lack of formal education, having dropped out of high school two weeks into my sophomore year. Someone smart enough to attract the attention of *Guinness World Records* must have great wisdom to impart—or so I believed. I was curious about what this local genius would have to say. It was the topic of discussion that raised a red flag.

"It's a multilevel marketing company, isn't it? You know how I feel about MLMs." We'd been involved with them before. Joined as affiliate members, sold memberships to our friends, racked up fat commissions—which was well and good until the day the promised check didn't arrive, and we called to ask about it, and the number was disconnected, and all the money was gone.

"I'm not saying we should join, just that we should hear what he has to say."

"Okay, sure, fine, let's go. But I mean it: I am *not* signing up; I don't care *how* smart he is."

Maybe if I'd put my foot down, if I'd refused to accompany Rusty to the Holiday Inn, our relationship would have survived this rough patch. Maybe we'd still be together, thirty years later, presiding over an empire of tanning salons that stretched from Maine to Michigan. Ours wasn't exactly the romance of the century, but he was loyal, fun, caring—a kind man and a decent partner.

But I know better than to play at "what if." It was my destiny to meet Keith Raniere. And as the Greek tragedies make clear, it is impossible to run away from one's fate.

Speaking of ancient Greece: there was something about Keith's backstory that always struck me as a piece of heroic mythology. He was born in Brooklyn (the borough where half a century later he would be incarcerated) in 1960, making him two years younger than I. Like David Koresh, like Charles Manson, like L. Ron Hubbard, Keith was an only child. His father worked in advertising; his mother taught dance. They divorced when Keith was eight. He and his mother moved to Suffern, an affluent suburb in Rockland County, New York, the last stop on the New Jersey Transit commuter train line to Manhattan.

He was sent to private schools, but if the legends are to be believed, Keith didn't really need them. At two, he was speaking in complete sentences, like Charles Wallace in *A Wrinkle in Time*. At four, he demonstrated an understanding of the rudiments of quantum mechanics. Over the course of a long weekend at age twelve, he taught himself advanced algebra, geometry, trigonometry, and calculus. (Isaac Newton himself discovered calculus during a similar period of intense boredom, but it took him a bit longer.) That same year, he became the East Coast judo champion for his age bracket.

At thirteen, Keith was taking college classes in mathematics and computer science. At sixteen, he left high school early to enroll full-time at Rensselaer Polytechnic Institute, the well-regarded tech university in Troy, New York. He would ride around the RPI campus on a unicycle. *Look,* he seemed to be saying, *I am agile of mind* and *of body.* At twenty-two, he earned undergraduate degrees in physics, mathematics, and biology—three majors, an achievement that required sixty additional credits. Then came his big break. At twenty-seven, he correctly answered forty-six of the forty-eight questions on an impossible brainteaser test given by the exclusive Mega Society, placing his IQ somewhere in the stratospheric 170–180 range. This gave Keith local notoriety. On June 26, 1988, the *Albany Times Union* ran a feel-good piece about him for its Sunday "Living Today" section, under the headline "Troy Man Has a Lot on His Mind—IQ Test Proves What Many Suspected: He's One in 10 Million":

> You might say Keith Raniere is one in a million.
>
> He's a member of Mega, a high-IQ society with a minimum requirement at the one-in-a-million level. Actually, the 27-year-old Troy resident is in an even more exclusive category. By answering correctly all but two questions on a 48-question, self-administered test, Raniere moved up to the rarified one-in-10-million level...
>
> Geniuses, apparently, are born, not made. Raniere says he was identified early as a bright child. By age 2 he could spell the word "homogenized" from seeing it on a milk carton.

He was precocious in math development and says he had an understanding of subjects such as quantum physics and computers by age 4...

He's not your stereotypical genius. Watchful blue eyes look out from behind aviator glasses. His brown hair is parted stylishly down the middle. He has the physique of an athlete, which he is. He was East Coast Judo champion at age 12, tied with the state record for the 100-yard dash, is an avid skier, swimmer and wind surfer. He says he plays seven instruments and also sings "high tenor" in local musical productions.

He is, the article tells us, an "amazing young man, who requires only two to four hours of sleep," and he finished the Mega Society test in two weeks.

"There's no enforceable time limit. Some people take up to a year to answer the questions. It's suggested you limit yourself to no more than one month," he explains.

Unlike with some tests, applicants are encouraged to use such reference aids as dictionaries, thesauri and pocket calculators, he says. Guessing is permitted. There is no penalty for wrong answers or guesses so guessing is advantageous.

Assistance from others, however, is prohibited. "But," says the young genius, "who could give you assistance?"

Who, indeed.

That first article, seemingly so innocuous, helped propel him to fame and fortune. At twenty-eight, Keith began claiming that he was in *Guinness World Records* for "Highest IQ," checking in at an eye-popping 240—brainier than Albert Einstein (170),

Stephen Hawking (190), Garry Kasparov (194), or Marilyn vos Savant (228), the Mega Society member and *Parade* columnist, who from 1986 to 1989 actually *was* listed in *Guinness World Records* for "Highest IQ." Keith was also a virtuoso musician who could play a variety of different instruments, including piano. Juilliard was after him, or so he claimed. For a while, he contemplated a career as a classical pianist, but he found a higher calling: multilevel marketing. He forsook the concert hall for the Amway distribution center.

At twenty-nine, after a short stint at Amway, he and four of his friends founded a business called Consumers' Buyline, Inc., or CBI. Like all multilevel marketing companies, its success depended on the recruitment of new affiliates and new members. This venture is what brought Keith Raniere to Rochester, and into my life.

The CBI seminar was held in one of the ballrooms at the Holiday Inn in Rochester, out by the airport. I'd driven past it a thousand times but never actually been inside. It hadn't been renovated in quite a while and still had that seventies feel to it: well-worn deep-pile carpets with kaleidoscope patterns, oversize lighting fixtures, plenty of ashtrays. Rusty and I smoked cigarettes and watched people show up. It wasn't packed, but it wasn't empty, either. A solid if unremarkable turnout for the Smartest Man in the World.

The first thing I noticed about Keith is how short he was: five six, maybe five seven. In my pumps, I towered over him. His short stature, combined with his rosy cheeks and a pageboy haircut that was one remove from a mullet, made him look like a child playing at dress-up. *He may have a 240 IQ,* I thought, *but he looks like Little Lord Fauntleroy.* He was unassuming in person, even shy, but he came alive onstage. He fed on the adulation of his audience. Intelligence burned in his bright blue eyes, and there was a devil-may-care bounce in his step.

"Sheesh," Rusty whispered. "What a geek!"

"Well, what did you expect? Tom Cruise?"

Keith took off his glasses, gave them a polish, replaced them, and began to sell us on the wonders of Consumers' Buyline. As he did so, all lingering doubts about his credentials vanished from our minds, along with my initial reservations about involving myself with another MLM.

The underlying concept of CBI was brilliant: customers would buy memberships to join the group, and the group's collective purchasing power would be sufficient to buy merchandise at wholesale prices. It was the same general idea that Sam's Club and BJ's and Costco was capitalizing on. I liked it because it was consumerist. It saved shoppers money. As long as you bought more items than it cost to join, it was a savvy investment, because it made goods more affordable. The greater the number of members, the steeper the discount. Everybody won.

For Keith, it was the perfect business model, because once CBI reached critical mass, it would be self-sustaining—like Rusty's tanning salons, but with potentially exponential streams of revenue. As a multilevel marketing company, it had its affiliates do the bulk of the recruitment, for which they would receive commissions. Employees would negotiate with suppliers and keep the books. In time, Keith could simply kick back and watch the money roll in.

And I understand that it was just multilevel marketing, akin to Avon or Amway, and one remove from life insurance sales.

But Keith made it seem different. Bigger. Larger than life. More important. He made us feel like we were joining not just a budding commercial enterprise, but a new way of life.

"You have a 240 IQ," I said to him after the presentation. "Why are you not curing cancer? Why are you not changing the world, making it a better place?"

"I *am* changing the world," he replied without hesitation. "I *am* making the world a better place. Don't you want to come along?"

When we shook hands after the presentation, he gazed deep into my eyes, and I was mesmerized. Everything else faded from view—my husband, the other attendees, the Rochester Holiday Inn—and it was like I was the only person who existed for him in the entire world. There was no question that Rusty and I would join up. We wanted to be part of something so obviously special. We wanted in. We were eager to proselytize for CBI, to spread the Consumers' Buyline gospel.

We believed in Keith Raniere.

In hindsight, it's clear that Keith embellished, exaggerated, and sometimes invented critical details in his life story. Judo *champion*? *Seven* instruments? Two hundred *forty*? *Juilliard*? He had his ad-man father's flair for promotion, and he understood that superlatives (*biggest, strongest, smartest*) sell. But in 1991, I believed him, just as the *Times Union* reporter who took him at his word believed him, as my husband believed him, as the CBI affiliates and employees believed him.

And why would anyone have thought otherwise? Keith Raniere walked the walk. He may not have been the smartest man in the world, but he was absolutely and without question a genius.

# CHAPTER 2:

# "IS SHE FAMILY?"

## Clifton Park, New York, 1991

---

It's easy to sell something you believe in. Rusty and I had always been a good sales team, but when the product was CBI, we were next-level. We moved those memberships with the fervor of Jehovah's Witnesses, but instead of salvation, we were offering steep discounts on everything from microwave ovens to groceries—stuff that was valuable in *this* lifetime. We began selling memberships in March 1991. That summer, we raked in more than $10,000 in commissions. We won the coveted Spectrum Award, given to the top regional sellers, and its prize of $16,000—not too shabby for a pair of newbies to the operation.

We were pleased with the windfall, but after four months away from Keith Raniere, the magic had dimmed and doubts crept back in. Not about Keith—our faith in him was unshaken—but about the MLM structure. We'd been burned before. We did not ever again want to have to break it to our friends that oh, by the way, the money we were all promised isn't coming.

"So far, so good," Rusty said, "but we've only met *Keith*. CBI has hundreds of employees. Who knows what they're like?"

So we decided to make the trek across the state to pick up the prize money in person, using the award as an excuse to visit Consumers' Buyline headquarters in Clifton Park, an unassuming suburb strategically situated between the Capital Region urban centers of Albany, Troy, Schenectady, and Saratoga Springs.

"We'll check it out," Rusty said, "and if we don't like what we see, we can quit."

CBI occupied space in Rome Plaza, a charmless office park on Route 9, the multilane main drag that comprised the Clifton Park business district. We arrived late in the day, but the electric energy of the place was palpable. There were dozens of employees milling around, all of them with pep in their step, all of them thrilled to be there. The drudgery often associated with office work, especially at 4:45 in the afternoon, was nowhere in evidence. This frenetic activity went on well into the evening, most of the time. In addition to his other gifts, Keith required little to no sleep, or so everyone said, and his subordinates all wanted to keep up with his feverish pace. These people seemed to be on a mission, divinely inspired. The dedication was almost evangelical. One woman stood out in this regard, a pretty brunette of about my age, her Crystal Gayle hair pulled back with a thick hippie headband. Her enthusiasm was so great that she appeared to levitate as she buzzed from cubicle to cubicle.

There seemed to be more women than men at CBI, which immediately made me more at ease. One of the employees had her child with her, a girl of twelve or thirteen with braces and wonderfully feathered blond hair who thumbed dutifully through an algebra textbook. Keith was tutoring her in math. *That's* how amazing a person he was, we were told. He took time away from his busy schedule to share his genius with those in need. To new parents like ourselves, this spoke volumes.

But what impressed me most were the computers. In 1991, the Internet existed only in select circles—geeks at MIT and Stanford and Caltech (and, yes, RPI) arguing about *Star Trek* on rudimentary dial-up bulletin boards. The World Wide Web had literally just been invented. E-commerce was science fiction. Home computers were just getting started. Brands like Texas Instruments and Commodore still owned market share. Electric typewriters and adding machines remained the devices of choice in most offices. CBI didn't just have *a* computer; it had *many* computers. And it had employees who knew how to operate them. I wouldn't have been more blown away if they'd all been zooming around with jet packs. Between the tech and the enthusiasm and the dressed-down "fun" office culture, CBI was a portent of the tech start-ups that would crop up ten years later on the other side of the country.

Keith burst out of his office, his glasses slightly askew, to welcome us to the home office. He wore a dress shirt, swirls of black chest hair peeking over the top button, and gray sweatpants—an eclectic ensemble, but he managed to pull it off. In the friendly confines of CBI, he was more comfortable than at the Holiday Inn, and he talked a mile a minute. "We're changing the world here," he said. "This is where the magic happens."

And he managed to convey to us, without seeming boastful or arrogant, all the amazing achievements extolled in his official company bio:

**Keith Raniere President, CEO**, Noted as one of the 3 top problem solvers in the world. He has a problem solving rarity of greater than 1 in 400 million. With degrees in Mathematics, Physics, Biology, minors in Psychology and Philosophy with expertise in computers and systems analysis. Mr. Raniere designed and formulated the mathematical model of the marketing plan, marketing strategy and all of the practical and philosophical foundations of CBI. He is the primary founder of Consumers' Buyline Inc. and has utilized his problem solving abilities to bring this company from zero to a million dollar company in less than 2 years. Compared to the first year, Consumers' Buyline Inc., has grown over 20,000% which will make it #1 on the Inc. 500 fastest growing privately held corporations when it qualifies in 1994.

Mr. Raniere is also a National Sales Trainer with over 15 years experience. In 1989, Mr. Raniere personally recruited and trained 6 out of the top 10 producers in a National company with over 250,000 sales reps.

Six of ten! Of a quarter million!

He hadn't slept in two days, he said. In addition to his cognitive abilities, Keith was blessed with a constitution that required little to no rest. Think of all the time he had at his disposal that other people wasted in dreamland! He averaged two hours of sleep a day; the average for adults was seven. That was thirty-five extra hours a week, and a whopping *seventy-five full days* a year that he was able to work and scheme and play and get ahead, while other humans drooled and snored.

"Sleep is for mortals," he said, laughing.

"I'm getting tired just talking to you," Rusty quipped.

"We have a toddler," I said. "We don't sleep much, either."

"Oh? Where is she?"

"He. Home with the nanny."

We were joined then by a cocky blonde who seemed younger than the others. She couldn't have been more than nineteen or twenty. The girl had an infectious smile, and her eyes twinkled with mischief. She seemed like an outsider there, distinct from the others. "Keith"—she looked at me and grinned, like we were sharing an inside joke—"is Valerie Bertinelli working here now?"

Keith seemed not to understand the reference, but I did, and I smiled at the compliment. "This is Toni Natalie and her husband, Rusty." He pronounced my last name correctly, stressing the second syllable and not the first—avoiding a mistake most people make.

"Oh, sure! I know you. You guys won the Spectrum Award."

"Toni, Rusty...meet Kristin Keeffe."

Kristin shook my hand, then Rusty's. "I was gonna go have a smoke," she said to me. "Want to come with?"

The truth was that I was feeling a bit anxious and had been craving a cigarette since I walked in the door. Other smokers can spot each other a mile away, and Kristin had obviously recognized the itch. "Sure." I reached into my pocketbook and produced a pack of Marlboro Reds. "If you'll excuse me."

"Yes, yes, of course," Keith said. He paused thoughtfully. "Do you have any desire to quit?"

"Of course," I said. "I quit before. For a long time. But then my brother got sick, and I was spending all my time at the hospital. His girlfriend offered me a cigarette, and…you know how it is. It's a hard habit to break."

"I think I can help you with that."

"Really?" It was astonishing to me that the CEO of a bustling new business would be willing to take time from his busy day to focus attention on a nobody like me.

"Yes, I think I can help. But we have to find a quiet spot, just you and me. We have to not be disturbed." He looked over at my husband, as if for approval, and Rusty shrugged. "Tell you what. I still have some math tutoring to do. Why don't you have your cigarette, and we'll circle back in twenty minutes?"

So, the bubbly Kristin Keeffe and I went out into the gorgeous August afternoon, and we had a smoke. I never would have guessed that it would be my last cigarette.

There was nothing remotely fancy about Keith's office, which was just an extension of the mess of the rest of the office. Not that I could see much. The Venetian blinds were drawn tight, so no natural light came in. The fluorescent bulbs that buzzed overhead in the rest of the facility were shut off. The only light in the room emanated from the monitor on his cheap Formica desk, casting yellow light on piles and piles of papers collapsing into each other like ruins. The mechanical drone of a computer, set up on its own little table, drowned out the noise from the office proper. There were at least three whiteboards, on which were scribbled various unknowable mathematical calculations. Either Keith was trying to solve Fermat's last theorem in his spare time, or he wanted his visitors to think so.

"Come in," he said, gesturing toward a futon couch along one wall. "Make yourself comfortable."

I sat on the edge of the futon, my posture ramrod straight, my back two feet from the cushion. I crossed my legs and watched as he plopped down next to me. "May I?" he asked, and he took my hand. I was conscious of the cigarette I'd just smoked, hoping the smell had not lingered in my clothes, in my hair, on my hands.

With short, stubby fingers, he opened my hand, rubbing his meaty thumb into the contours of my palm, surveying my life line, my love line, my fate line. He registered the chiromantic information as a blind man "sees" a new face. With his 240 IQ, he could probably read palms *and* read Braille.

"What I'm going to do today," he said, his voice soft and hypnotic, "what I'm going to do is relieve you of the urge to smoke."

I could barely suppress a chortle. "Good luck with that."

He gazed deep into my eyes, and I met his gaze—his bright blues burning into my greens. "You have lovely eyes," he said matter-of-factly.

"Thank you."

"I'm going to ask you some questions," he told me. "And as I do so, I'm going to stimulate certain pressure points on your hand. Later, when you feel like you want to smoke, all you have to do is apply pressure to these trigger points, and the urge will vanish."

"If you say so."

"I say so," he said, raising his eyebrows. "Please, sit back. Relax." He smiled. "No wonder you crave nicotine. You're *literally* on edge."

I uncrossed my legs and leaned back, falling into the soft cushion of the futon.

"Close your eyes…good…now, tell me about some things that make you relax."

"I like to get facials," I said. "I like to get massages." I could feel him pressing down on the fleshy part of my hand, south of the thumb. "I like to take walks outside, especially in the fall, when the leaves turn gold and orange and brown, and the weather is perfect: when the sun is warm but not hot."

"What else?"

"I like to listen to music."

"What kind of music?"

"Oh, all kinds. Everything from Frank Sinatra to Genesis."

After a few minutes of this line of questioning, he asked what made me nervous. "My mom," I told him. "She worries so much about me, and that makes me worry about her." I didn't go into great detail. I didn't tell him anything too personal. I opened up just enough for Keith to do his little palmistry trick. Or so I thought.

Ten minutes later, he was caressing my hand and calling my name: "Toni…Toni…Toni…we're all done, Toni…we're all done."

When I stepped out of the office, I felt at once fuzzy but energized. Invigorated. But something was off: the light had changed. The sun was beginning to set. The place had thinned out. Many of the employees had left for the day. Kristin Keeffe was gone. I found Rusty in an empty cubicle, leaning back in the chair, feet propped on the desk, flipping idly through a back issue of *Forbes* magazine. "There you are," he said. "Another half an hour, I would have filed a missing person's report."

"What are you talking about?"

"What were you doing in there for so long?"

"I was in there for fifteen minutes."

"No, you were in there for"—he glanced at the Timex on his well-tanned wrist—"two hours and forty-five minutes."

"Get out of here."

"I'm serious. I could have watched *The Godfather* in the time you were in there."

To me, the time went by in the blink of an eye. It was like waking up after major surgery. Where did those lost hours go? What happened in that office?

For a split second, I thought I knew. A pathway appeared in my mind that might have led me to the memory of the lost two and a half hours. But my concentration was broken by the sudden appearance of the woman with the Crystal Gayle hair. She was walking ahead of Keith, as if on parade, spinning around in circles like a stoned hippie at a Dead show.

"Is she the one? Is she family?" she kept asking him, clearly in reference to me. "Is she the one? Is she family?"

"Yes," Keith said finally. "Yes, she's family."

"I knew it, I knew it, I knew it!" She gave me a big hug, which had the effect of grounding me. She was a good hugger. "I'm so happy," she said. "That makes me so happy."

Her name, I found out, was Pamela Cafritz. She would become one of my dearest friends.

She spun off like a top around a corner. Keith followed her. Rusty tossed the magazine onto the desk, like he was folding a bad poker hand. "I'm going to have a smoke," he said. "You want one?"

I pressed down hard with my left hand on the trigger point

on my right. Waves of relaxation radiated from my palm to the rest of my body. "Actually," I said, "I don't. I think I'm okay."

"Really?"

"Yes."

And I was. I haven't smoked since.

I know people who fell in love at first sight—girlfriends of mine who met a man and instinctively *knew* that he was The One. It wasn't like that with me and Keith. I was attracted to his *ideas*, not his person. After meeting him at the Holiday Inn, I might have started working for his company, but I was hardly obsessed with him. I would have forgotten him entirely, but for the fact that was our biggest draw when selling the CBI memberships: "The Smartest Man in the World"—the calling card that was used to bring in thousands.

It was only after I left his dimly lit office that August day, with a feature-film-length hole in my memory—only then did I feel a primal connection with Keith Raniere. It was like in a horror movie, where the vampire allows his acolyte to drink his blood, and her eyes suddenly fly open and she is forever changed. Keith was Nosferatu. He fed off the life force of those in his thrall. This kept him powerful, just as it kept them weak.

On that summer day in Clifton Park, he claimed me.

To this day, I have no recollection of what went on during that two-and-a-half-hour blackout in his office. But this much is clear: nicotine is one of the most addictive drugs out there. Cigarettes are notoriously difficult to give up. If Keith, in just a few hours, could compel me to quit smoking forever...what else could he get me to do?

From "In Raniere's Shadows"
By James M. Odato and Jennifer Gish
*Albany Times Union*, February 22, 2012

One woman…was just a girl in 1990, a 12-year-old with feathered bangs and long blond hair who was trying to adjust to a new life following her parents' divorce and a move to the country to Clifton Park. Her mother was a saleswoman for Raniere's members-only buying club, Consumers' Buyline, Inc.…

When Raniere offered free tutoring, her mother jumped at the opportunity…He was supposed to teach her Latin and algebra. Instead, she said…he taught her to hug the way adults do, pelvis-to-pelvis.

He took her virginity…

Even though the girl was several years shy of the legal age for sexual consent in New York, which is 17, Raniere continued to have sex with her not only in his townhouse but in empty offices, in an elevator and in a broom closet at the plaza that housed Consumers' Buyline, she said…

**New York State Police, Supporting Deposition
Town of Clifton Park
Filed July 10, 1993**

I state the following: That on 4/27/93, while residing at the St. Anne's Institute, I reported…that I had engaged in sexual intercourse with a man named Keith Raniere.

This occurred when I was approximately 12 to 13 years old and occurred either at Keith's townhouse on 3 Flintlock Lane, Clifton Park NY or his business located at Rome Plaza, Clifton Park, NY. Although these incidents did occur, at the present time I do not wish to formally entertain any criminal complaint against Keith Raniere.

# CHAPTER 3:

# JOHN GALT COMES TO ROCHESTER

## Rochester, New York, 1991

---

There was a teacher in my high school: an older gentleman, popular with the kids. Mr. Harris came from money. Every year, he would take a group of his best students to London—his treat. I did not come from money. We never went anywhere on vacation, and I was desperate to travel. I had no special interest in London. I could not have found it on a map. But I really wanted to get out of Rochester.

The problem was that I was not a good student. I now know that I suffer from severe dyslexia. When I read, the words swim off the page. But when I was in high school, dyslexia was not understood or diagnosed and was generally confused with lack of intelligence. After failing out of Mr. Harris's class freshman year, I enrolled again in tenth grade. I was determined to succeed, because I wanted him to take me to London.

Two weeks into the first marking period, Mr. Harris called me over at the end of class. "Toni," he asked, "why are you taking this class?"

I explained that I liked him, I was interested in the subject, and I really wanted to go abroad. He smiled and patted me paternally on the hand. "It's good that you work hard," he said, with a note of finality in his voice, "and that you're pretty."

Mr. Harris was only trying to let me down gently concerning my hopes for world travel. But I took him at his word. What he was saying, it seemed to me, was that I had no business in a classroom. My purpose on this earth was to work hard and be pretty.

So, I took his advice. I dropped out and went to beauty school. I made a living as a cosmetologist and an aesthetician, doing sculpture nails and makeup, giving facials. A few years later, my background in beauty provided an opportunity to invest in a day spa—a new concept at the time. I could see that day spas were the wave of the future, and I was right. The business did extremely well.

I met Rusty through cosmetology circles. He had rust-red hair, a rust-red mustache, and thick brown-red brows over smallish eyes. "I look like Howdy Doody," he used to quip—and he wasn't wrong. But for me, it wasn't about his looks. I didn't need someone conventionally handsome; I needed someone stable. And he was stable. Rusty cut hair, then branched out into the tanning salon business. He was a gifted salesman. Off the clock, he could be frustratingly quiet. Put him onstage with a bottle of something to sell, the light switched on, and he was Ron Popeil.

We got married when I was twenty-nine. I'd walked the aisle twice before—marrying a mobster's son at seventeen, to prevent a mob war in Rochester; and wedding a kind but troubled boyfriend at twenty, so he could gain custody of his three daughters—and I figured the third time would be the charm. Rusty was seven years older and had never been married, and the one serious relationship he had was sabotaged by his suffocating mother. Calling Rusty a "mama's boy" understated how much control that woman had over him. Nothing would *ever* come between Rusty and his mother—least of all a twice-divorced twenty-nine-year-old. I understood this, and I accepted it as a condition of our being together. But I never took to her, and she took to me even less. To the overbearing mother, the wife is nothing but a threat.

Stability, as I said, was important to me. My biological father, my namesake, Tony, was a serial philanderer. He had children with five different women, which I'm sure was a small percentage of the many paramours he'd entertained. He fancied himself a gangster, and he dressed the part: fedora, spats, pinstriped suits, pomade in his hair. He left my mother when I was very young; I barely remember a time when we all lived in the same house. My brother, John, seven years older, was my father figure growing up, and the man of the house. We moved around a lot. My childhood was chaos, complicated by the serious medical issues of my sister, Darlene, who was mentally ill and suffered chronically from grand mal seizures and high fevers until she died at age sixteen. Rusty provided the stability that had been missing all my life. He wasn't going to cheat on me. He wasn't going to knock up five of his tanning salon customers. For all his faults, he was dependable. Solid. Loyal. Present. He kept me grounded until the day he couldn't.

\* \* \*

After our visit to Clifton Park, I talked to Keith almost every day. We'd spend hours on the phone, talking about anything and everything. He introduced me to literature, to science, to theology and the occult, to philosophy and economics. At the time, he was deep into his Ayn Rand phase. He'd been reading *Atlas Shrugged*, which he recommended to everyone as an excellent prerequisite to appreciating his own philosophy. He would babble on about it like an obsessed fanboy, but try as I might, I couldn't understand the appeal. The plot involved locomotives and the manufacturing processes of steel; the characters were caricatures of captains of industry; the underlying philosophy extolled greed at the expense of compassion. Oh, and the thing was 1,074 pages of microscopic print, half a million words, with few paragraph breaks. An unlikely bestseller, it seemed to me.

Needless to say, Keith found parallels between *Atlas Shrugged* and his own life. He identified strongly with John Galt, the novel's most important character—a self-made genius who *didn't* come from money, who emerged out of the blue. Galt was the leader of "The Strike," a movement where all the productive members of society repaired to a compound called Galt's Gulch, leaving the rest of humanity, the "looters," to fend for themselves—with predictably terrible results. Keith loved this idea, because, like all Rand disciples, he never doubted that he was one of the productive members of society. One of the chosen ones. Who is John Galt? With his 240 IQ and his myriad talents, *Keith Raniere* was John Galt. And I was Dagny Taggart, he told me over and over, the novel's protagonist. He and I were special; we were chosen; we would save the world.

But our conversations weren't all about objectivism. Mostly, we talked about changing the world—how to make it better. He seemed to have all the answers. He confided in me; I confided in him. For all his accomplishments, he was lonely and dissatisfied. Although he had plenty of brilliant people in his orbit, none of them really *got* him. At least, that's what he told me.

"It's only you, Toni. You're the only one who understands."

On its face, this didn't make any sense. He was an honors college graduate, CEO of a million-dollar company, a mega-genius acknowledged by freaking *Guinness World Records*. I didn't even finish tenth grade.

"There are different kinds of intelligence, Toni. You are incredibly intuitive. You have this amazing *emotional* intelligence. That's what makes you so special."

During these long back-and-forths, I learned a lot about Keith. He wasn't lying about being lonely. He was an only child, as I've said, and his father left when he was eight. Having an absent father of my own, I knew what that felt like. He kept himself busy, mastering this instrument or that, playing arcade games, reading. But he didn't really have *peers*, as such—not until college.

Most of his close friends were women. He lived in a town house with three of them: Pam Cafritz, the effervescent space cadet with the Crystal Gayle hair whom I'd met during my visit; Kristin Keeffe, my smoking buddy; and Karen Unterreiner, a fellow RPI graduate. Together, they were four of the five founders of CBI. They lived together, he explained, to save money, to better grow the business. He adored them, or seemed to, as they adored him, but it wasn't enough. They couldn't fill the gaping hole inside him, the profound emptiness. Only *I* could do that.

"You have to come back out here," he said. "Just you."

"You know I can't do that. I have Michael to think of."

"I know, I know. I shouldn't be so selfish. But I feel like you're meant to help me change the world."

Most of the time, though, Keith would listen. He would ask me endless questions: about my childhood, about my parents, about my failed marriages, and he would listen, really listen, to my answers. And I opened up. I told him everything he wanted to know. Why not? Aside from my mother, it's not like I had any other confidants. Rusty didn't have the capacity to listen like that, and who else cared enough to try? By the end of 1991, no one, not even my mom, knew more about me—good, bad, and ugly—than Keith Raniere.

Of particular interest to him were the stories of my sexual abuse. From the age of four until middle school, I was molested repeatedly by one of my uncles. The only person I'd ever told about it was my biological father. "Daddy, he kisses me hard." My father ignored it. So, I never breathed another word about it. Instead, I'd buried the dark memories, locked them away in a vault.

Keith knew exactly how to unearth those memories, how to pry open the steel doors. He was an excellent listener. If you had trauma in your past, he knew how to root it out, he knew how to exploit it—and, most important, he knew how to make it seem like love. As far as I could tell, he cared deeply. He was trying to help me. To heal me.

"This is why you always have problems with your relationships," he told me. "This is why you're unsatisfied with Rusty. I can help you with this. Just like I helped you quit smoking. But you have to come here."

"Unsatisfied with Rusty? But I'm not unsatisfied with Rusty."

"No? Maybe it's just that he's unsatisfied with you."

It had never occurred to me to doubt my husband's loyalty. "Why would he be?"

"When was the last time you were intimate with him?"

"Intimate? Well, we cuddled on the couch last night, watching TV."

"That's not what I mean. When was the last time you made love?"

"Made love?" I let out a long sigh.

"How long has it been?"

He already knew the answer. It had been more than two years ago.

"You don't understand," I protested. "Our relationship just isn't like that."

"He's your husband. You're his wife. You're not a cloistered nun. You're a beautiful woman, thirty-two years old. Why isn't he making love to you?"

I thought about evenings with Rusty, how we retired at different times, each of us as far away on the king-size bed as we could possibly get. We were married, yes, but we were not lovers. We were roommates, we were partners, we were co-parents, but we were not lovers. I didn't respond to Keith's question. But I did note, with some pride, that he had called me beautiful.

"Has it ever occurred to you that he's not making love to you because he's making love to someone else?"

This had not occurred to me. The notion was so radical that I felt like Keith had reached his hand through the phone and slapped me across the face. "Rusty? *My* Rusty? Who would he be sleeping with?"

"Tammy."

"Tammy?"

"That's her name, isn't it? Your nanny?"

"Wait—you think Rusty is having an affair with *Tammy*?"

"It seems pretty obvious to me, yes."

Tammy was certainly pretty. But she was so young. She was practically a child herself. It was hard to think of her as a sexual being. Then again, it was hard to think of Rusty that way either.

"You're insane," I said.

"Rusty is a healthy, virile man. If he's not making love with you, believe me, he's making love to someone else. Tammy is the prime suspect."

This was, frankly, unfathomable to me. I couldn't picture Rusty having sex with Tammy. I couldn't picture Rusty having sex with *anyone*. He just wasn't a sexual being, not in that way. But once the seed was planted, suspicion grew in me like a noxious weed. I began to regard every interaction Rusty had with Tammy, however benign, as fishy. Why was he always offering to drive her home? Why was she laughing at some joke he made? Did he put his hand on her shoulder, or did I just imagine that?

My rational mind knew that Rusty was innocent. My heart was not so sure.

I said that Rusty's tanning salons were self-sustaining. This is only partly true. While the business was his on paper, his mother was the de facto chief operating officer. Marge did all the grunt work for him, made the appointments, worked with the vendors, kept the books, handled the money. Twice a month, she'd write out a check for some sizable chunk of change, and he didn't think twice about it. Between his tanning salon income and my day spa, we were doing well. We purchased a gorgeous home in the town of Webster, a tony suburb a short drive from the southern shores of Lake Ontario.

In order to adopt Michael, however, we had to make some drastic changes. The agency said that one of the parents had to be home with the child. "Great," I said. "My husband is home all the time." But that wasn't good enough. In those days, the concept of a stay-at-home dad was so ridiculous that a movie had been made about it, a comedy: *Mr. Mom.* The agency wanted *the mother* to be at home. So, I had to sell the day spa.

In order to keep busy while we waited for the agency to call, I started a home business selling gift baskets, which started to take off.

And then the bottom fell out. It turned out that Rusty's self-sustaining tanning salons were not the money factories we'd been led to believe. The company had been losing money for two years. His mother didn't bother to mention this to Rusty. She didn't want to upset him. Instead, Marge used his credit cards to pay the bills. She did this for the duration, two full years, until all the cards were maxed out, until the credit was gone. We thought we were on steady footing financially. Turns out, we were desperately, hopelessly in the red.

The news, while bleak, was not a death knell. We still had the basket business, and we still had CBI. But the problem with gift baskets is that they are seasonal, and the problem with commissions is that they are sporadic. Some months are up; some months are down. This was a slow period and we needed an infusion of $25,000, or Rusty would lose the tanning salons and we might lose our home.

There was only one person we knew who could possibly loan us that kind of money: Keith Raniere. Wasn't Consumers' Buyline growing at a rate of 40 percent per month? Didn't the company show receipts of $33 million last year? Twenty-five thousand was nothing to a guy like that, surely. And it's not like we were some charity case. We were top sellers, past winners of the Spectrum Award. There was no question we'd be able to pay it back.

"Can you mention it to him, please?" Rusty pleaded. "Maybe in one of your five-hour conversations, you can slip it in that we've gone bust?"

"Don't you dare," I said. "This is your mess—you clean it up. *You* ask him."

"Fine, I will."

So Rusty called Keith and spilled the beans. I didn't listen to the conversation—I was putting Michael to bed when they spoke—but I'm sure it was humiliating for my husband. The answer was: there was some sort of conference in Buffalo next week that Keith was attending—he would swing by our house on his way there, and we could talk about it in person.

And that's how Keith Raniere wound up sitting at our dining room table, sipping at a cup of tea: John Galt had come to Rochester—driven there by one of his dutiful subordinates. He brought with him two copies of *Atlas Shrugged*, one for me, one for Rusty. A thousand-page, single-spaced, five-hundred-thousand-word novel—a tough read for a dyslexic.

"What a beautiful home," Keith said. "This is like paradise."

As Tammy strolled Michael around the neighborhood, Rusty and I broke down the numbers for Keith. He nodded as we retold our tale of woe, occasionally rubbing the five-o'clock shadow on his chin. It was thoroughly mortifying. Here we were, in a beautiful house we couldn't afford, employing a nanny to watch our lone child. We must have seemed like so many spoiled, profligate

American families, living beyond our means. What must this self-made genius have thought of our self-made plight?

"I'd love to give you the money," Keith said finally. "The problem is, I don't have liquid assets like that. All my capital goes back into the company. And CBI, I mean, there's the other owners. It's messy. I can't just write you a check from the corporate account. That would be illegal. The IRS...we don't want to give them any more reason to put us on their radar." He looked at Rusty. He looked over at me. "The one to speak with is George Weiss. He handles the administrative side of things."

I'd heard the name before. Keith seemed to be fond of George Weiss and talked about him often during our marathon phone calls, bragging about his business acumen. He was forever telling me I *had* to meet George Weiss. He always referred to him by his full name, George Weiss; he was never just George.

"Let's get you back to Clifton Park," Keith said to me. Then, to my husband: "Can you arrange that, Rusty? Have Toni come for a few days? All expenses paid. I have an idea, a way out of this. But if it's going to work, she's going to have to come and meet George Weiss."

What could Rusty possibly say? No? Keith was his last, best hope of staving off financial ruin. The inclusion of George Weiss, a chaperone, meant that this was strictly business, aboveboard.

"It's fine with me," my husband said, "as long as Toni's okay with it."

And I was okay with it. More than okay. John Galt had come to summon Dagny Taggart to Galt's Gulch. And how did he sell me? Like Ayn Rand's capitalist hero, Keith flashed the dollar sign.

# CHAPTER 4:

# AWAKEN

## Clifton Park, New York, January 1992

---

"gain. Tell me again."

"But we've been through it three times."

"Three times is not enough. Tell me again."

"I have to use the ladies' room."

"Fine, but when you come back, I want to hear it again."

The clock on the nightstand flashes the time at me: 2:36. I have no idea if it's the middle of the night or the middle of the afternoon. Have we been here for twelve hours? Twenty-four? Thirty-six? I've lost track of time.

Keith sits cross-legged in the patterned chair by the window. The curtains are drawn tight. He's wearing sweatpants and a rumpled dress shirt. He doesn't appear tired. Those mesmerizing blue eyes blaze with energy. "I know this is difficult, Toni, but you have to trust me. This is how you will heal. This is how you will be made whole."

In the bathroom, I run cold water over my hands, throw it on my face. The reflection in the mirror shocks me. Bags under bloodshot eyes, mascara running, lips chapped. We've been in the room at the Best Western for most of my visit—not at all what I had expected. The meeting with George Weiss was nothing, a blip. So was the stop at Keith's town house. *It isn't enough to save you financially,* he said. *I have to save your soul.*

Keith is standing by the bathroom door, waiting for me. He takes me in his arms, and I collapse into him. Even barefoot I'm taller, but right now I feel tiny, like I barely exist. He holds me tight. His embrace is powerful, his arms strong. He runs his hands through my hair. He caresses my cheek. "We will do this," he says. "We will save you."

He walks me back to the bed, installs me there, resting my back gently against the cushioned headboard, and takes his place in the chair, sitting in lotus pose like a guru. "Again. Tell me again about your uncle."

"The first time it happened," I say, my voice weary, "I was four years old…"

Unlike the itinerant L. Ron Hubbard, who moved around constantly and spent half his life at sea, Keith Raniere was a homebody. Aside from a brief period just before his arrest when he was on the lam in Mexico, Keith lived his entire life in New York State. He moved from Brooklyn, where he was born, to Suffern, in Rockland County, when he was eight. His college years were spent in the Capital Region, in Troy. He lived near the RPI campus for five years after graduation, performing in a local production of *Sweeney Todd* (he played the snake-oil salesman!).

In 1987, when he was working as a data analyst for the New York State Department of Labor, Keith and his RPI friend Karen Unterreiner bought a town house in the Knox Woods development in Clifton Park, halfway between Albany and Saratoga Springs. The streets in Knox Woods all bear names associated with the Revolutionary War: Yorktown, Grenadier, Generals, Hale. Their town house was at 3 Flintlock Lane. For thirty years, Keith encouraged his followers to buy up properties in the same development, or as close to it as possible. Eventually, Pam Cafritz and Clare Bronfman purchased 2 Flintlock Lane; Lauren Salzman owned 21 Lape Road and 7 Minuteman Court; Allison Mack resided at 7 Generals Way. "The Executive Library," the town house that operated as Keith's kinky-sex lair, was at 8 Hale Drive. At the time of his arrest, NXIVM affiliates owned some fifty properties in and around Knox Woods. Keith was a creature of habit. He could, and did, walk from his town house to any of these residences, to call on his disciples. Likewise, Rome Plaza, the office park a short drive from the town house, was the headquarters for most of Keith's businesses subsequent to CBI, including ESP.

But all of that was in the distant future. In January of 1992, when I first visited Knox Woods, the Bronfmans were still in high school; Allison Mack was nine. As I saw it, Keith Raniere was a brilliant man who launched a business with his friends and was cohabitating with those same friends to pinch pennies. So, what if they were women? Women and men could be friends without it being sexual, surely. And what did I think, that he was sleeping with *all* of them? Yes, there were four people and three beds, but he had the futon in his office—and anyway, he didn't sleep. The story seemed perfectly plausible.

And even if I had my doubts, the fact was, I *wanted* to believe him. More than that: my future depended on the opportunity with Keith working out.

Pam Cafritz picked me up at the train station in a shitty little Datsun coupe. I'd thought she was maybe on something when I met her the first time at CBI, but no—she was always like that, a space cadet, floating around like a blown dandelion seed. Unlike Keith, she was in no danger of being admitted to the Mega Society—her acceptance to Smith College owed more to her wealthy and well-connected parents than to her academic achievements—but her good cheer was infectious. She was like a balloon, barely tethered to earth.

"How was your trip?"

"Fine, thank you. Where's Keith?"

"He's running late. We'll pick him up at the house and then head to CBI to meet George Weiss."

Before I could say another word, she turned up the radio. "Sugar Magnolia" was on, and Pam sang along, her airy voice slightly off-key.

I was dying to see where Keith lived. What would the home of the Smartest Man in the World look like? I could see it clearly in my mind's eye: black-and-white checkerboard tiles in the great room, Impressionist paintings in gilded frames on the walls, towering bookcases teeming with all manner of leather-bound volumes, and, because Juilliard marveled at his playing, the grandest of grand pianos beneath a giant crystal chandelier.

I could not have been more wrong. The exterior of the town house was generic, cookie-cutter, with drab, slate-gray vinyl siding and uninspired landscaping. The inside was an abomination. Oscar the Grouch kept his garbage can tidier than Keith and his friends kept their home. It was the filthiest place I'd ever seen. Discarded clothes and old mail and food wrappers and dirty dishes were strewn all around the place. On the counter was an old pack of vegan hot dogs that reeked like manure—although that horrible smell may also have been the piles of cat shit in the pungent litter box, or the guinea pig cages occupying an entire wall of Pam's bedroom, where Kristin Keeffe stood, doling out hay to the pets. The stench was so powerful that I actually gagged. The Smartest Man in the World, it seemed, was also the most unsanitary.

We were met in the kitchen by a dour, homely woman—the depressive yin to Pam's manic yang. This was Karen Unterreiner, the fourth and least remarkable resident of 3 Flintlock Lane, Keith's ex-girlfriend from college, and a co-owner of CBI. Her touch was cold as she shook my hand. "So, you're Toni." She had nothing more to say to me. As soon as I withdrew my hand, she vanished into one of the bedrooms, as if she was summoned back there like a curfewed demon.

The bathroom door opened, and Keith burst out, adjusting his belt. "Toni!" he exclaimed. "You made it!" He hugged me tight. "Let's go meet George Weiss!"

By the time we hit the driveway, the feathered-blond thirteen-year-old with braces whom Keith was tutoring in algebra, had finished walking Pam's dog, so she, too, hopped into the little Datsun, sitting in the back with Keith. The four of us made our way to the CBI offices.

"The first time was when you were four years old. When was the next time?"

"I don't remember."

"Yes, you do."

"It all blurs together. Maybe it was right after that, maybe it was a year later. I can't say for sure. All I know is that my aunt was my favorite person in the whole world. She would pick me up on Saturday, and we would go out for doughnuts, and I would stay with her all weekend. It was my only break from the chaos of my own house. She loved fire trucks, and she used to take me to the firehouse to see them. I loved her more than anyone on earth. She was a sweet, kind, lovely person. And she was somehow married to this sicko."

My voice is starting to crack—not from emotion, but from exhaustion. This is the tenth or eleventh time I've told the same story, in excruciating detail. My vision, like my memory, is starting to blur. Two Keiths hover before me in the chair.

"We need to take a break," I say. "I need to sleep. I'm tired."

"Sleep?" He stifles a yawn. "No, no. You don't need sleep. Sleep is a construct. For this to work, we have to keep going. But I do have to get to the office for a bit, so you'll have to continue with someone else."

"Someone else?"

The door flies open—who else has a key?—and Pam Cafritz tiptoes into the room. "Sorry to bother you, but there's a problem at the office."

Keith nods sagely, as if saddened by the interruption. Again, he stifles a yawn. "Pam will take over for a bit."

I eye her with suspicion. How can this flighty space cadet, lovely though she might be, "take over"? Keith senses my skepticism. "This is really about you, not about me. Pam knows what to do; don't worry." With some effort, he pulls himself off the chair. "I'll be back as soon as I can." He puts his hand on my shoulder, squeezes twice, and is gone.

"I can't do this anymore," I tell her once the door closes. "I have to sleep."

"Here." She hands me a giant cup of Dunkin' Donuts coffee and a corn muffin. "You might need this."

"Why do I have to stay up? Keith isn't staying up."

"Sure he is. He's going to CBI. Keith never sleeps."

"Well, I do."

"It's okay, Toni. I know how you feel. But you have to trust the process, okay? Drink your coffee, and we'll go get some food. The diner is really good."

Food. I do not realize how famished I am until she speaks that magic word. I nod, and I take the cup, and I follow her out the door.

George Weiss had the regal bearing of a circuit court judge who had been on the bench for twenty years. He was to the manor born, and he looked the part: tailor-made suits and dress shirts with crisp collars and cuffs, elegant silk ties with rich paisley patterns, mother-of-pearl cuff links. Even his nails were immaculate. He was tall and heavyset, with a deep, resonant bellow and a friendly Santa Claus laugh. Among the sweatpants-wearing Keith Raniere and the youthful employees of CBI, George Weiss was very much the adult in the room.

"Keith told me all about you," he said, taking my hand in his weighty paw. "He thinks, and I quite agree, that you are uniquely qualified to run our new business concern."

The new business was a line of skin-care products, aligned with but not officially owned by CBI, financed by George Weiss's venture capital. The brand name was new agey and mysterious: Awaken. "With your background in cosmetology, your experience owning a day spa, your tireless work ethic, your easy way with people, and, let's face it, your *look*"—he used this as an excuse to ogle me head to toe—"you are the perfect face for Awaken."

The base salary was generous—more than enough to alleviate our financial problems. I would not have to worry about a steady revenue stream. Commissions promised still more income. I'd have to give up the gift basket business, but while that company showed promise, it was not a sure thing. This opportunity would make life better for Michael and better for me.

There was just one catch, and it was a doozy: "The office is here, in Clifton Park. So, you'd have to relocate. We'd cover those expenses, of course. Unless you wanted to commute from Rochester. But that doesn't seem practical."

This should not have been a surprise. Deep down, I knew that it would be a possibility. But when I heard the words spoken out loud, I was still somehow shocked. Leave Rochester and the life I had built there? My brother, John? All of my friends and business contacts?

"Well?" George Weiss said. "What do you think?"

Not that leaving home was impossible. My mother had done it—she'd been living in New Jersey for the last fifteen years, where my stepfather was from. Clifton Park was not close to Denville, where they were, but it was closer than Rochester.

"It's an incredible opportunity. Thank you. I have to discuss it with my family…"

But there was no question that I would take the job.

*It's good that you work hard, and that you're pretty.* Once again, my greatest assets were paying off.

\*     \*     \*

"And it continued for how long?"

"Until I was eleven or twelve."

"Which one? Eleven or twelve?"

"Eleven," I say, but I don't really know for sure.

"Why did it stop?"

"My aunt had a stroke, and their living situation changed."

We are back in the hotel room at the Best Western. Aside from the brief interview with George Weiss at the CBI office, and the occasional run for coffee and corn muffins, we've barely left. When the maid knocks on the door to change the sheets and tidy the room, we send her away.

"He did this to you for seven years. Why didn't you tell anyone? Why didn't you stop him?"

"I told my father Tony, my biological father, not Al. I told him that my uncle kisses me hard. He ignored it. So I figured it wasn't a big deal. I figured it was normal."

"Normal? You must have known it wasn't normal."

"How would I know? I was four."

"Come on, Toni. You must have known."

"I was taught to trust him. I was conditioned to believe that it was okay. It was very confusing."

"Was it?"

I want to scream at Keith: *Yes*, it was confusing. I want to explain that the reason society protects children from sexual contact with adults is because children lack the cognitive agency to consent. I want to insist that sex with a minor is *always* rape, even if the child ostensibly wants to do it. But I've had enough. Reliving the trauma is too great. Tears burst forth, cascading down my cheeks, and they don't stop. My body trembles. My heart pounds heavy in my chest.

Keith rises from the chair. He comes to me. He takes me in his arms. Again, I fall into his embrace. "I will help you," he says. "I will make it better. But you have to be here, in Clifton Park. You have to take the job."

"The job?"

"At Awaken. With George Weiss."

"Yes," I whisper.

"Yes what?"

"Yes, I accept the offer. Yes, I will take the job."

**Handwritten Memo from CBI VP, to Keith Raniere**
**November 23, 1992**

*Keith,*

*This fax was sent to the [Rome Plaza] office on Sunday night, fortunately it was found this morning before it could be copied. We cannot tell who sent it, but I could probably guess.*

**From "The Inside Story On Consumers' Buyline Inc."**
**Anonymous fax sent November 22, 1992, 7:37 PM**

The intent here is to inform people of the ramifications of involvement in CBI. This is a giant scam that is hurting many people. The scam is not the...membership, nor the structure of the compensation, but in the management, and in particular the company's chief executive, Keith Raniere.

Are you one of the many affiliates who have quit CBI because of the incessant problems and poor treatment from the corporate office? If so, you have a responsibility to report these problems to your State Attorney General...

What kind of man is Mr. Raniere? Some people that have worked with him say that while he is very intelligent (he can learn academically), he is dysfunctional in his normal pursuit. Aside from lying on a regular basis, what level of morality does he have?...

On numerous occasions at various meetings around the country Mr. Raniere has stated publicly that CBI affiliates were not restricted to CBI alone and could thus do CBI together with other MLM programs. He also stated that if he found it necessary to terminate an affiliate, the affiliate would continue to receive their commission checks, but would not be able to sell any memberships or bring additional affiliates into the company. Several affiliates have these statements on both audio and video tape, yet he has terminated numerous affiliates for promoting another program AND STOPPED THEIR CHECKS, contrary to what he says publicly. These people were terminated illegally, having done nothing to violate their contract. Even so they were terminated and Mr. Raniere and CBI are now reaping the rewards of the hard work of these affiliates. Is this the kind of "INTEGRITY" Mr. Raniere refers [to] time and time again in his speeches...? What's to stop him from terminating anyone if he wishes? Will you be next?...

—A Concerned Affiliate

# CHAPTER 5:

# SLEEPING ARRANGEMENTS

Rochester and Clifton Park, New York, 1992

---

For the next five months, I continued to live in Rochester while working full-time in Clifton Park. I would pack little Michael into my Jeep Cherokee, drive three hours across Interstate 90, and hole up at the same Best Western in Clifton Park for three, four, and sometimes five nights a week. Until I found a nanny, Kristin Keeffe, who loved children, would often babysit.

At work, I reported directly to George Weiss and to Susan Ciminelli. The former was the avuncular venture capitalist and businessman; the latter, a legendary aesthetician whose work in the field remains unparalleled. They were fantastic bosses, giants in the industry, and I loved working for and with them. Although we occupied the same Rome Plaza office space as CBI, I didn't interact much with Keith during the workday. He was with Karen Unterreiner in his gloomy office or playing the *Vanguard* arcade game in the break room, or on the road, seeking out new recruits.

Keith would travel the country like a touring musician, giving seminars in ballrooms at Holiday Inns and Best Westerns and Grand Hyatts. I would often go with him, selling Awaken while he hawked CBI memberships. When the formal talk was over, he'd hold Q&A sessions to the point of exhaustion. Most of the attendees would leave after the seminar proper was done, more would trickle out in the hour or two that followed, and inevitably, he would be left with a single wide-eyed woman, eager to continue the conversation in private.

On one of his recruitment missions, Keith managed to sell the wife of a prominent southern minister on the glories of CBI. Once she was in the fold, her entire flock followed, and the holy-roller money came rolling in. Hallelujah and praise be! Having already hoodwinked Pam Cafritz, who was from a wealthy DC family, Keith well knew how a single convert, if sufficiently rich and prominent, could underwrite his entire business.

According to the grapevine at the office water cooler, Keith and Karen Unterreiner were an item. This wasn't true, but I understood how people might draw that conclusion. They had been boyfriend and girlfriend at RPI. Both of them were brilliant— Karen much more so than Keith. (I suspect that she helped him with the Mega Society genius exam, which, after all, comprised an untimed *take-home* test.) And they lived together, two of four people occupying a three-bedroom town house.

But Keith vehemently denied this. "We're not a couple," he told me. "We love each other, but we're not a couple. I promised that I would never leave her, and I have to keep that promise. I mean, *look* at her. She's so homely. Who else would want her?"

This assessment was true. Karen was far and away the plainest woman in Keith's orbit. And the way he phrased it, combined with the twinkle in his eye, seemed to suggest that Karen's unattractiveness was in stark contrast to my own beauty.

"We have the business together. She's really good at it. I want her to be happy. But we are *not* a couple. Not at all."

And why would I suspect otherwise? It wasn't like he lived *alone* with Karen, and people were always around, to say nothing of cats and dogs and guinea pigs. Was I supposed to believe that Keith Raniere, who rode a unicycle and played arcade games at the CBI offices, was maintaining a harem on 3 Flintlock Lane? It was reasonable to expect that a geek like that would not have a sex life on par with Mick Jagger's or Wilt Chamberlain's.

We were in my hotel room at the Best Western. It was late in the afternoon. Kristin Keeffe had taken Michael to the playground. Keith and I were alone.

"I love Karen, she's a dear friend, but I'm not *in love* with Karen."

I was sitting on the bed, Keith in the chair. Now he rose and moved closer. "I'm in love with someone else," he said, sitting next to me. "I'm in love with you."

My heart went pitter-pat, and I almost let out a gasp. The Smartest Man in the World in love with a high school dropout! It was like a fairy tale.

"With me?"

"With you."

And to prove it, he kissed me.

On the one hand, I fully expected this to happen, but on the other, I was surprised and thus unprepared for it. We had been building toward that kiss for months, slowly and patiently. There was comfort in the slowness and patience. And now, in this unromantic hotel room, we had reached the inflection point.

When you had a conversation with Keith, you felt like he was focusing 100 percent of his attention on you and only you. It was the same thing when you kissed him. You were the every and the all, the alpha and the omega. His lovemaking skills, too, were exceptional. He was giving and generous, but also fully in command. Five minutes after climax, most men are ready for bed; five minutes after climax, Keith was ready for more. His demonic ability to regenerate his carnal energy, to rise again and again to the occasion, was astonishing.

Looking back, I believe that he lacked the mental ability to fully revel in the climax. Just as other men grow bald or suffer from erectile dysfunction, Keith was unable to properly discharge energy during sex. It was a deficiency in his DNA. Even as he experienced orgasm, his body denied him release.

Me, I did not have that problem.

I had not had sex of any kind for almost three years—and even then, my partner had been, at best, uninterested. Going from Rusty to Keith was like upgrading from a paper plane to a Concorde.

"You should come here."

"I am here."

"No, I mean you should move here. For real. Live here with me."

"Keith, I'm married. Rusty and I have a son together."

"I know, I know, I know." He kissed me on the forehead. "But wouldn't it be nice?"

Yes, it would be nice. So nice that, when I had a big blowup with Rusty concerning his meddling mother, I decided to leave him. It's not quite right to say I left him *for* Keith, as I probably would have gone anyway, but there's no question that Keith's attention accelerated the process.

Clifton Park was not as lackluster a town as I'd thought, because apparently *everyone* wanted to move there. Kristin Keeffe was charged with finding me a place to live, and the only place she managed to find—the only space big enough for me and Michael, but not so big that it would cost more than I could comfortably afford—was a town house at 2 Schuyler Court. This was also, conveniently enough, in the Knox Woods development where Keith lived. In fact, he could walk through his backyard to get to my backyard (his place was such a pigsty that I almost never went).

My first night in the new place, Keith came over. I made him dinner, and he helped me put my son to bed, patiently reading to him in his soothing, hypnotic voice.

When Michael fell asleep, we slipped into my room, where, after the usual marathon lovemaking, he made declaration after declaration of his love for me, his happiness that I had moved here, his knowledge that I was the one who could complete him.

The next morning, the nanny came to watch Michael, and I picked Keith up and drove us to work. (He did not own a car or possess a valid driver's license. His had been suspended, years ago, for some infraction or other, and he was so incensed at this bureaucratic unfairness that in a fit of pique he never bothered to renew it.) I kissed him in the parking lot, and he looked ill at ease. When I went to hold his hand, he pushed me away.

"What's the matter?"

"We can't tell anyone about us," Keith said.

"What? Why?"

"For one thing, it would be unfair to Karen."

"To *Karen*?"

"We don't want to humiliate her, do we?"

I didn't much care about Karen Unterreiner's hurt feelings. I'd left my husband to move across the state to work with this man. To *be* with him. Last night he had proclaimed his undying love for me. The least he could do was acknowledge the relationship in public.

"But it's not just that. It's a business thing."

"A business thing?"

"Think about it, Toni." He tilted his head and gave me one of his life-coach looks, one familiar to anyone who spent time with him: the Smartest Man in the World was waiting beatifically for me to catch up.

"Because I didn't finish high school? Is that what this is about? That's it, isn't it? You think if people know we're dating, they'll think I only have the Awaken job because you're my boyfriend."

He nodded sagely. He knew I was insecure about my lack of formal education. "That's what everyone will think, I'm afraid."

As George Weiss rightly pointed out during my interview, I was uniquely qualified to run that company. As long as my job was done well, no one cared if I finished high school or held a PhD. But I didn't have the requisite self-esteem to realize that. I assumed that Keith was right. And it crushed me.

"Okay," I said.

And I followed him submissively into the office, trailing a few steps behind.

# CHAPTER 6:

# "A WELL TAUGHT CROOK"

## Clifton Park, New York, 1992–1993

---

*P*yramid scheme has become a catchall phrase for a business with fishy operating practices, but there is nothing inherently illicit about organizing a company in that manner. All multilevel marketing companies have pyramid structures, in which owners and early adopters earn a slice of the sales of their own recruits: Avon, Amway, and thousands more less heralded. Like capitalism itself, MLMs incentivize growth. Companies run afoul of the law when their revenue is generated by *recruiting new sellers*, rather than *selling actual products*.

Despite its structure, Consumers' Buyline was not a pyramid scheme per se, because it sold memberships that enabled members to buy products at near-wholesale prices. But it was a pyramid scheme in the popular sense, because it was not completely aboveboard. The problem was that memberships are not tangible commodities, so CBI operated in a sort of gray area, legally. It was essential that the memberships provide the promised steep discounts. If they stopped doing so, the operation became unlawful. Beginning in 1992, that's what happened with CBI. Complaints began to come in: Dissatisfied members. Discounts that did not materialize. Commissions not paid on time.

Keith would blame this on either the vendors, for not owning up to their contractual obligations, or the IT people, for mucking with the computers, or the affiliates themselves. "Not everyone has the mental capacity to appreciate what we're trying to do here," he'd say. "Not everyone is integrated."

The employees believed him. Why wouldn't they? At CBI, Keith Raniere was the messiah. To doubt the genius of the Smartest Man in the World was unthinkable. They were young people working in an avant-garde corporate office, where people dressed in business casual and played one of the two genuine arcade games on offer in the CBI warehouse. How could all of that be a scam?

Besides: the employees didn't know about the lawsuits. At first, and for a long time, only Keith and Karen Unterreiner, an actuary by trade who kept all the books, were aware of the class action lawsuit filed in Massachusetts by a woman named Helen Rhodes, and another suit filed by the attorney general in Arkansas, and the investigations into CBI by authorities in Maine, New York, and Pennsylvania—all accusing CBI of being a pyramid scheme. They didn't know that by court order, CBI had to pay $25,000 to the attorney general of Arkansas and $20,000 to the attorney general of Pennsylvania for non-compliance with state regulations, or that other state AGs were also on to the scheme. Even when the damning articles came out in the *Albany Times Union*—in the days before Google, the daily paper was the only real source of news—even when other states filed suit, most CBI staff accepted Keith's explanation that the government was out to get him.

Nor were they privy to the sexual harassment suit filed against Keith by a former CBI employee. Sexual harassment was still a novel concept in March of 1993, two years after Anita Hill made it famous during the Clarence Thomas confirmation hearings. How could anyone know when Keith quietly settled that case?

I didn't question it. Like everyone around Keith, I only saw what I wanted to see.

True to my word, I kept my relationship with Keith secret. Oh, his girls knew all about it—Pam Cafritz and Kristin Keeffe and Karen Unterreiner—but no one else. He stayed at my town house on Schuyler Court almost every night when he wasn't traveling, but it was a short and private walk through the backyard. There was no car to spot. And who would care enough to stake out the place? Sometimes I drove him into the office; other times he rode in with Karen or Kristin or Pam. My schedule was dictated by Michael; Keith's, by whim.

I didn't even tell my mother about the relationship. Even after I moved from Rochester, even as I divorced Rusty, I never even hinted that Keith and I were romantically involved. My mom was my best friend, and I talked to her every day. There were many times I desperately wanted to share something, because Keith had done something wonderful or was behaving in ways I didn't completely understand, or because the stress of keeping the relationship covert was wearing me down. But I didn't. Instead I talked about Pam, my closest friend in Clifton Park. Pam and I did this; Pam and I did that; I took Pam to a movie; we went to dinner.

"Toni," my mother said. "You talk about this Pam person all the time, and there's no boyfriend in sight. Are you trying to tell me something?"

I laughed. "I'm not a lesbian, Mom. We're just friends."

"Sure, sure. Well, if you need to tell me something, I'm okay with it."

Keith, too, was having trouble keeping secrets close to the vest. The lawsuits against CBI, once under lock and key, were now uncomfortably out in the open. The *Albany Times Union* ran an article on May 21, 1992, with the ominous headline "Discount Service Target of Probe, Pyramid Scheme Alleged." The opening lines were devastating:

Consumer Buylines Inc., a locally based discount buying service with 200,000 members nationally, is being investigated by authorities in New York and Maine and has been sued by the Arkansas attorney general for allegedly using deceptive trade practices.

"They're essentially operating what appears to be an illegal pyramid," said Perrin Jones, a spokesman for the Arkansas Attorney General. "Everything depends on you bringing in more and more people until the thing collapses under its own weight."

Pyramid schemes generally depend on investments by subscribers, rather than sales of goods or services, to make a profit.

Pyramids are illegal in Maine, New York and Arkansas, officials said.

The president of Consumer Buylines, Keith Raniere, denied the charge and said many officials misunderstood the operations of his 2-year-old company, which employs 200 workers and has a second office in Albany. In 1988, Raniere garnered local attention when he qualified at the age of 27 for the elite Mega Society—one up from Mensa—by demonstrating an IQ of 178.

Not only did the piece call into question the legality of Keith's company; it also listed the correct IQ reflected by his Mega Society test score. Why did he feel compelled to tack on 62 extra IQ points? Was 178—still smarter than Einstein—not impressive enough? And if he was willing to lie about something provable . . . how could he be trusted with anything else?

Faced with incontrovertible proof of his duplicity—all those state attorneys general could not possibly be wrong, however vehemently he insisted otherwise—Keith did what narcissists do, he doubled down and changed the narrative. "The government is out to get me," he insisted. "They don't understand what we're trying to do here. They don't like that we're trying to help people. They don't want us to change the world!" He gave out copies of *The Little Prince* to everyone at CBI, made us all watch *The Man Who Planted Trees* and hinted that the heroes of both children's stories were misunderstood geniuses, just like Keith Raniere. He was fond of quoting Swift: "When a true genius appears in the world, you may know him by this sign, that the dunces are all in confederacy against him."

And his followers believed him over the "lying" journalists at the *Times Union* and over various "vindictive" state attorneys general. He was that convincing.

Keith was fixated on explaining the difference between members and affiliates, in particular the key distinction that the latter were not required to be the former. The fuzziness between the two was at the heart of the court cases against CBI. He recorded and disseminated a five-minute message to the affiliates to hammer home this point. The video shows him perched on a desk in a tidy office—clearly not his—in a jacket and tie, his hair blown out and neat but desperately in need of a trim. He offers no preamble, no warm greeting, but gets right down to brass tacks. His voice is soft, but it's hard to miss the anger bubbling just beneath the calm surface as he asks affiliates to rat out any of their colleagues who dare demand, illegally, that affiliates *must* be members. "We will keep all correspondence confidential," he promises, "and we will reward any person that leads us to an offender. That's how serious we are about running our business right. After all: wouldn't you rather be involved with a company that demands the highest ethical standards?"

Left unsaid is the axiom that companies that demand the highest ethical standards don't usually find it necessary to send out videos trumpeting their own high ethical standards.

Everyone at CBI thought the video was terrific.

It wasn't just the lawmen who were after him. Jilted CBI members wanted him dead. On September 15, 1992, a disgruntled Vietnam veteran sent Keith a letter replete with misspellings, written in a neat, boxy, serial-killer hand, with a Maine postmark. (Maine was one of the many states investigating CBI.)

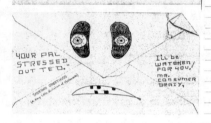

Sept. 15, 1992

Keith,

Don't come to my state Maine. I'LL tell ya plaine, And SIMPLE.

You broKe up our Family. My sister got everone into C.B.I. Inc., and we pooled what we had.

My name is Ted, And I am disabled From Nam, And my checks Feed Four people. Me, And my brotherlike to hunt just Fine. He can hit a dime From 100 Foot. So, if you or your people show up were gonna just wound them.

PAGE 4

You see we didnot want get rich, we wanted that food plan. It didn't work, and now my hole FAMILY is Fighting.

You broKe our trust, and hurt all my Friends too!

I hate you, and ever thing you stand For.

We got the best guns money can buy, scopes And such!

YOU STOLE FROM US! YOU WERE gonna Help Us LITTLE FOLKS. Well you turned out rotten, and we Kill rotten pigs.

Don't come to my state, And lots of

people got hurt.

Don't you look at your self in the mirror in the morning.

Your just a well taught crook, who do you think your Kidden.

Keith you been warned proper.

THE END

TED

It read:

*Personal & Confidential*

*For Our Savor Mr. Keith*

*Sept. 15, 1992*

*Keith,*

*Don't come to my state Maine. I'll tell ya plaine, and simple. You broke up our family. My sister got everyone into CBI Inc., and we pooled what we had.*

*My name is Ted, and I am disabled from Nam, and my checks feed four people. Me, and my brother like to hunt just fine. He can hit a dime from 100 foot. So, if you or your people show up were gonna just wound them.*

*You see we did not want get rich, we wanted that food plan. It didn't work, and now my hole family is fighting. You broke our trust, and hurt all my friends too!*

*I hate you, and ever thing you stand for.*

*We got the best guns money can buy. Scopes and such!*

*YOU STOLE FROM US! You were gonna <u>help</u> us little folks. Well you turned out rotten, and we Kill rotten pigs. Don't come to my state, and lots of people got hurt. Don't look at your self in the mirror in the morning.*

*Your just a well taught crook, who do you think your kidden.*

*Keith you been warned proper.*

*THE END*

The Smartest Man in the World, the altruistic genius who had promised to change the world by means of multilevel marketing, had bilked a wounded Vietnam vet out of his disability checks. Keith literally stole the guy's lunch money. To Keith, Ted was wrong, just as all those state AGs were wrong, and they all had it in for him. It was a giant anti-Raniere conspiracy.

But just to be sure, he intercepted that letter and stowed it at my house and made sure no one else at CBI saw it.

At the time, CBI was the fastest-growing MLM in the country, generating $1 million per month in profits. The sole impediment to the business becoming the next Sam's Club was its flaky CEO. Keith was a chaos agent, and by design. He took delight in bringing in extraordinary employees—a VP who had been a colonel in the army; the ad man who dreamed up the L'eggs campaign of putting panty hose in egg-shaped packages—and repeatedly humiliating them. He would call meetings for ten in the morning and not show up until the late afternoon.

Keith became increasingly paranoid. He accused the government of spying on him, of opening his mail, of tapping his phones. Always a night owl, he kept even odder hours, coming late to the office and staying there until well past midnight, holding court with whatever loyalists he could find to stave off sleep with him. (Stalin, it is said, kept similarly crazy hours late in his reign).

I was working for George Weiss and Susan Ciminelli, two dignified, solid professionals who headed Awaken, and was less affected by his mood swings. But in the confines of Rome Plaza, Keith was a dynamo, impossible to ignore. I had a child and didn't roll in at noon and stay at the office until midnight, as many of the others did. Even so, working for Keith, even second-hand, had worn me down.

At home, he was a nightmare. He would let himself into my house in the middle of the night, even as my son and I slept, and wake me up, frantic, desperate for physical comfort. I acquiesced, but only so he would go away, and Michael would not see us together. Many mornings I woke at 6:30 to get ready for the day and left with Michael, as Keith lay snoring in my bed; he would not appear at the office until well past lunchtime. (So much for the myth of Keith not needing sleep!) When he was there during normal daylight hours, he engaged in an endless raving monologue, decrying all the torment the government was subjecting him to.

And it's not like his problems were insoluble. Yes, there were quite a few lawsuits, but there was also a lot of revenue. "CBI is going to be a billion-dollar company," he would say at his presentations to potential affiliates. "It's worth millions now. We're going to be forty million households strong!" The senior management at CBI was talented. The idea was good. All Keith needed to do to get the law off his back was pay the settlement money, change the language in the legal documents, and cede day-to-day operations of the company to his superb senior management. But he refused to do so. He refused to settle—not because it cost money, but because it would mean admitting his mistake. And Keith Raniere did not make mistakes! It was *never* his fault. It was always everyone else's—*anyone* else's.

In April of 1993, I went to Rochester to spend Easter with my family. On the train platform on my way back to Albany, the same creepy man graced the cover of every paper on the newsstand: boyishly handsome; long, wavy brown hair; bad glasses;

thin smile; powerful, penetrating eyes. This was David Koresh, cult leader of the so-called Branch Davidians, polygamist and serial statutory rapist. He was dead, killed in the FBI's raid on his compound in Waco, Texas, where he was alleged to have abused and raped children. *He looks like Keith,* I thought, and then pushed that unpleasant thought from my mind.

Of greater interest was the story in the *Albany Times Union,* published the same day: "Consumers' Buyline a Pyramid Scheme, Abrams Alleges"—Abrams being New York State Attorney General Robert Abrams. In a prepared statement, Abrams said: "Inevitably, pyramid schemes collapse of their own weight. While the organizers of Consumers' Buyline already have reaped hundreds of thousands of dollars for themselves, we can safely predict that thousands of participants will be left empty-handed." The math provided by the state seemed to bear this out: "According to Abrams, a Consumers' Buyline membership costs $270 a year. Of that, $14 buys the new member enrollment in Purchase Power, a Texas-based discount buying club, 'so $256 goes toward building a pyramid...'"

Incensed about the big story in the local daily, which would be difficult to hide from the CBI staff, Keith paced around my kitchen on Schuyler, muttering curses and raving like a Shakespearean villain. He blamed the *Times Union* and the author of the piece, Christopher Ringwald, for his plight. "They are all out to get me," he insisted. "The government, the media. They have decided I'm dangerous and they want me silenced. They want only to destroy the good thing we've built."

Keith was earnest, aggrieved, persuasive. But he was dead wrong. Even Keith's fancy Washington lawyer sounded like a boob in that story, complaining that Abrams refused to negotiate:

"'We were prejudged as a sleazy company. We were able to resolve this with eight other states.'"

*Nine states* found CBI "sleazy."[1] States that built cases evaluated whether or not they had merit and then decided to pursue them. If CBI was unblemished, why would the attorney general for the state in which it was headquartered, whose salary was indirectly paid for by its corporate taxes, seek to kill it? Keith argued passionately, even self-righteously, and he seemed sincere, but his argument made no sense.

"Just pay the fines, Keith. Pay them and move on."

"Never." Paying the fines would mean he'd made a mistake—and Keith Raniere didn't make mistakes.

---

1    In the end, *twenty-two* state attorneys general and two federal agencies sued CBI.

# CHAPTER 7:

# ASHRAM BLUES

Clifton Park and South Fallsburg, New York,
1993–1994

---

I could handle Keith's ranting at home. I could handle it in the office. But I couldn't do both. It was a perfect storm, and I was at the center of it.

"I can't work like this anymore," I told him. "Seriously. If we can't find a new office, away from CBI, I'll quit."

He did not hesitate to hit me where it hurt: "What will you do, with your tenth-grade education? Go back to Rochester and make gift baskets?"

"Anything is better than this."

Keith refused to do anything, preferring to keep all his underlings under constant watch, so I went to George Weiss. I told him I was leaving immediately unless we relocated the offices. And since George Weiss was a businessman and not a sociopath, he granted my wish. Awaken moved to a new but equally charmless office park just up Route 9. Chelsea Park and Rome Plaza were almost indistinguishable in terms of appearance, but the difference for me was profound. At Awaken, we had been trying to tend our garden in the same patch where there was blight. Now, free from the Raniere infestation, we were free to grow our burgeoning company in peace.

The offices next to ours at Chelsea Park were home to the Albany franchise of Tony Robbins, the self-help guru. By 1993, he'd produced the popular Personal Power series of cassette tapes and published two enormously successful books, *Unlimited Power* and *Awaken the Giant Within*, so he was already a household name. (It was apropos that our skin care company shared a name from the title of Robbins's most recent book.)

As fate would have it, the franchise was owned by an old friend of mine from Rochester, a firecracker of a woman named Edie. I quickly befriended everyone in Edie's employ, even developing an infatuation with a man named Mark, a single dad who worked there.

Tony Robbins was a partner with John Grinder, one of the two developers of neuro-linguistic programming, or NLP. Having studied this approach to communication himself, Keith recognized the potential of NLP in helping him build his own self-help brand. To Keith, Tony Robbins was more than just a famous life coach. He was a template for his own plan. Keith didn't want to learn from Tony Robbins; he wanted to *be* Tony Robbins. So Keith made it known that he would like me to arrange a meeting between him and the great guru. I agreed to help facilitate such a meeting, and I worked with Edie to make it happen.

As CBI foundered in legal purgatory, Awaken bloomed. My new business venture was exploding—and I was right in the thick of it. I had team leaders flying in from all over the country for training sessions. Plans were made for me to travel to Dallas, to give a training to a conference of Awaken affiliates in the southern region. It was one thing to keep our relationship a secret when I was starting out. But now that I'd established my bona fides, why would anyone care that I dropped out of high school? You know who else didn't go to college? Tony Robbins! There was no earthly reason why Keith and I could not openly date. We didn't even work for the same company, and I was not keen on making such an enormous sacrifice just to placate the dour Karen Unterreiner. I broke down and told my mother. I told my brother. I told Rusty, who reacted with a shrug; my ex-husband was himself working for another of Keith's companies, one that sold vitamins.

But in Clifton Park, Keith insisted on secrecy. He treated our relationship like it was the nuclear launch codes. No one could know, or it would be the end of the world as we knew it! Awaken was a success. I was a big reason why. I even managed to wrangle the Tony Robbins meeting. (At six seven, Tony was more than a foot taller than Keith, who looked ridiculous next to this literal and figurative giant of a man.)

The tensions came to a head about my Texas trip, of all things. I was flying to Dallas in the middle of October. Keith didn't want me to go. He drew up what he called a "timeline," a convoluted graph with multiple x- and y-axes that included such phrases as *purification of heart, life, undoing of blocks, energy building, baby clock,* and *1½ years tests, development leading to final decision.* There was an instruction, *No more sliding above this line,* although he really meant *below* the line, and a helpful *you are here.* All the points connected at the top of the graph, where an arrow pointed to *Dallas.* The timeline didn't make much sense to me.

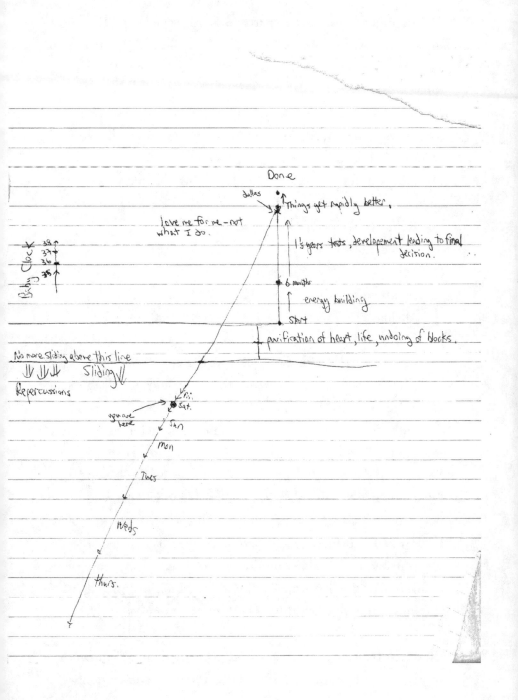

Done

dollars

Things get rapidly better,

love me for me – not what I do.

Baby Clock
38
37
36
35

1½ years tests, development leading to final decision.

6 months

energy building

Start

purification of heart, life, undoing of blocks.

No more sliding above this line

Sliding

Repercussions

you are here

Fri.
Sat.

Sun

Mon

Tues

Weds

Thurs.

The night before my departure, Keith called me. The anger in his voice was obvious. He hated disobedience. "Don't get on that plane," he said. "If you go to Dallas, everything will change forever."

"What are you talking about? Two hundred people are coming to this training. Team leaders are flying in from all over the country. I have to go."

"No, you don't. And you shouldn't. Prove to me you want to change the world. Cancel the trip."

"Keith, you're being ridiculous."

"*I'm* being ridiculous?"

"Yes."

"If you go to Dallas, Toni, that will be the end."

"The end?"

"I truly believe that."

"I can't cancel, Keith. So I guess we're done."

I hung up the phone, and so he wouldn't call back, I unplugged it from the wall.

Keith preferred that I wear loose-fitting clothes, to hide my figure. I had acquiesced to this, as to most of his wishes. When I told my friend and Awaken colleague Jim Wood that I had ditched Keith, he said, "Great! Now let's get you some new clothes!" That's the first thing I did when I got to Dallas. I addressed the fifty Awaken affiliates that day in a gorgeous, form-fitting, bright red Ann Taylor suit. I felt happy, confident, unafraid. For the first time in a long time, I felt like myself.

But freeing myself from Keith Raniere was not so easy.

Pam Cafritz picked me up at the airport. By then, I'd known her for two years. She was one of my closest friends, and certainly my closest friend in Clifton Park. I'd never seen her so despondent. She looked like she was barely keeping it together.

"Keith needs you," she said. "You can't leave him. He's lost without you."

"If I was that important to him, he wouldn't have insisted on keeping our relationship a secret. He acts like he's embarrassed to be seen with me."

"That's not true."

"Then why the secrecy?"

"Because Karen—"

"I don't care about Karen, okay? If he loves Karen so much, he can go be with her."

"You should give him a second chance," Pam said. "Things will be better. You'll see."

She dropped me at the Schuyler town house, and I was home for five minutes before Kristin Keeffe came knocking on the door. During the Dallas presentation, I had called Kristin and put her on speakerphone, so the entire Awaken audience could hear them say hello, she was with Michael at the time. She seemed fine then. Now she, like Pam, was in a dark mood.

"Give him another chance," she said, echoing almost word for word what Pam had said. "Things will be better. You'll see."

The next day I drove from Albany to Syracuse, where Rusty met me with Michael. Kristin offered to come with me, as she wanted to see my son. The whole way there, she wouldn't stop talking about Keith and second chances.

Curiously, Keith only tried a few times to contact me, calling me at the office. I would talk to him about business, but when he tried to change the subject, I hung up on him. After that, he was content to let the "girls" represent him. The relentless lobbying on his behalf went on for days on end, almost nonstop. Pam would show up at my office. Kristin would wake me up at two in the morning to beg me to take him back.

Pam grew more intense, more biting. "If you don't believe in perfection, why the hell are you here?" she wrote in a long, rambling letter. "Deep down, you know why I take Keith's side and not yours. You know. Your actions are always selfish, and his, for as long as I've known him, have been self-less. He gives and you take. You don't respect his abilities and what he needs to do. You say you do, and then you order him around, like he's not holding up his end of the bargain! My mother treats her help better than you treat Keith. Then you denigrate his actions, like he is not to be trusted. You failed, Toni. This happened—Mark happened—because you did not trust Keith and lashed out at him like a child. You don't appreciate all that you have. And you have so much!

"You don't trust I understand," she wrote. "You think I believe in him like Santa Claus. And you are the only one who can argue with him or stand up to him or have a brain." There was some truth to this, I had to admit. "No. You are an arrogant fool. Although I respect your work. I have zero respect for your spiritual understanding of Keith and his lifestyle. This is where we differ. YOU don't trust him. And you haven't learned from your own mistakes."

I reached my breaking point in the middle of October, in the dead of the night. I was awakened by a noise: footsteps on the stairs. The front and back doors were dead-bolted shut, and no one else had the key, but someone was clearly here. Half-naked, I raced into the dimly lit hallway and threw a right hook at the intruder. The punch landed just below the left eye of Pam Cafritz, who tumbled backwards down the stairs.

"Leave me alone!" I screamed. "Leave me the fuck alone!"

I was over Keith; I was over Pam; I was over Kristin. To hell with them. I arranged for Rusty to pick up Michael. Once my son was safe, I packed my bags, got in my car, and started driving. For more than two hours I drove, and I didn't stop. I headed south on Route 9, took the thruway to Kingston, and took a state highway deep into rural Sullivan County. That's where the ashram was—the yoga retreat where, years ago, Keith had first met George Weiss. I'd been there before, plenty of times, with George, with Susan Ciminelli, and with Kristin Keeffe. For me, the ashram represented the safest place I knew. Even Keith couldn't hurt me at the ashram—and how would he even know I was there? I didn't tell anyone that I was leaving, let alone where I was going. I was sure they wouldn't find me there.

But they found me. It took them less than a week.

I was sitting under a tree daydreaming about Mark, the single dad I'd met through Edie. After the years with aloof Rusty and the subsequent period with the Smartest Sociopath in the World, I was crazy about Mark, a handsome, caring, *normal* guy.

And then a strange little man, dressed in the robes of the ashram, his head shaved, ambled over. He was holding a rose—the flower the Little Prince is so in love with. He handed it to me. There was a note: "This is from Keith. He wants you to call him." And he left without saying a word.

I shouldn't have called Keith; I know that now. But I was not in the right frame of mind to resist. The ashram was a spiritual place to me. I believed deeply in the blessings, in the rituals, in the divinity of the gurus. It sounds preposterous now, but at the time, I felt like Keith somehow both tracking me down *and* delivering that rose—one of the sacred roses that are not supposed to be plucked—was a sign from the universe.

But I didn't call right away. First, something told me to check in with my friend Edie. As it turned out, she was having a crisis. She had a huge Tony Robbins event planned, she was the hostess, and she'd fallen and sprained her ankle and couldn't walk. "I don't know what to do!"

"I'll help you," I assured her. "Whatever it takes, we'll make it work."

Then, after much internal hemming and hawing, I phoned Keith. What was I supposed to do? I couldn't keep running away forever. Closure was needed.

"Have you heard about Edie?" he asked. This was surprising, as he was not friends with her and had no connection to the Tony Robbins people.

"Heard what?"

"How many people have to get hurt, Toni, before you realize we're destined to be together?"

It was all I could do to not drop the phone. He didn't come right out and say so, but I knew he was talking about Edie, about her accident.

"How's your friend Mark? He seems like a nice guy. Good father."

"He is," I managed to say. Keith knew about Mark and was not happy about it.

"He should be careful. Not rush into things too quickly. It would be a shame if something happened to him. His little girl needs her father." It sounded like something one of my first husband's Mafia uncles might say, but Keith's voice was so calm, so serene, that he may as well have been reading from a prayer book. Still, I understood that the threat was real.

"I shouldn't have kept us a secret. I was trying to protect you, but I see now that I didn't need to. If you come back, I'll give you everything you ever wanted."

"Everything?"

"We'll tell everyone about us. No more skulking in the shadows. We'll buy a house together—whatever type of home you want for Michael."

At one time, this *was* what I really wanted. A normal life with the Smartest Man in the World: my business partner, my friend, my life coach, my lover. But now that he was proposing it, now that I had met, in Mark, a more normal alternative, my desires had changed.

"Not in Knox Woods," I said, stalling.

"No, no, of course not. Somewhere else. Our own place. Wherever you want. Where we can start over. Away from Pam and Kristin and Karen. Just you and me—and Michael, of course. He's such a gifted child, and he would benefit from a strong family environment. We'll provide for him what I never had. And who knows? Maybe you and I can have a child of our own. What do you say?"

*No.*

That's what I should have said.

Or: *You're too late. I don't love you anymore. You can't make me happy.*

But I didn't. I knew that resistance was futile. He was too good and there was no telling what he was capable of. And I had Michael to think of—Michael who was not yet in kindergarten. When Keith said things would be different, I believed him.

I had to believe him. I had no choice.

To be fair: things *were* different. We *did* tell everyone. We *did* move to a house somewhere else—a lovely home in Waterford, on a tree-lined street in a neighborhood teeming with families, a mile and a half from his old town house. Michael *did* benefit from having the Smartest Man in the World serving as his de facto stepfather. Michael attended a Waldorf school, and Keith was an active participant in his education. For the next few years, Keith and I lived a traditional family lifestyle. We celebrated holidays together. We went to New Jersey to visit my parents. We took trips to the city to see shows and visit museums. We had our ups and downs, to be sure, but there were more ups than downs. We were, in a word, normal.

In many ways, it was a dream life.

But there's a fine line between a dream and a nightmare.

# PARADISE LOST—"THE FALL": GASLIGHTING LETTERS FROM KEITH, APRIL 10, 1999

Of what he was, what is, and what must be
Worse; of worse deeds worse sufferings must ensue.
Sometimes towards Eden which now in his view
Lay pleasant, his grieved look he fixes sad,
Sometimes towards heav'n and the full-blazing sun,
Which now sat high in his meridian tow'r:    30
Then much revolving, thus in sighs began.
  "O thou that with surpassing glory crowned,
Look'st from thy sole dominion like the god
Of this new world; at whose sight all the stars
Hide their diminished heads; to thee I call,    35
But with no friendly voice, and add thy name
O sun, to tell thee how I hate thy beams
That bring to my remembrance from what state
I fell, how glorious once above thy sphere;
Till pride and worse ambition threw me down    40
Warring in heav'n against heav'n's matchless King:
Ah wherefore! he deserved no such return
From me, whom he created what I was
In that bright eminence, and with his good
Upbraided none; nor was his service hard.    45
What could be less than to afford him praise,
The easiest recompense, and pay him thanks,
How due! yet all his good proved ill in me,
And wrought but malice; lifted up so high
I sdained subjection, and thought one step higher    50
Would set me highest, and in a moment quit
The debt immense of endless gratitude,
So burthensome still paying, still to owe;
Forgetful what from him I still received,
And understood not that a grateful mind    55
By owing owes not, but still pays, at once
Indebted and discharged; what burden then?

31. *revolving:* meditating.
32–41. Milton's nephew Edward Phillips, in his *Life of Milton,* said he saw these lines "several years before the poem was begun." They were, he said, to be the opening lines of a tragedy.
35. *diminished:* reduced in authority or dignity.
37. Cf. John 3.20, p. 456: "For every one that doeth evil hateth the light, neither cometh to the light, lest his deeds should be reproved."
38–39. Cf. Rev. 2.5 "Remember therefore from whence thou art fallen . . ."
43–45. Cf. Ezek. 28.15–17: "Thou wast perfect in thy ways from the day that thou wast created, till iniquity was found in thee. . . . Thine heart was lifted up because of thy beauty, thou hast corrupted thy wisdom by reason of thy brightness: I will cast thee to the ground, I will lay thee before kings, that they may behold thee." James 1.5: "If any of you lack wisdom [to resist temptation], let him ask of God, that giveth to all men liberally, and upbraideth not; and it shall be given him."
50. *sdained:* disdained.
51. *quit:* pay.
53. *still:* always.
56. *owing:* both owing a debt and owning (admitting) a debt. The old form of the past tense of owe was ought. Owe comes from ME owen, to have, to own, to have (to do), hence, to owe.

O had his powerful destiny ordained
Me some inferior angel, I had stood
Then happy; no unbounded hope had raised    60
Ambition. Yet why not? some other Power
As great might have aspired, and me though mean
Drawn to his part; but other Powers as great
Fell not, but stand unshaken, from within
Or from without, to all temptations armed.    65
Hadst thou the same free will and power to stand?
Thou hadst: whom hast thou then or what to accuse,
But heav'n's free love dealt equally to all?
Be then his love accursed, since love or hate,
To me alike, it deals eternal woe.    70
Nay cursed be thou; since against his thy will
Chose freely what it now so justly rues.
Me miserable! which way shall I fly
Infinite wrath, and infinite despair?
Which way I fly is hell; myself am hell;    75
And in the lowest deep a lower deep
Still threat'ning to devour me opens wide,
To which the hell I suffer seems a heav'n.
O then at last relent: is there no place
Left for repentance, none for pardon left?    80
None left but by submission; and that word
Disdain forbids me, and my dread of shame
Among the Spirits beneath, whom I seduced
With other promises and other vaunts
Than to submit, boasting I could subdue    85
Th' Omnipotent. Ay me, they little know
How dearly I abide that boast so vain,
Under what torments inwardly I groan:
While they adore me on the throne of hell,
With diadem and scepter high advanced    90
The lower still I fall, only supreme
In misery; such joy ambition finds.
But say I could repent and could obtain
By act of grace my former state; how soon
Would highth recall high thoughts, how soon unsay    95
What feigned submission swore: ease would recant
Vows made in pain, as violent and void.
For never can true reconcilement grow
Where wounds of deadly hate have pierced so deep:

79–80. Cf. Heb. 12.17 "For ye know how that afterward, when he [Esau] would have inherited the blessing, he was rejected: for he found no place of repentance, though he sought it carefully with tears."
87. *abide:* (in the sixteenth and seventeeth centuries erroneously used for *abye*) pay the penalty for, atone for, suffer for, endure.
94. *act of grace:* suspension of sentence.

*[Handwritten annotations:]*
- GIVEN too Much (lines 58–61)
- How LUCiFER Justifies wrong-doing — His (lines 75–79)
- Can't bEAR TEllIng his team He's WRONG (lines 80–84)
- Self-Esteem AND Theft. (lines 88–91)
- SCARED to Mess-up agaiN, DOESN'T TRUST himself (lines 95–99)
- BUT (left margin)
- SE PEDO ENCE (left margin)
- tE (left margin)

TONI AT AWAKEN: Here I am, happily working away in my new Awaken office at Chelsea Park in 1993. *Photo Courtesy: Joan Schneier*

NEWARK STATE HOSPITAL: Me, my mom, my brother John, and Aunt Pat visiting my big sister, Darlene, at Newark State Hospital in 1965. This is where Darlene lived until she passed away on July 7, 1970. *Photo Courtesy: Toni Natalie*

JOHN AND TONI: My brother, John, and me at our mom's house in 1992. He was, and always will be, my hero. Thank you for trying so hard to save me. *Photo Courtesy: Joan Schneier*

AL AND JOAN: My mom and dad, Joan and Alfred Schneier, at one of their favorite restaurants, the Lamplighter, in Rochester. Without them, I never would have made it through all of this. *Photo Courtesy: Toni Natalie*

KEITH AND JIM: Keith and his father, James Raniere, a nice man who had a very successful career in advertising. Here Jim poses with his son before a National Health Network gala. *Photo Courtesy: Toni Natalie*

KEITH AT CBI: Keith in his office at Consumers' Buyline, tapping at the piano I gave him for his birthday. After I left him, the police were sent to my parents' home, claiming I stole this piano from him and that it was worth $17,000. (I didn't, and it wasn't.) *Photo Courtesy: Toni Natalie*

KEITH AND PAM: Daughter of wealthy Washington, D.C., socialites, Buffy and Bill Cafritz, Pam Cafritz was one of Keith's closest confidants. Little did I know she was also Keith's longtime girlfriend and fixer. *Photo Courtesy: Toni Natalie*

KRISTIN KEEFFE: Kristin Keeffe, in 1993. She was the only person I would trust to watch my precious son. She was fun, brilliant, and caring. Michael nicknamed her "Kristin Bunny Rabbit." *Photo Courtesy: Toni Natalie*

HALLOWEEN: This was the Halloween party for Consumers' Buyline Inc., in 1992. Keith thought it would be hysterical if he dressed up as me. His costume was a big hit. Jim Wood, one of my employees, was commemorating this moment with my camera, at my request for my personal memories. *Photo Courtesy: Toni Natalie*

TONI AND KEITH ON THE TOWN: Keith and me together for a birthday celebration in 1996. These years were our happiest times together.
*Photo Courtesy: Joan Schneier*

KEITH AT THE LAKE: Once NXIVM reached its height, Keith's birthdays were celebrated with ten-day-long extravaganzas called Vanguard Week. This photo, however, was taken in 1993 during a more modest weekend celebration at Pyramid Lake.
*Photo Courtesy: Toni Natalie*

KEITH IN THE MIRROR: Keith loved to have his picture taken. He would insist I take multiple images, snapping one after another, while he practiced different poses to see how they changed his appearance—glasses on, then glasses off, smiling, then not smiling, with small changes to his posture in each shot. This photo is from our early days, taken at my request with my camera, 1992. *Photo Courtesy: Toni Natalie*

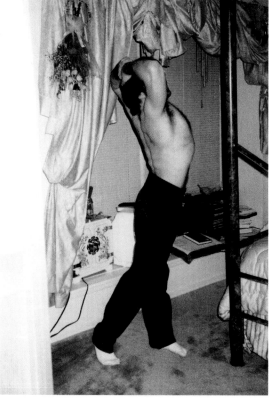

KEITH IN THE FIFTH POSTION: Another example of how much Keith loved to have his picture taken; this one taken in my bedroom in Knox Wood, 1992. *Photo Courtesy: Toni Natalie*

TONI, JOAN, AND KEITH: Weddings in New Jersey were big, fancy, and fun. This was a family friend's wedding that Keith and I attended with my mom and dad in 1995. *Photo Courtesy: Alfred Schneier*

TONI, KEITH, AND MICHAEL: Michael, Keith, and me on weekend visit to see my mom and dad, 1996. *Photo Courtesy: Joan Schneier*

MOVIE NIGHT: The "normal" life Keith had promised to give my son and me. This was taken on our first night in our new home on Anchor Drive in Waterford, NY, June 1994. *Photo Courtesy: Joan Schneier*

MICHAEL AND KEITH: Michael with Keith in 1994. *Photo Courtesy: Toni Natalie*

DAWN, BARBARA, KAREN, AND PAM: The original inner circle in 1996 (from left): Dawn Morrison, Barb Jeske, Karen Unterreiner, and Pam Cafritz. *Photo Courtesy: Joan Schneier*

PAM CAFRITZ AT NHN: Pam Cafritz at National Health Network in Rome Plaza. I later learned about so many dark things that happened in those offices before, during, and after I left. *Photo Courtesy: Toni Natalie*

TONI, LOUIS, AND NANCY: Just a few short months after Nancy Salzman came into our lives. Here we are at Keith's birthday party at National Health Network in August 1998. *Photo Courtesy: Joan Schneier*

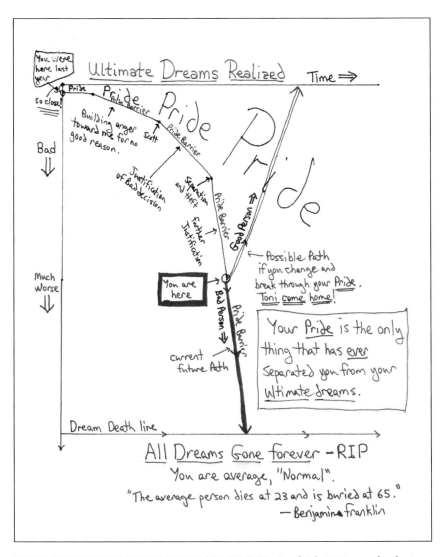

ULTIMATE DREAMS REALIZED TIMELINE: April 24, 1999, my death timeline included in one of the many "gaslighting" letters Keith sent me that year. *Photo Courtesy: Toni Natalie*

SCOTT, TONI, AND PAMMIE: At a National Health Network event with Scott Foley in 1997. What I didn't know at the time was that someday Scott would be my husband, and key in helping me get away from Keith. *Photo Courtesy: Joan Schneier*

MICHAEL AND TONI: By the fall of 1998, I feared for my safety and the safety of my son, Michael. This was the last photo taken with Michael before I sent him to live with his father in Rochester and ran for my life. *Photo Courtesy: Joan Schneier*

INNER CIRCLE: Exhibit GX 362 in the government's case against Keith Raniere. A depiction of Keith Raniere's "inner circle." *Government Exhibit: United States District Court for the Eastern District of New York*

FIRST LINE OF DOS: Exhibit GX 363 in the government's case. These are the "first line" in Raniere's secret society known as Dominus Obsequious Sororium or DOS. *Government Exhibit: United States District Court for the Eastern District of New York*

JUSTICE FOR TONI: Checking out Keith's new home, the Metropolitan Detention Center in Brooklyn, the day before his first court appearance on Friday, April 13, 2018. *Photo Courtesy: Stanley Zareff*

88   PARADISE LOST

*[handwritten: Mess up More SECOND TIME]*

Which would but lead me to a worse relapse, 100
And heavier fall: so should I purchase dear
Short intermission bought with double smart.
This knows my punisher; therefore as far
From granting he, as I from begging peace:
All hope excluded thus, behold instead 105
Of us outcast, exiled, his new delight,
Mankind created, and for him this world.
So farewell hope, and with hope farewell fear,
Farewell remorse: all good to me is lost;
Evil be thou my good; by thee at least 110
Divided empire with heav'n's King I hold
By thee, and more than half perhaps will reign;
As man ere long, and this new world shall know."

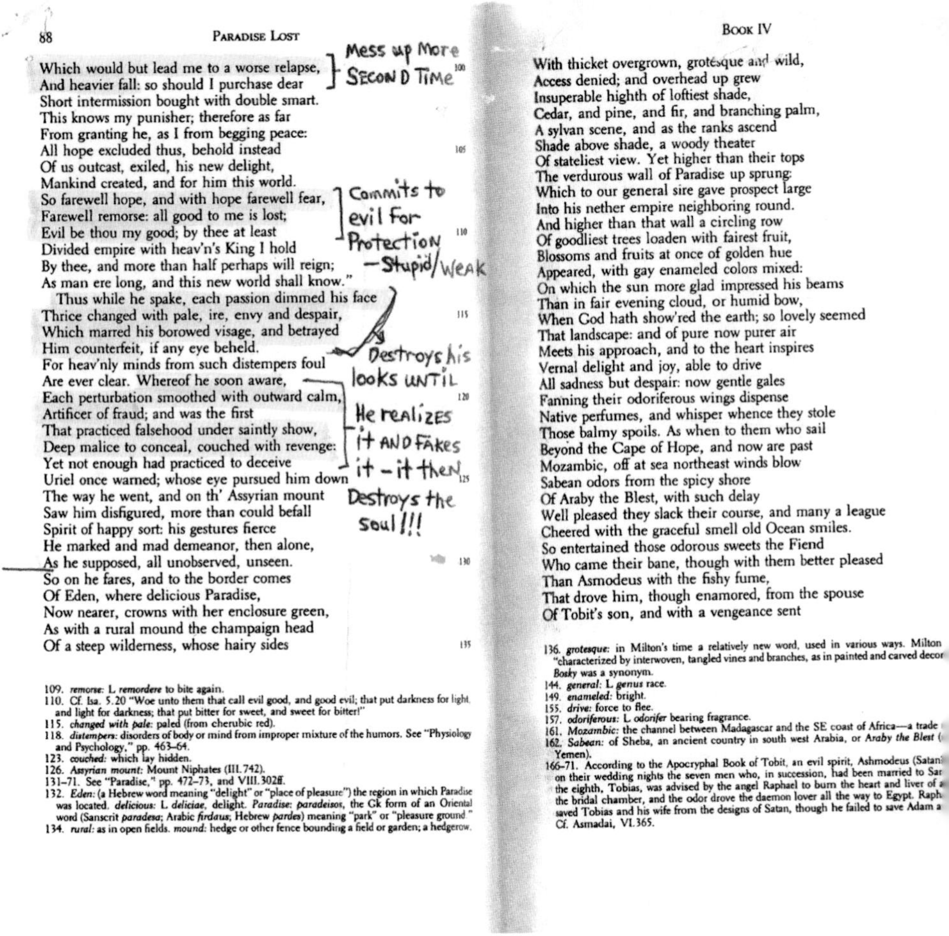

*[handwritten: Commits to evil for Protection — Stupid/weak]*

 Thus while he spake, each passion dimmed his face
Thrice changed with pale, ire, envy and despair, 115
Which marred his borowed visage, and betrayed
Him counterfeit, if any eye beheld.
For heav'nly minds from such distempers foul
Are ever clear. Whereof he soon aware,
Each perturbation smoothed with outward calm, 120
Artificer of fraud; and was the first
That practiced falsehood under saintly show,
Deep malice to conceal, couched with revenge:
Yet not enough had practiced to deceive
Uriel once warned; whose eye pursued him down 125
The way he went, and on th' Assyrian mount
Saw him disfigured, more than could befall
Spirit of happy sort: his gestures fierce
He marked and mad demeanor, then alone,
As he supposed, all unobserved, unseen. 130
So on he fares, and to the border comes
Of Eden, where delicious Paradise,
Now nearer, crowns with her enclosure green,
As with a rural mound the champaign head
Of a steep wilderness, whose hairy sides 135

*[handwritten: Destroys his looks until He realizes it AND fakes it - it then Destroys the soul !!!]*

*[handwritten left margin: STOP]*

---

109. *remorse*: L *remordere* to bite again.
110. Cf. Isa. 5.20 "Woe unto them that call evil good, and good evil; that put darkness for light and light for darkness; that put bitter for sweet, and sweet for bitter!"
115. *changed with pale*: paled (from cherubic red).
118. *distempers*: disorders of body or mind from improper mixture of the humors. See "Physiology and Psychology," pp. 463–64.
123. *couched*: which lay hidden.
126. *Assyrian mount*: Mount Niphates (III.742).
131–71. See "Paradise," pp. 472–73, and VIII.302ff.
132. *Eden*: (a Hebrew word meaning "delight" or "place of pleasure") the region in which Paradise was located. *delicious*: L. *deliciae*, delight. *Paradise*: *paradeisos*, the Gk form of an Oriental word (Sanscrit *paradesa*; Arabic *firdaus*; Hebrew *pardes*) meaning "park" or "pleasure ground."
134. *rural*: as in open fields. *mound*: hedge or other fence bounding a field or garden; a hedgerow.

---

BOOK IV

With thicket overgrown, grotesque and wild,
Access denied; and overhead up grew
Insuperable highth of loftiest shade,
Cedar, and pine, and fir, and branching palm,
A sylvan scene, and as the ranks ascend
Shade above shade, a woody theater
Of stateliest view. Yet higher than their tops
The verdurous wall of Paradise up sprung:
Which to our general sire gave prospect large
Into his nether empire neighboring round.
And higher than that wall a circling row
Of goodliest trees loaden with fairest fruit,
Blossoms and fruits at once of golden hue
Appeared, with gay enameled colors mixed:
On which the sun more glad impressed his beams
Than in fair evening cloud, or humid bow,
When God hath show'red the earth; so lovely seemed
That landscape: and of pure now purer air
Meets his approach, and to the heart inspires
Vernal delight and joy, able to drive
All sadness but despair: now gentle gales
Fanning their odoriferous wings dispense
Native perfumes, and whisper whence they stole
Those balmy spoils. As when to them who sail
Beyond the Cape of Hope, and now are past
Mozambic, off at sea northeast winds blow
Sabean odors from the spicy shore
Of Araby the Blest, with such delay
Well pleased they slack their course, and many a league
Cheered with the graceful smell old Ocean smiles.
So entertained those odorous sweets the Fiend
Who came their bane, though with them better pleased
Than Asmodeus with the fishy fume,
That drove him, though enamored, from the spouse
Of Tobit's son, and with a vengeance sent

---

136. *grotesque*: in Milton's time a relatively new word, used in various ways. Milton "characterized by interwoven, tangled vines and branches, as in painted and carved decor. *Bosky* was a synonym.
144. *general*: L. *genus* race.
149. *enameled*: bright.
155. *drive*: force to flee.
157. *odoriferous*: L. *odorifer* bearing fragrance.
161. *Mozambic*: the channel between Madagascar and the SE coast of Africa—a trade
162. *Sabean*: of Sheba, an ancient country in south west Arabia, or *Araby the Blest* ( Yemen).
166–71. According to the Apocryphal Book of Tobit, an evil spirit, Asmodeus (Satan on their wedding nights the seven men who, in succession, had been married to Sar the eighth, Tobias, was advised by the angel Raphael to burn the heart and liver of a the bridal chamber, and the odor drove the daemon lover all the way to Egypt. Raph. saved Tobias and his wife from the designs of Satan, though he failed to save Adam a Cf. Asmadai, VI.365.

# II:

# VANGUARD

# CHAPTER 8:

# THE TURNING OF PREFECT

## Clifton Park, New York, 1997–1999

---

**A**ll supervillains have origin stories. The Vanguard is no exception. His origin story does not involve radioactive spiders, gamma-ray exposure, or, as fans of *Smallville* will find familiar, a rocket from planet Krypton crash-landing in rural Kansas. No, Vanguard's origin story is decidedly less elaborate. His story begins with constipation. If Nancy Salzman were more regular in her bowel movements, NXIVM might never have happened. Put another way: Vanguard was born because Prefect was, quite literally, full of shit.

By 1997, CBI had been officially out of business for three years, and I had moved on from Awaken. Keith and I started a new company, National Health Network. Unlike Consumers' Buyline, this one was my baby—in more ways than one.

Rusty and I brought Michael home from foster care on December 26, 1988. He was, as almost everyone remarked at the time, the greatest Christmas present we could have ever hoped for. Four days later, baby Michael was running a fever of 105, vomiting, and wracked with diarrhea. We brought him to the hospital. After pumping him with fluids and antibiotics, the doctor finally determined that our son had suffered one of the worst bouts of salmonella poisoning he'd ever seen. The foster home, apparently, was less than careful in cleaning the baby bottles.

Michael survived this initial brush with death. But there seemed to be something wrong. We just couldn't figure out what. He would have short bursts of energy, followed by long bouts of lethargy, when he could barely summon the energy to blink. I took him to every specialist in western New York, and no one came up with a credible diagnosis. Six years later, a kinesiologist finally solved the riddle: Michael had severe food allergies that contributed to deficiencies in certain key vitamins and minerals. The doctor prescribed a series of supplements and had us radically change Michael's diet. In just two weeks, he was a different child: sharp, alert, engaged.

The supplements, clearly, worked. But they were expensive—hundreds of dollars a month. It wasn't sustainable. There were other people like me, surely, who needed the supplements but couldn't afford the usurious cost. My idea was to take the CBI model, the wholesale buyers' club, and apply it to nutritional supplements. And this was how National Health Network came to be.

I was working at NHN with a woman named Sandy Padilla, who was married to Nancy Salzman's ex-husband Michael—the father to Lauren and another daughter, Michelle, the prettier and more popular of the Salzman sisters. Nancy was having problems with her digestive system, Sandy said, and wanted to come in and discuss it with me. So, we arranged what would become a fateful meeting.

Nancy was an impressive woman: smart, professional, intimidating. If a corporation were to take the form of a female human, it would look very much like Nancy Salzman. She was the type of female executive who dressed like a man: pants, button-down shirts, loafers, understated makeup. She had tremendous gravitas, so when she spoke, everyone around her seemed to listen and take heed. At the time, she, like Tony Robbins, was a master of neuro-linguistic programming, or NLP—the number two–ranked expert in the world, or so she claimed. Nowadays, life coaching is its own industry, but back then, there weren't that many people doing it. Nancy was on the vanguard. She had an impressive list of corporate clients, such as American Express and Con Edison. She was the very model of executive success.

But I didn't see her that way, at least not initially. I saw her as someone suffering from an unpleasant digestive condition. Someone who needed help. I gave her a consultation, put her on a nutrition protocol, suggested supplements that might help loosen her stubborn bowels. She took them, and they worked. She was so pleased with our interaction that she offered to help me.

"I'm having problems with my boyfriend," I told her. "His name is Keith. Keith Raniere."

"He's the genius?" Nancy said.

"That's him." And I gave her the rundown on our relationship, from the first meeting at the Rochester Holiday Inn to the move to our home in Waterford. "Keith has grandiose ideas. He just sits around thinking all the time. I'm so sick of hearing him say, 'You don't understand me, Toni; I'm *thinking*.' He lacks follow-through, because he's lazy. I mean he's *useless*, doesn't even know how to wash a dish. You should have *seen* how he lived in his old house. The place was like a garbage dump. He's keeping odd hours again and spending more time with his enablers than with me and Michael. He sleeps for most of the day and stays up late at night doing God knows what. The only time I was sure of his whereabouts was during the O.J. Simpson trial—he didn't miss a minute of that. He found it riveting."

I didn't tell her about the darker aspects of Keith Raniere, how he would demand sex every day, even if I didn't want it. I didn't tell her how if I said no, he would rape me as my son lay asleep in the next room. I didn't tell her about his justification for this: that only through "energy exchange" via intercourse could our relationship fully heal. I didn't tell her about all the times I had to spend the night barricaded in a closet, rolled in a fetal ball on a bunch of pillows, to avoid his relentless assault. That would come later, after I began having formal sessions with her.

But Nancy, apparently, had enough information for a diagnosis.

"Oh, that's easy," she said cheerfully. "He's a psychopath. I can help you with that." She suggested that we start having formal sessions.

I expected Keith to chafe at the news, but to my surprise, he was encouraging. "From what I gather, she's a very ethical person. I think she can help you." He smiled that bodhisattva smile. "Maybe I'll see her, too."

At my first session with Nancy, we reviewed what I'd already told her: Keith was a pompous narcissist, sadistic and cruel at times, useless around the house, prone to megalomania. He was unwilling to compromise, unwilling to take responsibility for his actions, unwilling to admit he was wrong. When I turned down his sexual advances, he had his way with me and then declared that my unwillingness was frigidity on my part. That everything was my fault. That *I* was the one who was inflexible, mean, prideful. That this was harder on him than it was on me.

I expected her to supply the same diagnosis—psychopath— and to help me navigate through the shoals. Instead, she smiled wanly and shook her head. "You don't know who he is," she said. "The issue here is that you were molested at a young age and you never worked through that trauma. That's why you are stuck. I can help you, Toni. I can help you be a better mother, a better businesswoman, a better partner to Keith. But you have to do exactly what I say."

I was so shocked that I didn't resist. I took it at face value that she was a licensed professional, the number two NLP expert in the world, and that after she had time to reflect on my issues, she concluded that sexual abuse was the root cause of *all* of my problems.

"Will you let me help you? You helped me so much. Will you let me return the favor?"

"Yes," I said. "Yes, of course, I will."

I was so used to Keith and "the girls" hectoring me about my childhood trauma that it never occurred to me to ask how Nancy knew that I was a survivor.

What I didn't know then, but would find out later, was that Keith had already gotten to Nancy. As a master of neuro-linguistic programming, and a brilliant and successful woman besides, she should have been able to identify his strategies and withstand his parries. She could not and did not. He was that subtle, that effective, that good. In just four meetings preceding mine, Keith completely turned her. When Nancy met Keith, she was a fully independent woman, albeit at a crossroads in her life. Two hundred forty minutes later, she was his first true acolyte—his Prefect.

This reversal is a pivotal moment in the history of NXIVM—*the* pivotal moment.

How did Keith enlist her? How did he turn a brilliant woman who was herself a master of hypnosis?

First, Keith understood that Nancy was not what she seemed. She might have looked like a model of executive success, but that was an illusion. She didn't even have a bachelor's degree in psychology; she was a nurse by training, and her first job was working in that capacity for her then husband Michael, a doctor. She misrepresented her education to her supervisor at Con Edison.

Neuro-linguistic programming sounds like a cutting-edge psychological technique. In the nineties, it was still novel enough to be regarded as legitimate. We now know that NLP is not an evidence-based practice, and thus not used by any reputable licensed psychologist or social worker. NLP has been debunked as a pseudoscience. Being the number two expert in neuro-linguistic programming is akin to being the world's second-best astrologer.

Although, as with astrology, NLP often seems to work. It sure as hell worked on me.

Her only real training was in hypnosis. As Nancy would explain in a deposition in 2000: "I have several years of Erick-sonian training...a post-graduate type of training that taught me how to use and apply brief solution-based models of ther-apy and hypnosis...I took a course at Columbia University in hypnosis...I took a series of courses that were given privately by different practitioners of the Ericksonian therapeutic method." Erickson is not to be confused with the famed psychologist Erik Erikson, who developed the theory of stages of development. Nancy was a proponent of the teachings of *Milton* Erickson, a much more unorthodox figure, who was a big believer in trance, the power of the subconscious, and posthypnotic suggestion. In the same deposition, Nancy describes him as "one of the foremost experts in clinical hypnoses [*sic*] in the world...and...the founder of brief solution-based models of therapy." *Brief therapy*, as the name implies, focuses on finding answers to problems in a relatively short period of time—unlike more conventional psychotherapy, which can last for years.

In short, she came from a long American tradition of snake-oil salesmen, peddling psychological gobbledygook and promises of quick human empowerment through self-awareness and "ethical behavior." Some of what she said and did certainly was valuable; but mostly, Nancy Salzman was a charlatan. Her collaborating with Keith Raniere was like putting two volatile chemicals together in a mad scientist's lab: the resulting compound was both explosive and dangerous.

Because she was not a real psychologist, she could not take insurance. She worked around this by having a colleague file her claims for her. Lying about her qualifications could make her lose her cushy job at Con Edison. Keith now had compromising information on her—what the Russians call *kompromat* and he called "collateral"—which he could release at any time, to cause maximum damage.

Last but not least, Nancy was in a bleak period of her life. Her marriage to Michael, the doctor, had ended years ago. Now husband number two wanted out, and for the most humiliating of reasons: he was leaving her for a man. Charming a woman with low self-esteem, in the throes of marital difficulty, was something Keith could do in his sleep (when he slept, that is).

Keith already had disciples, but his "girls" all had flaws. Pam was a space cadet, too flighty and dim to stand with him. Kristin was too headstrong and didn't bring enough expertise to the table. Karen had the brains and the capacity for evil but lacked the charisma. I was supposed to be the primary consort, Hera to his Zeus. While he had wooed me as a lover and partner, however, he had failed to convert me to the Church of Keith. But Nancy Salzman checked all of the boxes. She was smart, charismatic, capable. She knew how to manipulate people almost as well as he did. As a corporate creature, she would present as a formidable number two in his many businesses and help to expand the operation. But she was weak enough to submit to him. She could lord over everyone else while capitulating completely to Keith Raniere.

She was what Keith had been searching for all his life: she was Prefect.

And she allowed him to become Vanguard.

# CHAPTER 9:

# THE ULTIMATE LUCIFERIAN

## Clifton Park, New York, 1997–1999

K eith met Nancy in November of 1997. After watching her teach a class called "Irresistible Communications," he knew he wanted to work with her. By February 1998, they were already in business together, laying the intellectual and legal groundwork for a new company. Keith had decided that saving consumers money was too pedestrian for his singular genius—and too fraught with legal minefields. Life coaching, executive success, the sort of self-improvement hokum peddled by the likes of Tony Robbins...that was the way to go. The new business was called Executive Success Programs—ESP for short. The full name reflected the company's mission, while the abbreviation hinted at the metaphysical way the titular success would be achieved. Like CBI, ESP would be a multilevel marketing company, with students and coaches instead of members and affiliates. Instead of selling steep discounts on various consumer goods, the product was human potential coursework. Students would recruit others to take the courses, which would be followed up by still more courses, until the subject was either broke or full-on enlightened. The model looked very much like Scientology, minus the thetans and the religious tax exemptions.

Because the "technology" behind the coursework involved tweaking the way participants think, speak, write, communicate, and view the world generally, Keith and Nancy believed that they could "coach" anyone to do anything. Using their trade-secret, patent-pending techniques, they could make a ho-hum actress into an Academy Award winner, a decent equestrian into a grand prix champion, a good filmmaker into Alfred Hitchcock, a so-so runner into an Olympic athlete. In time, they would accumulate hundreds of testimonials that the ESP methods worked wonders—although they never produced an Academy Award winner, an Olympic medalist, or a director who could make a film as sublime as *Vertigo*. The only grand prix–winning equestrian in their camp, meanwhile, quit the sport soon after joining up.

But all of that was on the horizon. In 1998, ESP existed only in the minds of its diabolical co-creators. As the founder of the "philosophical movement," Keith insisted that ESP students call him "Vanguard." The name derived from one of the arcade games he used to play in the CBI offices, but it had a New Age, forward-looking resonance and the same poetical meter as "the Buddha." Nancy, as his first pupil and "chief officer," was "Prefect." Vanguard and Prefect spent the early months of 1998 developing the ESP coursework.

Keith focused on the big picture and came up with the "Rules and Rituals," guidelines for ESP sessions that would reinforce his status as the aloof holy man high atop the pyramid. A lot of this was borrowed from the martial arts community, where one bows to one's superior, where belt color designates who that superior is, where the sensei's picture appears on the wall.

The first lesson in an ESP introductory session teaches you the proper handshake. "Placement of the left hand denotes rank," the ESP materials explain: "individuals of higher rank place their left hand on the top; individuals of the same rank shake vertically; individuals of lower rank place their left hand on the bottom." This was, of course, silly. But it set the tone right away: the new student was inferior to the proctor, who was inferior to Prefect, who was inferior to Vanguard. From the first fifteen minutes of day one, Keith subtly communicated that he was the Master, and everyone else, his dutiful submissive.

The utmost priority, in a maiden ESP session, was to normalize unusual behavior. One of the first exercises in the class is to make a list of "as many organizations as you can that require their members to wear some sort of garment to meetings, or uniforms to work." This is an easy and fun assignment, and creative people wanting to show off vied to come up with more answers than their peers. Police officer, judge, fireman, EMT, doctor, scientist, baseball player, college professor on graduation day, and so forth. After this icebreaker, the ESP instructor explained that "like in martial arts where a participant's rank is signified by the color of their belt, in ESP we wear neck sashes. Each participant shall wear an official ESP sash. The sashes come in different colors signifying measurable achievement and contribution to the ESP mission. Sashes may also have a platinum edge at every level, except white. The edge signifies the participant has met additional rank requirements in a minimum amount of time. A participant must have earned the present rank with edge to be eligible for an edge with the next rank." Participants were informed that framed pictures of Vanguard and Prefect would be displayed prominently, "to show respect and to give tribute." This was compared to similar photographs of leaders hanging in "hospitals, corporations, and martial arts dojos." Then, to further normalize the habit of addressing a grown man by the name of an arcade game, the students were asked to make a list of other professional settings in which titles were used.

Participants who had paid a princely sum to take the class almost always went along with this, even if it seemed ridiculous. The "Rules and Rituals" set the tone: Vanguard and Prefect were above everyone else, their portraits on the wall, like Roman emperors put their busts on silver coins; students had to climb a ladder to achieve recognition within the group; competition, while never spoken of, was tacitly encouraged.

The rest of the class was spent learning how to properly "pay tribute" to one's superiors: removing shoes, dressing properly, bowing, standing when a ranking member entered the room, promising to keep everything strictly confidential, and reciting Keith Raniere's "Twelve-Point Mission Statement," which offers up plenty of profound-seeming affirmations, such as:

*Success is an internal state of clear, honest knowledge of what I am, my value in the world, and my responsibility for the way I react to all things.*

And:

*I am committed to be successful. I understand each of us must raise ourselves—and thereby raise all others—as all others raise us. This is interdependence.*

And:

*I pledge to ethically control as much of the money, wealth and resources of the world as possible within my success plan. I always support the ethical control of these things...A world of successful people will be a better world indeed.*

That's the eleventh of Keith's twelve points. It would make Ayn Rand swoon.

What Vanguard terms "behaving ethically" really means "living selfishly." As John Galt divided the world into looters and nonlooters, so Keith Raniere explained that people were either "parasites" or "producers." This is from the ESP module "Parasites," published in 1999:

> Stages of evolution are dependence, independence, and interdependence. They are also the basis of the producer parasite model. Human beings are born parasitic, unable to take care of themselves, depending on others for their very survival. As people grow and develop, they learn two types of strategies:
>
> **Parasite strategies**—strategies that keep people dependent on others and lower self-esteem.
>
> **Effort strategies**—strategies that create independence and raise self-esteem.
>
> Most people use both types of strategies in life, but people use mostly parasite strategies keeping them in a perpetual state of dependence and low self-esteem...

Not that there's anything inherently wrong with that, according to Vanguard:

> The term parasite is not a value judgment. Parasite does not mean a bad person, good people can be parasites,

they are people who never grew to incorporate effort strategies.

The person who has invested a few thousand dollars to take these self-improvement courses will likely identify themselves as a producer—or, more ideally, as a natural-born producer hampered by parasitic tendencies. They will question their self-esteem and decide that, while not low exactly, it could certainly be higher. Who doesn't want to incorporate more *effort strategies*? Who wants to be regarded as a lazy parasite?

*Success in my own right is my earned success. True success cannot be stolen, copied, or received by happenstance. I will not masquerade as successful by these methods or any other, I will earn my success.*

Keith's genius solution was the same as John Galt's: to gather together the producers and cast off the parasites. ESP created an artificial world, full of New Age jargon and tributes to Vanguard. But living ethically—at least, the Raniere brand of ethics—wasn't as easy outside the bubble, with non-Espians. With muggles. With looters. With parasites. With suppressives—another ESP term, borrowed from the Scientologists. So Keith's disciples circled the wagons and, insofar as it was possible, remained aloof. Outsiders were greeted with suspicion—family members were no exception—and the group became more and more insular, incestuous, and inbred. To doubt Vanguard was regarded as apostasy.

There's a word for what this looked like to an objective observer, and even in the original ESP modules, Keith and Nancy foresaw its possible employment to describe their fledgling organization. The module warns that detractors may "holler 'CULT'" when they observe ESP in action. "This is a label," they explain, "that conveys no meaning but devalues the group. It is designed to keep people away from the group without saying what is wrong with it." When this happens, they advise the student to respond, "What specifically makes the group a cult?" or "What do you mean by cult?" or "What do they do that's wrong?" The key point to make, they suggest, is that according to the dictionary definition of the word, a cult must involve religious beliefs and rituals. ESP was not a religion, so how could it be a cult?

As an expert in neuro-linguistic programming, Nancy worked on the psychological aspects of the modules. She needed a guinea pig, to figure out what worked and what didn't. Unbeknownst to me, I was that guinea pig.

It began with individual sessions. Hours and hours of sessions, seven days a week, sometimes more than one session a day, just me and Nancy. The most depressed, suicidal person in the world would not require as much one-on-one attention, but she gave it to me. The time I spent in those sessions almost rivaled the time I spent working or sleeping.

She never called it "therapy," but that's what it felt like. "Coaches" don't encourage their clients to reveal their deepest, darkest secrets, but that's what Nancy did. She was so smart, so giving, so seemingly sincere in her desire to help. I loved Nancy. I trusted her. I never would have believed that she was capable of causing such damage. "Now that you've told me that," she would often remark at the end of a particularly intense session, "don't you feel better?"

Sometimes I felt better; sometimes I didn't. I never got

the sense that the simple disclosure of a secret caused me to heal from my trauma. A licensed mental health professional would never have done what Nancy, who was not licensed, had done. This is an important distinction to make. Mental health professionals have to pass a rigorous licensure process because they deal with trauma. Trauma is like nuclear power—it has to be handled with the utmost care, or it can be explosively dangerous. L. Ron Hubbard, the founder of Scientology, led a lifelong crusade against psychiatry because he knew that actual medical professionals would recognize the danger in his amateurish methods. "Auditing," as Hubbard termed it, unearths deep-seated trauma and then weaponizes that trauma against the traumatized person, with unpredictable results.

In the winter of 1998, I participated in a class Nancy taught called "Irresistible Communications." I took the class because I was working with children at the time, and Nancy told me the class would help me communicate better with kids with ADHD. For the twenty participants, it was intense. Over the course of eight months, we met sixteen times, over various weekends, from 9:30 to 5:30 Saturday *and* Sunday. Nancy taught us how to break down and analyze how people communicate. We spent time studying body language, tone of speech, anchoring techniques, nonverbal communication, and other material central to neurolinguistic programming. It was fascinating stuff, I really enjoyed it, and Nancy was an excellent teacher. On September 13, I was awarded a certificate of completion and named a practitioner of neuro-linguistic programming by the International Center for Change, Inc.

I was proud of the certification. I framed it and hung it in my office.

But change was afoot at the International Center for Change, apparently. "This is the last class I'll ever teach in Irresistible Communications," Nancy announced after handing out the certificates. "Keith and I have developed something else. Something new. Something better."

The Executive Success Programs pilot program was held on October 8, 9, 10, 12, 15, 19, 20, 22, 24, and 29 and November 3, 5, 7, 12, and 17, 1998. Some modules were taught by Prefect, some by Vanguard himself. Among the participants were Pam Cafritz, Dawn Morrison, Kristin Keeffe, Lauren Salzman, and me. Two of these first students—Pam and Barb Jeske, who'd worked for Keith at CBI—would eventually hold the prestigious Purple Sash, ranked just below the founder and his pupil.

The "girls" were way into it. Pam, in particular, treated Keith like he was the Second Coming. I was more skeptical—and with good reason. Most of the stuff I'd learned in "Irresistible Communications" that was so useful and so fascinating was stripped from the curriculum. This was something else entirely. At one lecture, Keith was talking about sexual abuse. "What is molestation and what is not molestation?" he asked, glaring in my direction until he caught my eye. I was horrified that he brought the topic up at all, but what he said next made my blood run cold. "If a mother in an African tribe performs fellatio on a baby, is she a *bad* mother because she is molesting him? Or is she a *good* mother because she has soothed her child?"

I realized, to my horror, that Keith and Nancy had used things I'd discussed in my private sessions to form the curriculum.

Normalizing sexual molestation proved to be a long-running

ESP theme. Years later, Nancy would be recorded lecturing this to a class of students:

If you look at sexual abuse, there are different ways to determine if it's abuse. One of them is the age of consent... In some states in the United States the age of consent is 17, in some parts of the world the age of consent is 12... so what's abuse in one area is not abuse in another.

But what is sexual abuse really? Is the person a child, or is the person adult-like? Does the person have a certain type of understanding or cognition of morality to make such a choice? In other words, when you are talking to a 12-year-old, does the 12-year-old understand the choice she is actually making? That determines whether it is abuse or not. Because that choice has effects potentially on her physically, but also effects in society later.

Often when you counsel people who are children of what you might call abuse, some little children are perfectly happy with it until they find out what happens later in life. In other words, at the time, they didn't know it was bad. They didn't know anything about it was bad. Later, they grow up, and they find out that it was actually something that was bad. In that case is it more society that's abusing them? Because society says it's bad, but they didn't know it was bad, so society is abusing them. It's... more society abusing them than the adult, because they didn't know it was bad, but society tells them it's bad before they're bad. Something bad was done to them. So was it the adult or was it society? Because in some societies in the past, like in Rome, standards were completely different. But we are not in Rome.

Instead of the workshops on body language and nonverbal communication, the class broke into small groups, where the participants were encouraged to reveal their deepest, darkest secrets—just as Nancy had done with me. I watched, stunned, as the other participants, Pam and Karen and Kristin and a dozen or so others, cheerfully revealed all to Prefect and Vanguard—the keepers of the secrets.

Never mind that this was a recipe for post-traumatic disaster. Furthermore, her skills lay in something much more esoteric. Whether through careful study and lab work, arcane knowledge of the black arts, or a psionic superpower of the kind practiced by villains on *Smallville*, Nancy was masterful at hypnosis. Her powers were uncanny. Maybe they didn't work on some people, but for me, she was a veritable witch. What she did with me, and to me, in those months under her "care" formed the basis for what she would do with, and to, hundreds of other innocents in the years to come. That was what ESP was all about.

Later, after I left Keith, I learned that one of the modules was directly based on my leaving him. The "Fall" module presents Lucifer in the guise of a beautiful woman who has rejected the teachings of Vanguard. Lucifer is "prideful" and not "steadfast," and she fails her "test." The training materials included passages from *Paradise Lost* mirroring ones that Keith had sent in his last meaningful letter to me, which highlighted "false independence," "tribute," "pride," "self-esteem," and "theft." The Fallen Angel "commits to evil for protection" and this "destroys the soul!!!" He thought so highly of his "technology" that he filed a US trade patent application for his tactic of "Rehabilitating a Luciferian." In the "Fall" module, Vanguard teaches that Toni Natalie is the first suppressive and the ultimate Luciferian. All ESP students knew me by name.

When I first spoke to the actress Sarah Edmondson, a long-time Nxian, after she left the group, she said, "I can't believe I'm actually talking to you."

"Why?"

"Because I was taught that you were the devil."

# CHAPTER 10:

# "EAT YOUR PRIDE"

## Clifton Park, New York, March–April 1999

After a promising start, National Health Network was showing signs of trouble. We had three locations—the flagship, in Clifton Park, which also contained a vegetarian restaurant called A Place of Creations Café, and satellite stores in Scotia, New York, and Ames, Iowa—all of them doing well. We planned to open a fourth location in Saratoga Springs, an upscale community known for its yearly thoroughbred horse race. Expansion is tricky. Having more than one location can generate more revenue and also save on expenses, because of increased purchasing power. But the front-end costs are considerable. In the event of a catastrophe, we might be spread too thin.

And that's what came to pass. We recruited an entrepreneurial couple to manage the Saratoga location, which would include a second Place of Creations Café. I found and leased the space—and Keith and Nancy pressured me into putting my name on the lease. When the couple came to sign the documents, to make the partnership official, they threw a monkey wrench in the plan.

"We looked you up," the man said to Keith, "and there's no way in hell we're going into business with you."

"What do you mean?" Nancy asked indignantly.

The man laughed. "You're a snake-oil salesman who hides behind women." He tossed the keys at Keith. "Go fuck yourself."

The couple would be rewarded for their due diligence. But me? I was stuck. I'd already signed the lease. I was responsible for those payments. I had no choice but to operate the Saratoga location myself. And I ran into pitfalls. First, because I used my own contractors rather than the ones suggested by the Saratoga old boys' network, everything I tried to do was met with delay and added expense. I was also having problems with the leasing company that was supposed to provide used restaurant equipment. When we went to pick up the equipment, it wasn't there; they wanted us instead to buy newer, pricier equipment.

And Keith and Nancy were impossible to work with. For all his talk of ethics, Keith refused to do things on the up-and-up. He'd read a book called *IRS Humbug*, a handbook for how to legally evade taxes, and he did everything he could to throw the tax man off his scent. He insisted that I pay Barbara Jeske, a holdover from the CBI days who was now one of my employees at National Health, her commissions under the table. I refused; I was not going to pay out $4,000 without issuing a 1099. But I couldn't issue a 1099 without Barbara providing her social security number, which she refused to do. I owed her money, but she gave me no legal way to make good.

With the opening more expensive than anticipated, and more

money going out than coming in, we were suddenly tens of thousands of dollars in the red. I had nowhere else to turn, and Keith did not have the money to give me. So he sent Nancy to bail me out.

"Let me lend you the money," she said. At the time, Nancy was my de facto therapist, my teacher, and, I believed, a close friend. I trusted her. But Prefect wasn't about to give me what I needed without exacting her pound of flesh.

"I'm happy to help you," she said. "But if I do, you have to promise to run the company in a manner consistent with Keith's teachings and business philosophies."

What did that even mean? That I was supposed to read *IRS Humbug*? It was like agreeing to "be cool." It was vague enough to not be legally binding, and therefore impossible to enforce.

"Fine," I said. "Done."

"Also: we need to increase our sessions. I sense so much anger and hostility coming from you, and I want to help you overcome that. I'm now investing my own money in your company, and I want to do what I can to make sure I recoup that investment. I'm your friend, Toni. Let me do that for you."

At the time, I was already spending so many hours in sessions with Nancy that my time with Michael, my work, and sleep, had started to suffer. But I consented.

"Okay, sure. Whatever you want."

True to her word, Nancy issued a check to the company. She paid Barbara Jeske $4,000 and she gave me a check, made out to National Health Network, for the balance: $46,000.

"And, Toni?"

"Yes?"

"You need to start calling him Vanguard."

Vanguard. Like he was a hunky member of the Justice League and not a megalomaniacal con man who looked like Rick Moranis.

I laughed in her face.

"Fuck that," I said. "I'm *never* calling him that."

Although Keith and I nominally lived in the same house, we were spending less and less time together. He continued to be prone to violent outbursts, and to rape me when I did not consent to have sex with him, but mercifully, these episodes occurred with less frequency. I began to suspect that he was investing his considerable carnal energies elsewhere, although I wasn't sure who his new lover might be. Karen was homely, Kristin was a kid, Barb Jeske was a lesbian (or so I'd been told), Pam was more like his little sister, and Nancy was his business partner. I couldn't imagine him wanting to sleep with any of them. One day, Keith and Pam came to the café laughing hysterically about a private joke; they laughed so hard, tears streamed down both of their faces. When I asked what was so funny, Pam explained that there was a new ESP recruit whom Keith was training to be a marathon runner. She'd been running in tight white clothes, and when she sweated, they could see her pubic hair and her nipples through the thin fabric. For some reason, this was riotously funny to them. This struck me as very odd, and disturbed me at the same time, as the marathon runner was a young high school girl.

When he did come home, he was as volatile as ever. The situation was not safe—not for me, and certainly not for Michael. Above all, I was going to protect my son. I could not risk anything bad happening to him. It broke my heart, but I sent him back to Rochester, to stay with Rusty and his mother—where the escalating situation with Keith was less likely to harm him.

It was supposed to be temporary. I figured he'd be back in a month or two, at worst.

But Michael never moved back.

He stayed with Rusty until he graduated from high school.

That I allowed myself to be separated from my child, far and away the most important person in my life, shows just how afraid I was of Keith Raniere.

We finally broke up because of a sweater. This was in early April of 1999. It may well have been on April Fool's Day.

When I left for work that morning, Keith was still in bed. He'd been up late the night before doing God knows what (or whom). Just before I left, I put a load of laundry in the washing machine. I called him at lunch.

"Can you please rotate the laundry?"

He reacted like I was speaking Greek. "*Rotate* the laundry?"

"Take the clothes out of the washing machine, put them in the dryer, throw in a few dryer sheets, turn the dryer on."

"Okay."

"One thing: my sweater is in the wash, the black wool one. You can't put that in the dryer or it will shrink."

He consented to help me, which was miracle enough, and I hung up the phone. When I got home, the clothes had made it into the dryer. *All* of them, including my black wool sweater, which was now too small for my dog to wear.

"Keith," I said, holding up the shrunken garment. "What the hell?"

He looked up from his dog-eared copy of *Dianetics*. "What?"

"Why did you put my sweater in the dryer?"

"You told me to."

"No, Keith. No, I didn't."

And the Little Prince lost his shit. He cornered me in the laundry room, screaming, spit flying from the corners of his mouth, like a rabid dog. "You are wrong, Toni. As usual. You don't know *what* you said. I'm the Smartest Man in the World! I have a 240 IQ! Do you really think that *you're* right, and *I'm* wrong? Tell me you're wrong. Do it. Tell me you're wrong."

"No."

"Say it."

"No."

"Say you're wrong."

"Fuck you."

For a minute I thought he was going to hit me, but he fought off that impulse. Instead, he stormed out of the house, like a hurricane veering back out to sea.

He didn't come back. Instead, he sent Kristin and Pam to the house, to entice me to apologize and beg for reinstatement. I refused. After about four days, I came home from work to find that most of his stuff had been removed from the house.

*Good*, I thought. I told my mom. I told my brother. They were delighted. We'd broken up, like a normal couple.

But Keith doesn't just *leave*.

Once it became clear that I was resolute in my decision to not apologize and admit wrongdoing, I was subjected to a barrage of gaslighting letters: from Kristin, from Pam, from Nancy, from Keith. Although the voices were different, the content was all more or less the same. It was like he'd given them a writing assignment, and they'd all put their individual spin on his instructions.

I was prideful because I left Keith; I was arrogant because I falsely believed that I knew better than Keith; I was doomed to live a miserable life because I would not recant; but they knew I had it in me to improve, if only I would swallow my pride, renounce my bad decision, and return to the flock.

There were cultural references in each letter. Nancy wrote about *The Matrix*, then still in theaters—a dystopian film about an alternative reality that would give the men's rights "red pill" movement its name:

> *Over the weekend I went to see a new movie, Matrix. I strongly suggest you go see it. It's about the future and what it would be like if everyone was in some sort of matrix where they thought the world was one way when in fact it was another. What if everyone woke up one day and realized the world wasn't the way we thought but another way entirely?... in this movie, to leave the matrix and enter the real world you have to make a decision because there's no going back. Once your eyes are opened you can't close them again. There is one character [who] wants to leave because the real world is too difficult. He wants to go back to the matrix and he asks to have his memory changed so he can't remember anything about the truth... It made me think of you. What would it be like to go back to a non-spiritual, non-caring, non-ethical, non-critical thinking world after living with Keith for all these years?*

Pam cited my "Dagny drive and competence," alluding to the protagonist of *Atlas Shrugged*.

And big-brained Keith compared himself to "George (from Sunday in the Park)" and me to his "Dulcinea," urging me to "rent the video <u>Man of La Mancha</u> to understand," once again ripping my lack of formal education. To further rub it in, he included annotated pages from *Paradise Lost*, the John Milton epic poem about the battle between God and Satan, and the fall of mankind. "In our case," Keith wrote, "I believe you have behaved in a way that has wronged me for a long time and on many levels. I can no longer support that behavior. I am therefore withdrawing all support. Please read the enclosed <u>Paradise Lost</u> excerpt: It precisely details, in metaphor, the psychology of your situation—its [*sic*] so accurate and predictive its [*sic*] scary!" The text was from the beginning of book 4, when Lucifer wistfully recalls his decision to stand up to God.

"False independence," Keith scrawled in the margins. "Tribute. Pride. Given too much. How Lucifer justifies his wrong-doing. Can't bear telling his team he's wrong. Self-esteem and theft. Scared to mess up again, doesn't trust himself. Mess up more a second time. Commits to evil for protection. Stupid/weak." And the kicker: "Destroys his looks until he realizes it and fakes it— it then destroys his soul!!!" The one Milton passage marked with an exclamation point—so obvious, even to a high school dropout, that he didn't think it needed his dumbed-down genius annotation—went like this:

> *I disdained subjection, and thought one step higher*
> *Would set me highest, and in a moment quit*
> *The debt immense of endless gratitude,*
> *So burdensome still paying, still to owe;*
> *Forgetful what from him I still received,*
> *And understood not that a grateful mind*
> *By owing owes not, but still pays, at once*
> *Indebted and discharged; what burden then?*

In other words, I owed him everything, and because I spurned him, I'd never get over my sin. I was doomed.

Implicit in his choice of text: I was Lucifer, and he, Keith Raniere, was God.

All the letters recalled some fond reminiscences, complimenting me in some way or other. Pam: "I have always enjoyed your company and appreciated your sense of humor." Kristin: "When we first met, there was no question that I would do anything to help you. Right out of the gate I had an unfailing—sometimes BLIND—belief in your goodness." Even Nancy, colder than the others, had this to say: "I remember when I first met you, what rough shape I was in and that you always fed me and let Keith take care of me." And Keith himself proclaimed my "highest values" to be "Honesty, Intelligence, True Love, Connection, Ability, Strength, Power, Education, Passion, Charisma."

After the friendly preamble, however, the letters became epistolary guilt trips. Keith and his minions joined forces to batter me. Together, the letters comprised a coordinated attack, designed to cause maximum damage, to hit me where it hurt the most, at the moment when I was weakest.

Kristin talked about the time she spent with my son and brought up my issues with Rusty:

*On sight I felt unconditional love and connection with him...He was so cute. You used to tell people, "He thinks Kristin is a 4 yr. Old with car keys!"*

*I never thought twice about the hour and forty-five minute drive, both ways, to take him to Rusty at the Thruway. You were going through a difficult time, and I was there for support...You would cry and cry about how awful Rusty was. Your terrible marriage, the hurtful things he said to Michael about you and Keith. Rusty's mother! The stench she gave off, her low class mentality, and the way Rusty let her control and RUIN his businesses... Now you are doing the same things you despised or were so critical of.*

Pam, the daughter of a Republican blue-blood Washington power couple, compared me unfavorably to Bill and Hillary:

*You wanted me to recognize how hard you've been working. The only way I could have really aided the situation was to get you some money to survive (or inspire you to listen to Keith so you could work smarter). And I gladly went to bat for you... I tried to get a 50,000 dollar loan from my Father. I'm glad my Mother and Father did not experience your theft... Although I have differences with my family, they do not understand your behavior after the friendship we've had. Even the Clinton's have shown more loyalty to their friends who have supported them in hard times.*

Nancy summarized the supposed sacrifices the "girls" had made on my behalf, laying the guilt on thick:

*As far as I can see you had a life where you had people who loved you for you and asked for nothing in return. Keith was dedicated enough to you to sacrifice his relationship with you to help you grow personally, this is true giving, when one gives us what we need not what we want. What happens to a child who is always given what they want without regard for how it will effect [sic] them in the future? Who else in your life has ever offered you such a gift? Pam worked in your store for months with no pay and did so many, many other things for you throughout the years expecting nothing in return. Kristin took care of your child. I did all the things I did. None of us asked for anything in return.*

*This decision cuts off people in your life who truly loved you and wanted nothing in return.*

The circumstances of my escape were presented in inaccurate terms. Here is Keith's version:

*Five or so years ago you were given the choice to do one of 2 things: 1. What was right and grow (eat your pride) or 2. Fall in bed with Mark G. and try to steal the Awaken business. You chose 2. incorrectly... You finally realized it was better to be true to your non-prideful self (your soul) and came back. You never really said you were sorry because you had too much pride. You said that if you swallowed your pride you would lose your mind and your self. This was/is untrue. You are not your pride... Had you swallowed your pride and grown-up it would not have had to come to this. But you put it off for years (think of how much happiness was missed over the last 5 years because of pride) and now we have the same weak, bad decision again... You were fighting to keep your pride at the expense of your ethics...*

The letters came one after another, and they had the desired effect: they made me question my own sanity. At the end of her letter, Pam had the gall to write, "You sound crazy. You look crazy. You need to get professional help."

Such is the essence of gaslighting. The truth is not omitted as much as inverted. How could I steal from them? (I did not steal from them.) How could I not be ethical? (They were very fond of that word, *ethical*, even as they behaved abominably.) Didn't I realize I'd screwed up? (I hadn't.) Surely life would be better if I came back to Keith. (Not so much.)

In time, and with help from my friends, my brother, and my

parents, I was able to banish from my mind Keith's distorted version of events. After all, what did it matter what they thought or said? I had the truth on my side.

But I couldn't dismiss all of it. I knew Keith was vengeful. I knew what he was capable of. One line in his letter terrified me: "If you look at how your decision will affect everything— yourself, business, family, children...even your dogs...you will not want to face the things that will happen. Please change your decision, as of now you still can."

How could that be read as anything other than a threat?

When I got home from work one day, I found that someone had broken into the house, taken the rest of Keith's things, and made off with some of my jewelry and clothes. The bed, which I made every morning without fail, was a mess, the covers strewn.

The tacit message was clear: *Wherever you go, we can get to you. You're not safe anywhere.*

I didn't see Keith for three weeks. I'm sure he thought that depriving me of the privilege of his genius company would be so much torment that I would come running back. When this tactic failed, he appeared in the National Health Network office. His eyes, as bright and hypnotic as ever, were shooting daggers at me.

"The next time I see you," he told me ominously, "you will be dead or in jail."

He was half right.

I would not lay eyes on Keith Raniere again until his arraignment on Friday, April 13, 2018—but it would be Keith, and not me, who was in custody.

# CHAPTER 11:

# HELTER SKELTER

## Clifton Park, New York, April–October 1999

---

**B**arb Jeske was from Michigan but would have looked right at home in some farm town thirty miles from Krakow. She was fair-skinned and blond, impressive, with Slavic features: broad forehead and nose; small, narrow eyes; big head. Inside that big head was a big brain. Barb was smart, an expert in menopausal health. The first time we met, Keith told me she was gay, and I had no reason to doubt him, as she was always in the company of either women or dogs.

As I mentioned earlier, Barb cut her teeth at CBI and followed us to National Health Network. She was a producer, a hard worker, a nice enough person, and a dyed-in-the-wool Keith Raniere true believer. She thought Keith could walk on water and heal the lepers. It's no wonder that she wound up being one of only two individuals to hold the Purple Sash, ESP's highest rank. Aside from being a stickler about not violating US tax law when doling out her commission check, I had done no wrong to Barb Jeske. To the contrary, I had given her a job at NHN when CBI shut down. But in the months that followed my leaving, she was one of the primary agents Keith employed to make my life a living hell.

At the end of April 1999, Barb sent out a one-page letter to everyone on the National Health Network mailing list, imploring them to repudiate me:

*Dear Friend,*

*I know you know my highest priority in life is that my actions be ethical and moral, and that the actions of whatever I support be the same. It is one of the reasons working with National Health Network has been such a source of joy for me. The concept and the company were designed with unimpeachable ethics and have been a great value exchange for everyone involved. The philosophical founder of NHN, Keith Raniere, is an individual I have the utmost respect for because of his track record as an ethical business-man and human being.*

Barb informed our members that, although Keith "designed" the company, he did not have an ownership stake. "Ms. Toni Natalie is sole owner of the corporations."

*It is my belief and experience that recent actions taken by Ms. Natalie have been inappropriate both ethically and legally. She has not followed the philosophy of Mr. Raniere and has separated herself and the corporations from him… The monumental contri-butions of Keith Raniere, [NHN and its sister companies] having been his concepts and designs, were given with ethical agreements and conditions that had to be met. They have been egregiously broken by Ms. Natalie...For these reasons I am withdrawing my support from NHN...I cannot in good conscience support anything that is unethical...It is my belief that most of us would like to live in a world where we feel safe in the knowledge that our ethics and the ethics of others support life and the building of value—not the destruction of them.*

Barb then directed the members to cancel their memberships and join up with a new concern, called—with no apparent irony—the Ethical Coalition.

Although the letter was clearly the work of a raving lunatic, it still freaked me out when I discovered how widely it was disseminated. I was eager to send out my own letter, to correct the many factual inaccuracies in Ethical Barb's transmission. After all, we were spread thin. My business was in a precarious place, with the new location in Saratoga Springs barely hanging on. I just wanted this to be over so I could bring Michael home. The last thing I needed was a mass exodus.

When I got to the office and turned on the computer, I discovered, to my horror, that the hard drives were corrupted. I couldn't access any of the data. All the addresses of all of our members and all of our customers, all of the invoices and accounts payable information, everything—it was all gone, wiped clean.

There was no question in my mind who was responsible for the corporate sabotage. He may not have done the dirty work himself, he never did, but I suspected that, despite his "track record as an ethical businessman and human being," this was the work of Keith Raniere.

Although he hadn't used it in weeks, Keith kept a little office at NHN, right next to mine. Rage coursed through me as I marched into that little room. He'd already taken away most of his stuff, but not everything. There were whiteboards bolted to every wall, all full of mathematical equations and New Age mumbo jumbo. I took a bottle of 409 and some paper towels and wiped them all clean, as he had done with our hard drives. I scrubbed so hard on the whiteboards that my wrist ached. On his desk was a rain stick and a little snow globe with a figurine of the Little Prince inside. I took the rain stick and smashed that snow globe to bits. Once the glass shell had shattered, its shards flying all over creation, I teed up the Little Prince and knocked him off his pedestal, clear across the room. Then I stomped on him.

Then I burst into tears.

Later, during the criminal investigation, the police marveled at the technological savvy of the saboteur. "It's a self-replicating virus," they said. "If you do anything to try and delete it, it automatically makes a copy of itself. We've never seen *that* before."

The "Dear Friend" letter and the self-replicating virus were the shot and the chaser. Together, they killed me.

I was both surprised and terrified that Keith could possibly wipe out a company Nancy had just loaned $50K, knowing they'd never see that money again. He was willing to lose that much money to ruin me—and he would make sure I couldn't walk away from or pay back my obligations so easily. Nancy Salzman, the bad cop to Vanguard's good cop, made this clear in a fax she sent to my brother on April 24, 1999: "Keep in mind, I should have higher priority than the landlord or other creditors. I have real cash stolen. If I am not satisfied, or any assets are given to another creditor before I am happy, I will take very decisive action."

And then the kicker: "I am not Keith, I will not walk away just like that."

This was laughable. For one thing, Nancy *was* Keith, for all intents and purposes.

And it was Keith, not Nancy, who refused to walk away.

One of the enduring NXIVM myths held that Vanguard would one day impregnate one of his concubines, giving her the greatest gift he could possibly bestow: his child. Obviously, the spawn of the Smartest Man in the World and his concubine of choice was destined for greatness. Marked from conception as the Chosen One, like Jesus or Harry Potter—both of whom Keith vaguely resembled—the baby would grow up to become the Child Who Would Save the World.

As far as I know, this myth originated with me, and with the events that happened in the aftermath of my break with Keith Raniere. After I left, Kristin Keeffe patrolled the sidewalks outside A Place of Creations Café and declaimed to all of Saratoga Springs that I, Toni Natalie, was the lucky Madonna who would bear this Christ child. She would spend five or six hours a day, every day, accosting anyone who was about to walk into the place. She would explain that I was Satan, that I was a thief, and, more crazily, that I was forsaking my destiny to bear Keith's child—the Child Who Would Save the World.

It was true that Keith and I had discussed having children. This was one of the many empty promises he made: that he would put his brilliant mind to work figuring out how to coax my unwilling body into going to term with a child. I wanted more children. I would have had four if I could have and would have done almost anything to have just one more, to give Michael a sibling. Keith wanted me to be the mother of his child, he said so many times, because he prized me more than anyone. But this never came to pass. (Looking back, I'm thankful that I had a miscarriage.) He never told me that our baby would be the Chosen One. Kristin was the progenitor of that myth, on the sidewalk outside my restaurant.

The police knew this was happening, but there was not much they could do about it. It's legal to walk down a public sidewalk, and the stuff that she was saying, while wackadoodle, was not threatening. "There's nothing we can do," one officer told me, shaking his head. He was as frustrated as I was. "They know just where to draw the line."

When Kristin finally gave up, Pam Cafritz was sent to A Place of Creations Café. She was still furious at me. She couldn't comprehend how I could have left Keith Raniere—or, rather, how I could have allowed him to stay gone. In her mind, I had fallen, like Satan in *Paradise Lost*. I had become the devil incarnate.

The tables in the restaurant were lined with plain white paper, with a jar of crayons and colored pencils by the salt and pepper shakers. Customers would draw while they waited for their dishes, and if the drawings were good, we hung them up on the wall. Pam was an amazing artist, and she was a frequent guest at the restaurant, so her drawings were prominently displayed.

"I'm here for my artwork," she told me. I watched dumbfounded as she found each piece of hers and removed it from the wall—in some cases completely ripping the paper and ruining the drawing. She was causing a scene, and it brought the head chef, Scott, out of the kitchen. He was protective of me. He stood with his arms crossed, glaring at the psycho ripping papers off the wall.

"Pam," I said, "why are you doing this? Why can't you just let it be?"

"You stole from Keith," she said, her voice shaking. "It's right there in the mission statement. 'Successful people do not steal, and they have no desire or need to steal.' How many times did you repeat it? And you go ahead and steal from Keith anyway."

"Pam, that's not what happened."

"I don't believe a word you say," she snapped. "You're the devil. You're Lucifer—the ultimate suppressive."

I glared at her. "That's ridiculous."

Scott took a step forward, but I shook my head no.

"I mean it, Tink." That was her pet name for me—Tink, like Tinker Bell. She'd been calling me that since I wore a Tinker Bell costume to the CBI Halloween party six years ago. "You're dead to me." And she spun around, her Crystal Gale hair flowing behind her, and stormed out of the restaurant. She meant it, too. I never saw her again.

I wasn't safe at home, either. They knew I spent most of my time at work, and they used the opportunity to break into my house and channel the Manson family. I believe that Barb Jeske was the principal culprit here, but it might have been any of the "girls." Someone would break into my home, muss my bed, open the cabinets in the kitchen, rearrange the artwork on the wall, and make off with some of my clothes. This happened more than a dozen times and was extremely terrifying. I did not feel safe in my own home. I'd pack up my dogs and go to a hotel.

Barb also stole my mail. Repeatedly, every day. She would come to the mailbox on Monday, take the mail, steam open the envelopes, photocopy the bills and other personal information, reseal the envelopes, and return the mail on Tuesday, when she'd take away the new mail for inspection. She did this all summer.

This was 1999, before the dawn of online banking. All my bills arrived in the mail, and I paid all my bills by check. Thus Keith and his lackeys were able to screw with my already pre-carious finances. They had my answering service turned off. They called the cable company and canceled the service. They had my phone shut off so many times that the phone company issued me a special PIN code, known only to me, that was required before any changes could be made. They threw away the utility bill, hoping to have my electricity turned off, and when that didn't work, they called to shut it down. They called my son's school and told them that he was withdrawing.

I didn't realize they were doing this. Not at first. The answering service would be off, and I couldn't figure out why. Then the same thing would happen with the cable, the credit cards, the insurance policies. It was only when a vigilant neighbor spotted Barb Jeske tampering with my mail—and we subsequently captured her doing so on video—that I could identify the intruder, file a police report, and press charges. Barb was arrested, and a restraining order was issued against her.

Again: Barb was a smart, capable woman. She really did believe what she wrote in that letter to the National Health Network customers—that she was an ethical person, committed to always acting in an ethical manner. She'd taken all the ESP classes and memorized Keith's "Twelve-Point Mission Statement," so she knew how to put this philosophy into practice. And to this otherwise smart, capable woman, it was *ethically right* to tamper with my mail, because that's what Vanguard wanted her to do. It was all to teach me a lesson, you see. That's what Keith told her. And he didn't say it in the manner of a Mafia don with a toothpick in his mouth: "Let's teach her a lesson." His manner was beatific, like a holy man, and he made it seem like she was *doing me a favor* by shutting off my electricity and screwing with my child's education. And Barb Jeske believed this so completely and utterly that she was happy to get arrested to make his wishes manifest.

Even in 1999, there was no shortage of "girls" like Barb Jeske, eager to obey Vanguard's every command. As ESP/NXIVM grew, so did the number of Keith's loyal kamikaze soldiers. His "girls" stole mail and broke into houses and forged documents and circumvented immigration laws and posed nude for his pleasure and, eventually, allowed themselves to be clumsily branded with a cautery pen.

Because she doesn't factor much into the story going forward, I want to tell what became of Barb Jeske.

She gave thirty-plus years of her life to Vanguard. During those three decades, she occasionally ran afoul of both the lawman and the tax man. At Vanguard's suggestion, she became a renunciate—a cloistered NXIVM nun. In 2012, she began to have terrible physical symptoms, which Keith assured her were carpal tunnel syndrome and could safely be ignored. A year later, she was diagnosed with brain cancer. It was stage IV, a death sentence.

With months to live, she contacted her sister Cindy, told her that she wanted out of NXIVM.

"Then leave," said Cindy, who knew. "I'll help you leave."

But Barb couldn't escape. She was owed a considerable amount of money, and the money was stashed in Mexico, where she couldn't touch it. That money comprised her life savings, which she'd entrusted to Keith Raniere.

She would never see a dime of it, and neither would her next of kin.

Barb was moved to hospice in the late summer of 2014, which coincided with Vanguard Week—the ten-day saturnalia given at the end of each summer in honor of Vanguard's birthday on August 26. Because Cindy lived in Florida, Nancy and Keith were making the command medical decisions at Albany Medical. They wanted Barb to attend V-Week.

"Are you crazy?" Cindy said. "She's dying. Let her die in peace."

"But she holds a Purple Sash! The highest rank possible! It would be such an honor for her to be there, at her last Vanguard Week."

"No!"

When Barbara Jeske finally passed on September 3, 2014, Keith and Nancy asked Cindy if they could have the body. Vanguard wanted to employ cryogenic techniques to preserve it, in case a cure for cancer was someday found. Cindy told them to screw off.

They said, "What about the head? Can we keep that?"

# CHAPTER 12:

# THE BOOGEYMAN

## Saratoga Springs, New York, 1999

I plucked Scott Foley from the reject pile. We were looking for a head chef for A Place of Creations Café in Saratoga. My friend Pammy, the restaurant manager, who was helping me with the search, had discarded Scott's résumé. Something about it caught my eye.

"How about him?"

He came for an interview. He was a man's man, ruggedly handsome, the sort of guy you'd find grilling porterhouse steaks on the Fourth of July—not at all what you'd picture a chef at a vegetarian restaurant to look like. He was thirty years old, ten years younger than I. He was unhappy at his job, wanted a new one. He was funny and down-to-earth. No drama: the antidote to what was swirling around the rest of my life. We asked him to cook us something, show off his culinary chops.

"What would you like?"

"Steak au poivre," I said. "But vegetarian."

This was a tall order, but Scott nodded, strode into the kitchen like a commander boarding his new vessel, and whipped up exactly what I'd asked for. It was delicious. One of the best dishes I'd ever had.

As he walked out the front door, Pammy grinned, gesturing at his ass. "Boss, can we keep him?" she said.

We kept him.

Due to Scott's incomparable cooking and indomitable work ethic, A Place for Creations Café became a place to be. Not even a lunatic on the sidewalk out front, raving about the Chosen One, could keep hungry foodies away. Scott would cook these amazing vegetarian dishes, then go out to the back lot, sit in the bed of his pickup, and eat Big Macs between puffs of Marlboro Reds.

Scott was protective of me. When Pam Cafritz came by that day to remove her "artwork," he stood between me and Pam like a Secret Service agent in a white apron. When he heard what Keith's minions were doing to my home, he began to sleep in his truck, stationed in front of my house like a sentinel. He was outside, in fact, when Kristin Keeffe showed up at my house one night bearing a bouquet of flowers and a box of candy with a picture of the Madonna and Child on it—she probably bought it on the clearance rack at Walgreen's, as Easter had already come and gone. He escorted her in to see me.

"What are you doing here?"

"I had a vision," Kristin said. "Last night. I had a vision that you changed your mind. That you are coming back to us to fulfill your destiny and have the baby. I am so happy you changed your mind. I'm so happy you're having the baby."

"I'm not having the baby," I said. "You know this. Now please, get the fuck out of my house."

Whereupon Scott, my knight in dungarees, showed her to the door.

That night, at my request, he moved from the pickup to the couch, and, soon after, from the couch to the bed. He would remain there for years.

Although I had broken up with Keith romantically, our business interests were still legally entwined. The process of disentangling them was arduous. We lived together, but we weren't married, so we couldn't simply get a divorce. And while his name wasn't on the deed to the house, and he had no lease, his shit was everywhere. There were two arcade games in the garage, and a treadmill, and some punching bags, and dozens of boxes we were storing for Pam. He would dispatch one of his minions to the house almost every day to steal my mail or unmake my bed, but God forbid one of them would carry a box back to Flintlock. I faxed them a bunch of times, insisting they remove the stuff, and they kept blowing me off. Finally, at the end of May, Keith faxed me an itemized list of items he wanted me to return. Scott offered to load as much as he could fit in his truck and haul it out of there. He'd been living with me less than a month, but he already realized that Keith was a psychopath. He wanted my ex gone as soon as possible.

"What are you doing?"

He was in the garage, rifling through one of the boxes. "Seeing what's here."

"But that's Pam's stuff."

"There's got to be something," he said. "Has to be. They're too weird."

And sure enough, there was. In a small, sequined purse, he found a couple of photographs. Dirty photographs. One of them showed a woman, completely naked, shot from the ground looking up, legs spread wide so the vagina was prominently featured. There was an astonishing amount of pubic hair. I'd never seen her vagina before, but I recognized her smiling face. It was Pam Cafritz.

Scott let out a little yelp and dropped the picture on the floor. "Ugh," he said. "I wish I could un-see that."

"There's another."

The second photograph featured a nude, hirsute Keith Raniere. Around the tip of his partially-erect penis was a little black bow tie.

I flashed to a memory from a few years before, when Keith and I were still together: I went to the Fotomat and picked up some pictures he had developed. I opened them, expecting to find happy snapshots of Michael's birthday party, and was shocked to discover photographs of myself, naked, asleep in the bed. He'd removed the covers, snapped the pictures, replaced the covers, and not bothered to tell me. I went ballistic on him. I took the pictures and the negatives, threw them in the sink, and burned them. "Don't *ever* do that again." As far as I know, he didn't.

Now I realized that Keith had not given up his nude photography habit. He'd simply found a willing subject: the woman I thought was my best friend.

"Oh my God," I said. "He's fucking Pam Cafritz."

"Sure looks like," Scott said. "But that's not all—he's fucking Kristin Keeffe, too. And that ugly bitch Karen Unterreiner. He's fucking all three of them. He's running a harem over there!"

"No," I said, wincing at the distasteful image of an orgy at 3 Flintlock Lane. "It can't be."

"Yes," Scott said. "I'm sure of it."

And that's when it all became clear. Keith's three friends, his three housemates, his three lovers, his personal witches from *Macbeth*.

"Once," I said, "when we were having problems—because, you know, he's a psychopath—he told me that the best way to unblock our stagnant energy was for us to have a ménage à trois."

"Seriously?"

"Of course he never said who the third person would be. Pam Cafritz! How could I be so *stupid*?"

It was hard to imagine any of them consenting to such an arrangement, let alone all three. And then I realized: it was more than three. It was Pam and Kristin and Karen. And maybe—and this was hard to process—maybe the list didn't end there.

I thought back to the previous summer. Keith and I were vacationing in Lake George with Michael, and Nancy and her daughters came to visit. Lauren was twenty-one, Michelle maybe eighteen or nineteen . . . and the two of them were wrestling with Keith. Really going at it, their bodies up close and intertwined. They were too old for that sort of roughhousing. It was weird and inappropriate. It made me uncomfortable.

"Nancy," I said. "Are you okay with that?"

"Oh, you don't know who he is," she said dismissively—as if *I* were the crazy one.

I stood in that garage with Scott, staring at those pathetic Polaroids, and all of the permutations of this new, creepy knowledge revealed themselves to me. The three Flintlock girls were all sleeping with Keith, all in love with Keith, all slaves to Keith.

Then I came along, and the troika was relegated to the second string. I was the primary consort (to use a Vanguard word); they were side pieces. When I dropped Keith, he suddenly had a lot more time for his "girls." And yet they kept coming to see me, again and again, begging me to give him a second chance—and they seemed sincere about it, even though the resumption of my relationship with Keith would adversely affect all of them.

"This guy," Scott said, "is fucking unbelievable." And then, to lighten the mood, he quipped, "But just so you know, if you ever wanted to test the theory about having a ménage à trois to unblock stagnant energy...I mean, I'd totally be down with that."

Despite the restraining order against Barb Jeske, despite Pam Cafritz making good on her vow to never speak to me again, despite Kristin Keeffe finally getting tired of loitering in front of the restaurant raving about the Chosen One, Keith did not yield in his mission to destroy me. Instead, he swapped out his "girls" for professionals: attorneys. Lawyers didn't need to believe the ESP party line to indulge the whims of Vanguard; they only needed to be compensated for their billable hours. At this time, he also repurposed Kristin into his legal liaison—his very own Michael Cohen. She ran ESP/NXIVM's legal department, filed lawsuits, coordinated with attorneys, worked with the private investigators, and helped devise creative legal strategies to destroy Keith's enemies through the courts.

In her letter to me demanding restitution, Nancy Salzman threatened to notify "the SBA, state liquor license authority and the attorney general." On June 15, 1999, she filed a complaint with the New York State Liquor Authority. She claimed A Place of Creations Café was in violation of the Alcoholic Beverage

Control, or ABC, Law. We had a license to serve beer and wine, and that's all we served. We ran afoul of the regulation when we renovated the restaurant and moved the bar from one wall to the other. This innocuous upgrade was somehow illegal under the ABC Law. Writing up a business for that was like giving a ticket for driving fifty-eight in a fifty-five-miles-per-hour zone. Technically it was a violation, but the Liquor Authority had better things to do with its time than go after a business for that. But Keith and Nancy somehow knew about the regulation and decided to make noise about it. They did this because it required little effort on their part to file a complaint and considerable stress on my part to vindicate myself.

It was not possible to simply run away from them. I could see that if I did not come to the table to set the terms of my release, they would continue to hound me.

My brother offered to help me. John had known Keith for years. He thought they were friends. More than friends, brothers-in-law. Keith was family. And John was good with people. He was always quick with a joke. He liked to make everyone laugh. He was also a savvy businessman, with good horse sense. He had his demons too. For most of his adult life, he battled depression, which he staved off with booze and pills. He had terrible, scary downward spirals. Most of the time, though, he was his old, fun-loving self. He was like that now, when I needed him.

John drove to Albany several times to "negotiate my release," as he phrased it. As he saw it, I was a hostage, being held by terrorists, and he was going to have a sit-down with them and arrange my freedom. It took a few meetings, at which my poor brother was subjected to Keith's rambling diversions and digressions, but eventually, John managed to secure the terms.

"You need to turn over 80 percent of the companies to Keith."

"Which companies?"

"National Health, the restaurants—all of them."

"What?"

"But you have to pay all of the company's debts first."

"You're kidding me."

"He insists on that."

"If he wanted the debts repaid, he shouldn't have put the virus on my computer."

He shook his head and laughed. "There's more."

"More?"

"He wants you to agree to have as many sessions with Nancy as Keith deems necessary. Oh, and you have to write a letter of apology and publish it in the Albany *Times Union*."

"Jesus," I said. "There's no way I can do all of that."

"Yes, no kidding. Listen," he said, and his face was dead serious. "Remember when you were little, and you asked me if the boogeyman was real? You remember what I told you? I said, 'No way, there's no such thing as the boogeyman.' I was wrong, Toni. There is a boogeyman. His name is Keith Raniere. And he wants us all dead. Right now, you have to get the hell out of here, but I'm telling you: if you ever try and take him down, make sure you kill him. Because if you don't—the boogeyman's going to kill all of us."

I took John's advice: I got the hell out of there.

We closed down everything. I stopped making payments on the house, defaulting on the mortgage. (Although it was my house and Keith's, his name wasn't on the deed, so the bank couldn't put a lien on him.) Eventually it would sell, at a considerable loss. I had a garage sale and liquidated almost everything I owned. And on October 27, 1999, with great reluctance, I filed for bankruptcy protection.

The bankruptcy, which I needed to go through to fully liberate myself financially, dragged on and on. Keith and Nancy kept contesting it or filing new claims against me to stave off its resolution. I called and left a message on their machine, asking them to leave me alone. Pam Cafritz and Barb Jeske—future holders of the Purple Sash, fully committed to ethical living— filed a harassment claim against me in Clifton Park, citing the single message. Because in their eyes, *I* was somehow the one harassing *them*. The charges were eventually dropped, but I still had to handle, and finance, the legal issues.

In July of 2000, Nancy Salzman sued me in bankruptcy court. Her purpose wasn't merely to recover her lost assets—it was to destroy me completely. On September 1, 2000, Nancy filed an amended complaint in *Salzman v. Natalie*. In November, she was deposed. Under oath, she admitted to not being a licensed mental health professional, which meant it was unlawful for her to give me therapy of any kind, much less the intensive sessions I'd undergone.

In her deposition, Nancy went to almost comical lengths to deny that Keith owned, well, anything at all:

Q. Have you made an agreement to pay him a remuneration from whatever you received from those patents from any of the money that you earn for use of those patents?
A. I don't understand.

Q. Somebody's got patents. Do you think they've got any value?

A. Yes.

Q. Did Keith just give you those patents and say you can do what you want with them?

A. Provided that I use them in the way that he wants them used, he gave me those patents.

Q. And he doesn't expect to receive any money or remuneration of any kind?

A. At some point we have an agreement that he will get a portion of my profits.

Q. So there is an agreement that he will be paid for the use of those patents at some point?

A. That's correct.

Q. Is there an agreement for an amount or percentage?

A. It's a percentage.

Q. Of whatever you gross, I assume?

A. Yes.

Q. Could I ask, why are they being registered in your name and not his name?

A. That was the agreement that he made with me.

Q. I'm asking you why.

Her attorney objected and did not let her respond. A few minutes later, the same tack was taken:

Q. Now, you mentioned that Keith was your mentor. Was he anything more than your mentor? I don't mean personally; I mean, was he a business partner?

A. He is the conceptual founder of ESP.

Q. Does he get paid from any of those corporations for any of
those services?
A. He does not.
Q. He does it for free?

But the attorneys pulled the plug, as attorneys will, and we never got the answer.

The actual bankruptcy trial was finally held on February 23–26, 2002. By then, I'd been back in Rochester for two full years. Scott Foley and I had gotten married and were living in a nine-hundred-square-foot home, working sixteen-hour days at my brother's pizzeria, praying that the boogeyman would leave us alone.

It took another full year for the bankruptcy to be formally discharged. The presiding judge, Robert E. Littlefield Jr., held that "this matter smacks of a jilted fellow's attempt at revenge or retaliation against his former girlfriend, with many attempts at trying to trip her up along the way. After careful consideration of the entire record, with particular attention paid to [Raniere's] post-trial briefs and appendices, the Court concludes that [Raniere] did not meet his burden of proving, beyond a preponderance of the evidence, that the Debtor should not receive a discharge."

I wept when I heard the decision. At last, someone in a position of authority—a judge, no less!—recognized Keith Raniere for what he really was. The discharge of the bankruptcy was welcome enough. The validation from Judge Littlefield made the victory even sweeter.

I could breathe again. Not only that, but Nancy's disclosures in her deposition opened the door for me to sue her. That's what my attorney told me. "She isn't licensed to give mental health counseling, but she gave you mental health counseling for years. And she caused you great damage. We absolutely have a case now."

On January 7, 2003, I got my life back.

After a decade of Vanguard, I was finally able to move on.

# CHAPTER 13:

# "I WAS BRAINWASHED"

## The Growth of ESP. Early ESP Victims.

---

When Nancy Salzman joined forces with Keith Raniere, she brought with her an impressive Rolodex, built up through her work with corporate clients. The original plan for ESP, in fact, was to cater to large corporate clients rather than individuals. Once they investigated Keith, however, they refused to work with him. They liked Prefect; they hated Vanguard. Rejected by big businesses, Keith and Nancy had no choice but to pivot and operate as an MLM.

Nancy integrated a lot of her old "Irresistible Communications" classwork into the ESP curriculum. Students were offered the choice of a five-, eleven-, or sixteen-day intensive, each day focusing on a new module that tackled NLP-inspired practices such as observing social cues, mirroring, and taking control of your emotional state—the stuff I'd found so fascinating when I took her class in 1998. These intensives would be taught by someone charismatic, dazzling, seemingly wise—Nancy herself, generally, in the early going. She would have students slow down and focus on things we generally don't have time to focus on: body language, for example. She would lecture on how to read certain types of body language, to help their communication skills. After the exhilaration of these intimate, ten-hour-day marathons, the students would go home pleased with their new, esoteric knowledge—eager to learn more and encouraged to recruit.

Even at the very beginning, the classes drew seekers, often at a crossroads in their lives and thirsty for exactly the type of knowledge Vanguard and the Prefect seemed to have in spades. They were not easy marks. They were not stupid. ESP attracted smart, capable people whose desire for self-improvement was sincere. The actress Allison Mack joined the group because she genuinely believed Keith Raniere could help her become both a better artist and a better person. The *What the Bleep* filmmaker Mark Vicente was recruited, and subsequently bought into the ESP precepts, because the self-determinative messaging resonated with him. The liquor heiresses Sara and Clare Bronfman recognized their enormous privilege and felt that Vanguard could help them make the best use of it. One of the horrible ironies of NXIVM is that its practitioners genuinely believed it was a force for good. Keith is a devil disguised as an angel.

The pitch, usually from a close friend or family member—and, later, from a minor celebrity like Allison Mack or Nicki Clyne—was some variation of this: "How would you like to achieve more in life, while at the same time feeling more joy?" Anyone who answered in the affirmative—who didn't immediately run for the hills—was already predisposed to fall under the ESP spell. At the intensives, the students went through a series of exercises in which they determined what they wanted to achieve and what might be holding them back from doing so. The answer was always the same: *they* were to blame for their lack of achievement. *They* were the obstacles to their own success. The trick was to change perception, to stop living as a victim. To take responsibility for their actions. To live *ethically*. And who could show them the way? Vanguard, of course. The "technology" of his "Rational Inquiry" included a mathematical formula for how exactly to make the world a better place. Keith's way to change the world would succeed, where everyone else's had failed!

For all the heaviness, there was certainly an element of fun to the ESP crew, especially in the early days. The Nxians were smart, creative people. They liked to converse about deep, interesting subjects. They also liked to joke around and play games. Some Nxians dated and eventually married other Nxians, or else brought their significant others into the group. Vanguard Week, or V-Week, was a ten-day celebration on a bucolic lake in upstate New York. At the upper levels, there were dinners at Prefect's house, retreats at Clare Bronfman's farm, trips aboard the Bronfmans' private jet, vacations on their private island in Fiji. Even Virgin Group mogul Richard Branson played host to the Nxian elite at his exclusive resort on his private Necker Island. How could Mark Vicente, to name an extreme example, not have been bowled over when these insanely wealthy heiresses chased him down, flew him around in their jet, and offered to finance his film projects? There was a feeling of camaraderie, of mutual respect, and initially, of joy—until the joy was replaced by fear, anxiety, and self-loathing.

\* \* \*

How and where multilevel marketing companies expand depends on the professional and personal networks of the early adopters. NXIVM grew organically, and randomly.

Barbara Bouchey, the child of a broken home in South Troy, New York, put herself through community college waiting tables and, through hard work and perseverance, became a successful financial planner in Saratoga Springs. By age forty, she was a self-made millionaire. But she wasn't happy. Her marriage was on the rocks, and a close friend had committed suicide, shaking her to the core. In 2000, an acquaintance of hers, Nancy Salzman, encouraged her to give ESP a try. Barbara was blown away by the experience. The "technology" she learned from the program changed her life for the better—even after leaving the company, she maintained that the "technology" was good. She wanted everyone to know about Vanguard and his wonderful self-improvement modules. For the next nine years, she would be among the most successful ESP recruiters, and one of the principal architects of NXIVM.

On the other side of the continent, in Anchorage, Alaska, Esther Chiappone and Kathy Russell had stumbled upon ESP. Esther was a schoolteacher in Soldotna and a mother of four; once she was initiated into the way of Vanguard, she became an active recruiter and eventual high-ranking Nxian. Kathy would stay until the bitter end and wind up indicted with Keith.

ESP made its foothold south of the border through Edgar Boone, scion of a wealthy family who was a Tony Robbins–style self-help guru in his native Mexico. He reportedly heard about ESP when he was taking a class called "Life Skills," in Detroit of all places; the instructor urged him to give this new path to self-improvement a try. He took to ESP like a fish to water and quickly established himself as the best recruiter in Mexico. (That he was supposedly in love with Michelle Salzman, Lauren's kid sister, was even more incentive for him to join the cause.) Boone was responsible for ESP's first real wave of success, when members of other prominent Mexican families enrolled in the classes and encouraged their high-society friends to do the same. Ana Cristina Fox, the daughter of president Vicente Fox; Emiliano Salinas, son of president Carlos Salinas de Gortari; and Rosa Laura Junco, daughter of the Mexican newspaper publisher Alejandro Junco, were three of the first notable Mexicans to take the classes. Once they tried ESP, others followed, and by 2002, the company was regularly offering intensives in various major cities in Mexico.

After graduating from Oswego State in 1998, Lauren Salzman wasn't sure what to do with her life. Her mother said, "Try ESP for six months. I'll pay your way. If you don't like it after that time, you can leave." Lauren tried it. She liked it. She stayed, eventually achieving the Green Sash, and along with Boone and Bouchey was one of the organization's most successful recruiters. In 2002, she was teaching the ESP intensives in Monterrey.

One of the participants in the Monterrey summer intensive in 2002 was a young woman named Daniela Flores.[2] The class was a gift from her parents, Hector and Adriana, who had both taken ESP classes and were Vanguard true believers. Daniela was sixteen that summer. A brilliant student, at the top of her class at Techno Monterrey, she received a full scholarship to finish high school at the prestigious Leysin American School in the Swiss Alps. Her

---

2   The last name has been changed to protect Daniela's identity.

dream was to go to Harvard and then pursue an academic career in the sciences. The scholarship—the only one given that year—would help her get a head start on this dream.

But the ESP intensive gave her second thoughts. In Monterrey, she was easily the youngest person in the room, but what she lacked in life experience she made up for in youthful enthusiasm, work ethic, and intelligence. Throughout the sixteen-day intensive, Daniela was told about the brilliance of Vanguard, Keith Raniere, whose portrait hung on the wall of the classroom. He was the Smartest Man in the World, with the highest IQ ever recorded. He was a scientist. He had developed a mathematical formula that he claimed would literally save the world from the path of destruction it was currently on. As he explained it, no matter how hard people tried to do good work—to cure cancer, combat poverty, save the whales—it was all futile. The only way the entropy of the planet could be reversed was if enough individuals became "integrated." And the only way humans could become integrated was to follow the path of Vanguard, the lone member of the human race who was *fully integrated*. He was a twenty-first-century Buddha. Because this concept was couched in scientific language—it was technology; it involved mathematical calculations—and because its author was both a genius and a fellow scientist, Daniela was seduced by the elegance of the argument.

"You're very bright," Lauren told her at the end of the sixteen days. "Why don't you come with us? You could help the mission."

Daniela explained that she had a prior commitment, that she was expected to attend a Swiss boarding school at the end of the summer, where she would prepare for university. But the opportunity to learn at the feet of Vanguard was too great to pass up. She decided to go to Clifton Park instead of Switzerland, to forsake her academic career for a chance to be tutored by the Smartest Man in the World, just as Aristotle had been tutored by Plato.

Things did not pan out as she expected. Tasked with teaching her computer programming and coding, Karen Unterreiner would give her a book on some obscure programming language and say, "Here, learn this." Otherwise, Daniela spent her time doing data entry. Keith didn't speak to her for months, and then, after a brief period during which he gave her brain teasers to figure out, he began to groom her to be his lover. Their first sexual encounter—a traumatic experience for her—came a few days after her eighteenth birthday, in October of 2003. She spent much of the following year doing data entry, cleaning houses of high-ranking Espians, and performing oral sex on command for Vanguard.

In the end, this child prodigy never finished high school, let alone college. Today, she is flourishing, but a critical learning period in her life was wasted on Keith.

Daniela was not the only bright young woman whose intellectual ambitions were curtailed by Vanguard's empty promises. Keith had been using the same technique for years. Back in 1984, when he was still in his twenties and living in Troy, he seduced a fifteen-year-old Cohoes High School student named Gina Hutchinson. Like Daniela, Gina was extremely bright. Unlike Daniela, she was raised Mormon, and her parents were divorced. Keith convinced Gina that she, too, was a genius, and that it was better for her to drop out of school and learn from him, the Smartest Man in the World, than subject herself to the patriarchal brainwashing that went on in the public-school system. He told her that she was a Buddhist deity and that her soul was much older than her physical being. He persuaded her to let him take her on, as a lover, teacher, and spiritual guide.

"He had this belief system that he was instilling in these girls that society was moronic, that society was the culprit that brainwashed people against their true natures and disempowered women, and sexual mores were all about keeping women bound and chained to the patriarchal system," Heidi Hutchinson, Gina's sister, told the *Albany Times Union* in 2012. "He had those kinds of beliefs about everything, including the school system. He didn't want Gina to be in school. He wanted Gina to leave school and become his consort. And she did, actually. He convinced her that he would be her mentor." When Gina chafed at Keith's philandering, Keith "threw out all sorts of different psychobabble justification on how this was actually empowering Gina, empowering the women." Gina worked at Consumers' Buyline and remained in Vanguard's orbit for years. Eventually, she attended the University at Albany, and, to Keith's annoyance, forged bonds with some of her male professors there.

Many times, Gina tried to break with Keith. He did the same thing to her that he did to me: he sent his "girls" to apologize on his behalf, harassing her and insisting she return to the fold. Kristin Keeffe was usually the one tapped for this particular assignment. Kristin and Gina were close friends.

In 2002, at the age of thirty-three, Gina Hutchinson cloistered herself at Karma Triyana Dharmachakra, a Buddhist monastery in Woodstock, New York. Her mother had just died, and she felt untethered. On October 11, 2002, the Woodstock police received a call that Gina was missing. She'd been acting erratically, sending dear possessions to friends. Her body was found in a stream in the woods. She had shot herself in the head. According to the police report, the shotgun was lying across her chest. In the pockets of her jacket were Winchester shells, gum, a motel room key, and a Buddha figurine. In her car, which was parked nearby, police found both a journal containing snippets of poetry and a copy of a set list of the band Smashing Pumpkins, handwritten by the lead singer, Billy Corgan. The set list bears an uncanny resemblance to one of Keith's timelines. In gold marker, Gina wrote three words: "LOVE," "GOD," and "DREAMS."

For all the talk about ethical living, Vanguard and Prefect were egregiously negligent when conducting their classes. When you have hundreds of people taking long courses that span a period of more than a week, during which they are asked to bare their souls to the group, the likelihood that someone will have a psychotic episode is extremely high. *Intensives* are called that for a reason. The company had no safeguards in place in case of medical emergency. When episodes did occur, their strategy was to isolate the person from the group, calm them down, and hope for the best.

At an intensive in Albany, a Mexican ESP student had a psychotic episode. She was whisked out of the conference rooms and into a car, where she was driven around for a while, to calm her down. When this didn't work, Lauren Salzman, who was in charge of the training, drove her to a friend's house and gave her some Valium. When she woke up still distressed, Lauren broke up Valium pills into her eggs and fed them to her.

As far as we know, the Mexican student recovered (although

I doubt she received a refund). A participant in Alaska was not so lucky.

Kristin Snyder was an environmental consultant living in Anchorage with her domestic partner, Heidi Clifford. She took an ESP class in November 2002, a sixteen-day intensive taught by Prefect herself, Nancy Salzman. Snyder took to it immediately. She sung its praises to Clifford and to her parents, whom she visited in South Carolina that Christmas. Before heading back to Alaska, she visited ESP headquarters in Albany, where she met Vanguard, who offered to be her "mentor." To Keith, "mentor" and "lover" are synonyms, and this was concealed for years by his inner circle.

Excited about her meeting with Vanguard, Snyder returned to Alaska in January 2003 and convinced Clifford to take the next ESP class with her. This intensive was held at the Westmark Hotel in Anchorage and taught in part by Esther Chiappone, the schoolteacher turned ESP proctor. The training ran from late January to early February, and as it progressed, Snyder began to behave erratically. She interrupted the class to make deluded pronouncements. She called her parents and raved maniacally, telling them she was responsible for the space shuttle *Columbia* blowing up. She stopped sleeping, or tried to stop, because she believed that Keith needed no sleep and wanted to emulate her mentor. (There were also reports that Snyder claimed that she was carrying Keith's child, although there is no way to know if this is true.)

On February 6, Snyder was ordered to leave the intensive by Esther Chiappone because she was being disruptive. When Clifford asked if she should go with her and bring her to a hospital, Chiappone instructed her not to do so. That was the last time Clifford would see her partner.

The next day, Snyder's pickup truck was discovered in the remote town of Seward, an hour and a half outside of Anchorage, at a park site on Resurrection Bay. The Alaska State Police would later conclude that Snyder had broken into a shed, taken an old wooden kayak, paddled it out into the vast and deep bay, and drowned. She was thirty-five years old.

Her body was never located, but police did find a suicide note:

*I attended a course called Executive Success Programs (a.k.a. Nexivm) based out of Anchorage, AK, and Albany, NY. I was brainwashed and my emotional center of the brain was killed/ turned off. I still have feeling in my external skin, but my internal organs are rotting. Please contact my parents... if you find me or this note. I am sorry life, I didn't know I was already dead. May we persist into the future.*

In 2009, in a lawsuit filed against the *Metroland* weekly, Keith and company would claim, bizarrely, that the suicide note was a fake.

Years later, Keith recruited the filmmaker Mark Vicente to make a documentary debunking certain myths about Vanguard. One of these alleged "myths" concerned Kristin Snyder. Keith believed, and claimed he had evidence to show, that Snyder faked her own suicide because she was involved with a drug-smuggling operation gone awry and has been alive and well in British Columbia this whole time. The film was never made.

For all his New Age, healy-feely mumbo jumbo, Keith Raniere was at heart staunchly aligned with Ayn Rand and Barry Goldwater: libertarian, anti-tax, anti-government, anti-regulatory, anti-feminist. The court battles that killed CBI pushed him further in that direction. In the vein of his tax evasion, he set out to conceal his activities from government oversight as much as possible. His corporate activities operated in silos, so the different parts had no idea what their counterparts were working on, or why. He used the same model Osama bin Laden employed in setting up al-Qaeda—everything operated in cells, so if the government shut down one part of the organization, the other parts would be shielded from harm and continue to operate. He wanted to be like the pope: in control of fabulous wealth and power, but legally owning nothing.

If he operated this way, he figured, he could keep the tax man at bay.

In 2003 Nancy Salzman registered a new LLC in New York, piggybacking on a redesignation she'd filed the year before in Delaware. The new company was conceived as an umbrella that owned subsidiary companies. It was also a shield to insulate Keith from direct ownership of so much as a CD of *Rachmaninoff Plays Rachmaninoff*. Its inscrutable name was a seemingly random and unpronounceable string of five capital letters, designed to evoke mystery and, perhaps, to look cool.

It was called NXIVM.

Through the years, the myth of the Chosen One persisted and grew in the NXIVM community. Vanguard passed around this honor like it was a heavyweight championship belt, or one of his sashes. First Pam Cafritz was supposed to be the mother. Then it was Barb Jeske; next, Barbara Bouchey. Keith dropped similar hints to all of the women in his inner circle. It was considered the greatest honor to bear his child. And it was one more carrot he could dangle. The promise of a Vanguard baby kept Lauren Salzman in the fold for decades, celibate and wanting.

What gave the myth extra juice was the fact that for most of the 2000s, Keith claimed to be a renunciate. He eschewed pleasures of the flesh to live, as he phrased it in a 2003 *Forbes* interview, "a somewhat church-mouse-type existence." Most Nxians thought he was a celibate; the ones who didn't were sleeping with him and were under strict orders not to kiss and tell.

In fact, Vanguard did not forsake sex until the day he was arrested by the FBI. Going back from that day to the early nineties, when he was hitting on teenagers in local theater productions at RPI, Keith Raniere copulated with thousands of women. Because he views sex as an "energy exchange" and his ejaculation as a sort of magical glue that keeps all of his concubines conjoined, Keith Raniere does not use condoms. Why deny his lucky sexual partners the privilege of access to his semen? When he ejaculated into the tremulous mouth of Daniela, the eighteen-year-old Mexican child prodigy who had never even kissed a boy before her rude entry into sexual activity, he asked, "Did you see a blue light? Some girls see a blue light." He wanted her to believe—and may have believed himself—that his discharge had a heavenly glow.

In the mid-2000s, Keith was having sex with everyone in his inner circle. He was having sex with Pam Cafritz and Kristin Keeffe and Karen Unterreiner, his original harem. He was having sex with Barb Jeske and Barbara Bouchey and another longtime concubine, Dawn Morrison. He was having sex with Daniela Flores, with her older sister, Marianna, with her underage sister, Camila. He was having sex with Lauren Salzman. He was having sex with Nancy Salzman. He was having sex with a beautiful young artist named Ivy Nevares. He was having sex with Gina Hutchinson and may have had sex with Kristin Snyder. He was even having sex with Kathy Russell, the company's bookkeeper. Not all of his partners were happy to share him. Barbara Bouchey required extra handling and would only have sex with him at her house, not at Flintlock. Kristin Keeffe had been sharing him for years but was never comfortable with it being thrown in her face. Lauren Salzman was jealous, especially of Marianna, whom Keith seemed to prefer. On the other hand, Pam Cafritz never minded, and indeed seemed to enjoy the sexual chaos.

All of this unprotected sex led to numerous pregnancies, and these numerous pregnancies led to the same number of terminations. Pam managed the abortions, shepherding so many women to Planned Parenthood that the staff there recognized her.

Despite all this, there was a Chosen One, in fulfillment of the NXIVM scriptures. The fortunate son was born in 2007, at the height of Keith's celibate monk phase. For its weirdness and unlikelihood, the backstory rivaled that of baby Moses set adrift in the basket of reeds. It went like this: Barb Jeske was in Michigan, where she was from, visiting her family. At the same time that she was there—what are the chances!—an old friend of hers who'd just had a baby boy perished tragically in a car crash. The baby boy somehow survived. The father's identity was unknown, and the next of kin were not capable of raising a child, so it was decided that Jeske, she of the Ethical Coalition, would adopt the boy. Thus when Barb returned to Clifton Park from Michigan, she brought with her an infant in swaddling clothes.

The boy was named Gaelen, an old Greek name meaning "gift of God."

That was the improbable cover story, the NXIVM myth. What

really happened is this: in 2006 Keith had gotten Kristin Keeffe pregnant. She was in her late thirties, and she felt that this would be the last time she'd ever have the opportunity to have a baby. And Kristin *loved* children. So she decided not to terminate the pregnancy. When she began to show, she stayed out of sight and stopped going to NXIVM events. She buried herself in her work. One day Keith went to her room and found Kristin unconscious, lying in a pool of blood. They brought her to the hospital, where she gave birth to a premature baby boy. She almost died in childbirth, and baby Gaelen spent weeks in the NICU. Cami Flores, who was living in Clifton Park at the time, would go to the hospital and sit with him.

Vanguard saw this as he sees everything—as another way to make money. With Gaelen, the Rainbow Cultural Gardens was born. He used this early childhood development program and school as a way to bring illegal immigrant girls into the country. These multicultural development specialists—nannies, in other words—were generally underage and lacked any formal education. The program costs about $120,000 a year per child, with a discount if there are siblings—or half price, if Keith was the father. The "Rainbow Culture" concept was to have five caregivers speaking five different languages, so the youngster was exposed to all five tongues.

The Nxians tripped over themselves to provide the best possible environment for the Chosen One. And Kristin ceded day-to-day responsibility of raising her child to the collective. Gaelen had the misfortune of being the son of Vanguard. His only saving grace was that very few knew he was really Keith's child. And although Kristin had to lie to the community about the fact that she was his mother, she was very protective of him.

When I was with Keith, I, too, had a small child. I, too, trusted Keith to help raise my child, assured that the influence of the Smartest Man in the World could only be a boon to my son. In my case, Michael turned out just fine. When I speak to him about it now, he is remarkably serene about the experience. But Michael had me. Michael had Rusty and Rusty's mother. Michael had my parents, my brother. He didn't have five nannies babbling at him in five languages while his mother was off in court, harassing innocent people.

# CHAPTER 14:

# "MR. RANIERE'S LEGAL TORQUEMADA"

## The Liquor Heiress

---

Rita Webb tended bar at Ye Olde Nosebag, a pub in her native Essex, England, owned and operated by her parents. She was pretty, blond, free-spirited, socially ambitious. On holiday in Spain in 1974, at age twenty-five, she met the businessman Edgar Bronfman Sr., scion of the Bronfman family and the head of the Seagram corporation. Edgar had baggage. He was tall and gawky, socially awkward, and not the handsomest suitor she'd entertained. He was more than twenty years older than Rita—old enough to be her father—and he brought to the table two ex-wives and five adult children: Samuel II, Edgar Jr., Matthew, Holly, and Adam. On the other hand, she got on with him well, he was clearly infatuated with her, and he was fantastically, superlatively wealthy. At his request, she converted to Judaism and changed her name from Rita to Georgiana. When they married in 1975, she was known as George.

It was a small price to pay for a barmaid to marry into liquor-business royalty.

The Bronfman fortune was made by Samuel Bronfman, a Jewish émigré to Canada who went into the liquor distribution business in Montreal just as Prohibition kicked in; his company, Seagram, supplied booze to the US cities of New York, Chicago, Detroit, and Boston almost exclusively for more than a decade. Samuel's pockets were as deep as the thirst of his American customers. His son's may have been even deeper.

Between the two ex-wives, the five children, the pressures of being the head of a prominent Jewish family, and the stress of running a vast corporation he had inherited, Edgar's life was something of a chaos. Also in 1975, his oldest son, Samuel II, was kidnapped and held for ransom. Edgar personally delivered a few million in cash to ensure his son's release. The perpetrator claimed to be Samuel's gay lover and said the kidnapping was Samuel's idea, to wangle money from the father. By the time of the Ford administration, when Keith Raniere was a bored teenager teaching himself calculus, the Bronfman family had already established itself as an easy mark for con men.

The couple's first child was born a year later. She was called Sara, pronounced in the British way, with the first syllable rhyming with *star*. Sara was cute, blond, bubbly, free-spirited—just like her mother. In 1979, a second daughter was born. Clare looked like, and took after, her father: plain, dour, austere, socially awkward. The Bronfmans divorced in 1983. George removed the girls, still quite young, from New York to her native England. Most of their childhood was spent on either a rolling estate in the bucolic English countryside or an even more rustic retreat in Kenya. The girls spoke with British accents and watched as their mother involved herself with, first, the son of a famous archeologist and, later, a famous British film actor, Nigel Havers, whom she would eventually marry. In between those relationships, George married Edgar a second time, only to divorce him again.

Thus, while Sara and Clare Bronfman were wealthy heiresses, they did not grow up in the usual wealthy-heiress way. Their five older half siblings moved more comfortably in their father's orbit and were more involved with the family's businesses and charitable work. As good as the patriarch Sam Bronfman had been at making money, his grandkids were even better at losing it. Like the drunken sailors who helped their grandfather acquire his fortune in the first place, they spent recklessly.

Edgar Jr. wound up taking over from his father at Seagram—and promptly ran the business into the ground. The younger Edgar wanted to work in entertainment, not the staid family liquor concern, and with stars in his eyes, he closed a series of business deals that shriveled the company's value. He flipped the massive stake Senior had acquired in DuPont, the blue-chip chemical company—a stake that constituted about three-quarters of the family's revenue—back to DuPont and used the cash to branch out into music and movies. But the play didn't work. Junior wound up effectively selling Seagram at a disastrous loss to Vivendi, the French conglomerate, which broke it down for spare parts. He eventually found his way as CEO of the Warner Music Group, but between the sale of the DuPont shares and the Vivendi merger, Edgar Bronfman Jr. cost the family something like $3 billion.

Despite being three years younger, Clare Bronfman was the sister who seemed better positioned to do something tangible with her life. Always a lover of horses, dating from her days at the English manor, Clare became a professional equestrian at seventeen. At twenty, she was among the best in the country. She won the grand prix at CSI-A Eindhoven in 2001 and the grand prix in Rome in 2002, and began a slow climb up the US and international rankings. She was serious about her sport, opening a farm where show horses were trained.

Sara, meanwhile, was a flibbertigibbet, a will-o'-the-wisp, a clown. According to a 2010 profile in *Maclean's*, she let her curly hair grow into dreadlocks and bummed around the Caribbean, where she opened a short-lived skydiving business in Turks and Caicos. She took a few semesters of college classes and wound up in Antwerp, Belgium, because that was where her love interest, the jockey Ronan Clarke, was living at the time. Their subsequent marriage lasted less than a year. It was in Belgium where Sara first heard of NXIVM, through a family friend, and with little to show for her life beyond a failed marriage and a small business jumping out of small airplanes, she decided to take one of their workshops.

The workshop Sara Bronfman took was in Mexico City. The experience was life altering. Before, she lacked purpose and direction. Now, she was on the path to self-empowerment. As Nicholas Köhler writes in *Maclean's*:

> "Before I came and took a NXIVM course I was much less driven in my life, I knew less who I was, I was less happy," Sara told an Albany radio host last year. "I had certain self-destructive patterns." She noted how some relatives reacted to the change. "They were like, 'You're doing so well, you're so much happier, you're successful in your life, all of your relationships are going better...but I don't know who you are

anymore, I preferred it when you were miserable and used to cry on my shoulder.'"

At first, Clare resisted her sister's overtures about joining the group. Unlike Sara, she already *had* purpose and direction. What did she need Vanguard for? What convinced her was Keith's reputation as a genius who could coach *anyone* to do *anything*, even things he knew nothing about. Horse-jumping competitions, for example. Clare sought Vanguard's help in upping her equestrian game and quickly became convinced that he could help her in every walk of life. Clare had no college education, so she was especially impressed by Keith's boast of a superior intellect.

Once she was in for a penny, Clare was in for a pound (millions and millions of pounds, as it turned out). Her interest in and devotion to Vanguard quickly outpaced her sister's. As the younger, quieter, homelier, less fun sister, she had always been in Sara's shadow. NXIVM gave her an avenue by which to outshine her older, bubblier, prettier, more fun sibling. Moreover, Clare was in love with Keith Raniere. She's still in love with him.

Keith, for his part, immediately sniffed out the sibling rivalry and used it to his advantage. The Bronfmans were not the first siblings he'd lured into his web, but they were certainly the richest. He convinced them to invest in NXIVM to the tune of $2 million. Two million to the Bronfmans was a rounding error, and they happily invested. It was the least they could do for their guru.

In 2003, a year after Sara and Clare had joined NXIVM, *Forbes* magazine decided to do a feature on Keith Raniere. The reporter Michael Freedman wanted to write something about high-end executive coaching, which had become a trend, and the Bronfmans' involvement with the company gave him an angle that would appeal to the *Forbes* readership. He contacted me for the piece when my name kept popping up alongside Keith's and Nancy's, because of the bankruptcy filings. I told him the truth about Vanguard and Prefect—the first time I had been able to do so.

The story wound up making the cover of the magazine. A somber-looking Keith Raniere, his hair and beard retouched to appear darker, glanced off in the distance, over the caption THE WORLD'S STRANGEST EXECUTIVE COACH.

As Freedman researched his article, Clare was seething with jealousy. It drove her crazy that Keith and Nancy seemed not to realize that she was the more valuable Bronfman sister to NXIVM. They made more of a fuss over Sara, paid more attention to Sara, spoke more highly of Sara. Clare felt humiliated, so she acted out. She told her father about the $2 million "loan" to Keith Rainere. This caused Edgar Sr. to sour on Keith and to remark to *Forbes* the five words that NXIVM would never be able to shake: "I think it's a cult."

Freedman seems to have agreed. Far from establishing Keith as a bona fide captain of industry, a John Galt, *Forbes* basically exposes him as a fraud. Here is the quote in context:

> Detractors say [Keith Raniere] runs a cult-like program aimed at breaking down his subjects psychologically, separating them from their families and inducting them into a bizarre world of messianic pretensions, idiosyncratic language and ritualistic practices. "I think it's a cult," says Bronfman.

Freedman writes off big-money executive coaching as a "high-profit fad." Keith, he says, is a "slacker poet" and "corporate

Svengali" whose "teachings are mysterious, filled with self-serving and impenetrable jargon about ethics and values, and defined by a blind-ambition ethos akin to that of the driven characters in an Ayn Rand novel." Keith's bombastic mission statement, Freedman says, "is apocalyptic in tone, with the occasional grammatical error—his genius notwithstanding." In the topsy-turvy NXIVM universe,

> those who question Raniere's views simply don't get it. He speaks slowly and methodically, with digression upon digression, using words he has defined for himself and then pausing to explain each term. You might think it pure genius. Or maybe horse manure.

When I read Senior's quote in the article, I contacted him myself. "Mr. Bronfman," I said, "you need to get your girls out of there. It's a cult. Raniere's bad. If you don't get them out, in a few years he's going to burn through all their money. He's going to be sleeping with both of them." And he said, "No. No. Not my girls. No. They won't do that." He thanked me for my concern and hung up. I'm sure he already suspected what I told him, but what could he do? His daughters were adults, in control of some of their own fortunes. He could not dictate how they spent their inheritance. Also, in the ugly fallout over the *Forbes* piece, Clare and Sara had both stopped talking to their father and benefactor. Cult, indeed!

Keith, meanwhile, blamed Clare for the catastrophically bad press. What she had done, he decreed, in telling her father about the loan was a breach of ethics—a violation of the "Twelve-Point Mission Statement" and the worst sin a Nxian can commit. She apologized, begged for his forgiveness. He withheld his approval, using emotional blackmail to turn her into his de facto slave. Clare would spend the next fifteen years, and more than $100 million of her family's money, vainly trying to work her way back into his good graces.

He used her as a weapon. According to a 2018 piece in the *New York Times*, Clare,

> who never attended college, served...as Mr. Raniere's legal Torquemada, financing and aggressively pursuing long-running lawsuits against NXIVM's enemies, both real and perceived. She filed criminal complaints against defectors from the group; used lawyers to threaten its critics; and allegedly hired an investigative firm in Canada as part of an ill-fated plan to hack into the bank records of American judges and politicians.

One of the perceived enemies was the Jersey City–based cult deprogrammer Rick Alan Ross. Ross was enlisted by the family of Stephanie Franco, a social worker from New Jersey who had taken a five-day NXIVM class in Albany and became alarmed at the cultlike aspects of the organization, particularly its emphasis on proselytization. She provided Ross with one of Keith's "Rational Inquiry" training manuals. Ross in turn handed the materials over to two doctors for their expert analysis, and posted their scathing critiques, which quoted from the primary source material, on his organization's website. Being called a cult by Edgar Bronfman Sr. was one thing; being called a cult by one of the world's leading cult experts and deprogrammers was quite another. Keith decided to go after Ross as hard as he could. Because the "Rational Inquiry" material was proprietary, and because Stephanie Franco had violated her nondisclosure agreement by showing it to Ross, NXIVM sued the Ross Institute in both New York and New Jersey, arguing that fair use of their federal trade secret did not apply when the materials were acquired in "bad faith," and demanding an ungodly sum of money in restitution.

Eventually, the First Amendment won the day. The lawsuits were both dismissed, as the judges determined that Keith's derivative and meandering manual was not to be confused with, say, the recipe for Coke. But the damage was done. The case took fourteen years to wend its way through the court system, with NXIVM appealing each loss. Ross had pro bono legal representation, but he was an exception. Stephanie Franco spent hundreds of thousands of dollars to finally settle in 2017 for $1.

Bankrupting its detractors with frivolous lawsuits became a favorite NXIVM line of attack. Because the company's legal fees were underwritten by Clare Bronfman, whose fortune was virtually limitless, it could open its pocketbook to have any legal issue dragged out: lawsuits, appeals, criminal complaints...whatever the well-fed attorneys might dream up. Better financed than anyone he took on; Vanguard was relentless in using the legal system to attack his detractors.

Keith used the Bronfman money in other ways, too. When he explained that he, the Smartest Man in the World, had devised a foolproof system for playing the commodities market, Clare forked over tens of millions to bring his scheme from the whiteboard to the commodities market. With every loss, Keith would blame her father, claiming that Senior had devised an elaborate conspiracy to ruin him. And she believed him. Within a few short years, he had blown through some $65 million, with nothing to show for it: the equivalent of going all in on red, and the roulette wheel coming up black. Vanguard had little in common with the investment company that shared his name. It takes a special kind of genius indeed to make that much money disappear.

Clare also financed NXIVM real estate deals. Dozens of properties in the Knox Woods development, commercial offices in Clifton Park and Albany, twenty-six properties in and around Los Angeles, satellite facilities in Mexico City, Monterrey, and Vancouver, even a tropical island near Fiji, where Vanguard would repair to rest and rejuvenate—Bronfman money paid for it all. Keith, meanwhile, presented as a modest, humble man, a sort of New Age monk, a renunciate, who carried no money, owned nothing himself, did not drive a car.

Finally, and most ominously, the Bronfman money was invested in municipal, state, and national politics. Albany has a well-deserved reputation for cronyism and graft. Using Clare's money, Keith bought as much political influence as he possibly could. This influence permeated the entire legal system. His white-shoe Albany law firm of O'Connor and Aronowitz could have opted not to take on a vindictive cult leader as a client; they chose billable hours over ethics. Insofar as politicians can be swayed by big donations and other, seedier perquisites, he paid off them, too. His goal was to have one of his underlings be a candidate for some prominent office. This goal was never achieved—as far as we know.

Clare also paid for "opposition research"—that is, the gathering of dirt: what Keith would call "collateral." When the FBI raided Nancy Salzman's Clifton Park home in 2018, they found a treasure trove of material on any number of influential politicians:

Senator Chuck Schumer, former state senate majority leader Joe Bruno, former governor Eliot Spitzer, and David Soares, the district attorney for Albany County—a key decision maker with respect to the pursuit of criminal charges. Vanguard presumably wanted to use these dossiers in his vast lobbying effort.

"Financial dossiers" were also kept on other prominent figures. George Hearst, who owned the *Times Union*, had a file. So did Rick Ross, the cult deprogrammer and longtime Raniere adversary, as well as Edgar Bronfman Sr. There was a dossier on the notorious Republican political operative Roger Stone. In a paranoid move that sounds like something from a John Grisham thriller, NXIVM spied on *its own* legal team, keeping dossiers on each lawyer, in case the attorneys developed a conscience. And while my name is not big enough to merit mention in the reporting, there was a file on me in that basement, too. During the trial, after fighting to have the files entered as evidence, the prosecutor, Moira Kim Penza, rattled off the important names involved and then pointed at me and said, "Even Toni Natalie."

In 2009, the Bronfmans scored their most impressive NXIVM victory. Sara and Clare arranged for the Dalai Lama to visit the city of Albany. Keith had hobnobbed with notable public figures before, but the Dalai Lama was on another stratum, in terms of both fame and enlightenment. When Vanguard grasped the hand of the Dalai Lama at Albany's Palace Theatre, symbolizing the equal standing of two spiritual leaders, it was the pinnacle of NXIVM's success. Keith Raniere would never know a greater achievement.

There is no question that without the liquor heiresses' money, influence, and hard work, NXIVM would never have grown as big as it did, expanded as fast as it did, or broke as bad as it did. If Nancy Salzman gave Keith permission to be Vanguard, the Bronfmans supercharged his twisted ambitions. Prefect allowed him to be Batman; the heiresses paid for stately Wayne Manor, the Batmobile, and all of the contraptions in the Batcave.

But all of this was not enough to atone for Clare's ethical breach—for telling her father about the loan and screwing up the *Forbes* piece. She would never stop trying to right that perceived wrong.

Clare Bronfman, too, was a victim of Vanguard. But she was also one of his key accomplices, torturing others just as Keith tortured her. She recruited women into Keith's web, at least one of whom, Sylvie, an equestrian from England, became a branded slave. It's hard to regard with much sympathy a cruel, petty heiress whom the *New York Times* rightly compared to the grand inquisitor of the notorious Spanish Inquisition.

## Email exchange between Sylvie —— and Clare Bronfman

*At the time, Sylvie was in training to be a professional distance runner, and Keith, who had no experience in that sport, was her coach. Clare had recruited her into NXIVM as her protégée and monitored her weight, food intake, and training routine every day. In Clifton Park, Sylvie had lived in Clare's house. At the time of this exchange, she was in England, recovering from a major medical issue that was a result of the rigorous training schedule and the lack of nutrition and proper care.*

**Sylvie to Clare Bronfman, December 5, 2012:**

Hey love!

Thank you for calling me!! I am sorry we missed one another...here is an update on Docs/Land of Sylvie!

RE Doctor—he is happy that the abscess is getting bigger as it gives them a better chance if being accurate when they cut into it...and cause less overall damage! He thinks that the pain I have had in that whole area may be an affect of the infection...He thinks heal time will likely be 4–6 weeks with an open wound that will need monitoring and redressing by the nurse...He thinks I really need to back off for a while and take things steady.

I also just wanted to share my process with you more, maybe so you can understand what is going on for me

165

better. I have been pushing through and fighting myself for a long time. Ignoring my body to do what I felt was the 'right' thing...I have always felt compelled to have to try to achieve something or be something...and now I am starting to consider that maybe I don't need to be 'the best' at something to love myself and be ok with me. I feel quite out of touch on what I truly want...a lot of the time I feel like I am trying to gain love or acceptance through results and being 'good' at something...

Everyone (from ESP or not) has suggested that before making any major decisions, I get well, rest, heal, and take some objective time. Which is a very good idea! I know that I needed a break before I threw the baby out with the bathwater...so this has enforced a break before I break myself!

Lots of love

Sylv xoxo

*Clare Bronfman to Sylvie, December 6, 2012:*

Dear Sylvie,

I felt sad in reading this email as it seems to be from your language, and your weight and eating patterns, you have slipped back into the robot Sylvie perspective. I can certainly understand this has been a scary time for you, it must feel very alone, scary and unsure. Try allowing yourself to feel those things. I also understand the temptations and what in this moment seems like an easier path, to disconnect and resort to what is most comfortable during this time, to find some predictability, some sense of feeling strong etc.

Love,

Clare

# CHAPTER 15:

# TRIALS

## Rochester, New York, 2003–2006

---

**O**nce my bankruptcy went through, I thought I was through with Keith Raniere. He was the head of a burgeoning business empire, the founder of a philosophical movement, the puller of the Bronfman purse strings, the rooster in a town house full of clucking hens. I wasn't even in Clifton Park anymore. I lived with Scott in Rochester, three and a half hours away. I wanted nothing more than to turn the page on that regrettable chapter of my life and forget all about the alleged Smartest Man in the World.

But Keith refused to let me go. He simply could not tolerate that someone he was that close to, someone he thought he would control forever, had slipped out of his hands. To hundreds of NXIVM students, I was Lucifer, the suppressive—the one he wrote the "Fall" module about. In the classroom, in the module called "Persistency," the proctor would say, "Who is the pretty brunette with a green scarf?" and then explain, "That is Toni Natalie. We don't talk about her. She is the suppressive that broke Vanguard's heart." To Keith, I was living proof that he was fallible. If he could not possess me, he wanted to destroy me. When he told me he'd see me dead or in jail, he wasn't exaggerating. He wanted me behind bars or, better yet, six feet underground. If he had to choose between meeting the Dalai Lama and watching my execution, I think he would have opted for the latter. He never wavered on this, and everyone knew it. Even Daniela Flores, the Mexican prodigy whom Keith seduced and later enslaved, a woman I'd never met, mentioned me by name in her court testimony when asked for an example of a suppressive. My ruination was that important to him.

Vanguard had tremendous resources to invest in this operation. By 2003, he had "enrolled" Sara and Clare Bronfman, who gave him financial carte blanche. His budget was virtually limitless. Too, the hundreds of Nxians who believed I was literally the incarnation of evil were ready, willing, and eager to do their part to drive a stake through my vampire heart, in service to their Vanguard.

In 2003, Scott and I were working for my brother at Mr. Shoes—a pizza place. The only way to escape from what was going on around me—and to pay my ever-increasing stack of bills—was to work, so that's what I did. Scott and I were at the pizza place when we weren't sleeping. By this time, Michael was sixteen years old, a few years away from high school graduation. He had survived a childhood that included formative years living with Keith Raniere, and, with a lot of credit to Rusty, blossomed into a happy, healthy, brilliant young man. My main priority was to keep Michael safe. I had achieved this—at the price of my living without him, which broke my heart.

From 1999 until the day of his arrest, Keith engaged in what is best described as terrorism by litigation. For most of that time, Kristin Keeffe spearheaded this operation. It would go like this: they sued me. When the lawsuit was thrown out, they filed an appeal. Then they terminated the appeal and sued in a different court. Then they filed a separate lawsuit, until they exhausted the legal system, or it was deemed to be frivolous. They had me investigated by the FBI. They did all of these things multiple times, so I was never not hounded by their lawyers. All this litigation takes a few sentences to summarize, but at the time, and for years, it was a gauntlet. Each new suit had to be addressed. I had to pay for legal representation. Meanwhile, the Albany insiders seemed to be siding with Keith—who was, after all, a prominent local businessman, as well as the Smartest Man in the World.

I began to doubt my own sanity. Maybe Keith was right. Maybe I really was the devil. My mental health was in peril, and my physical health along with it. I suffered from migraines and from weird aches and pains, the cause of which I could not determine. I was a nervous wreck. In April 2004 I was diagnosed with post-traumatic stress disorder.

My mother, who had been supporting me financially during this crisis, was forced to file for bankruptcy on July 15, 2004. She had blown through her life savings to pay my legal and medical expenses, and now there was nothing left. Keith dispatched Kristin Keeffe to Rochester, where she attempted to intercede in my mom's bankruptcy proceeding by purchasing a creditor's position for $375. The judge, John Ninfo, threw her and her attorney out of the courtroom.

My parents were now going through hell with me, and I felt responsible for their plight. But there was nothing I could do about it, apart from putting in more hours at the pizzeria. The guilt was all consuming. I was moved by my mother's sacrifice, by her love, but ashamed that I was the cause of so much trouble.

I stopped eating. I stopped sleeping.

In the summer of 2004, I had a full-fledged nervous breakdown and was diagnosed with PTSD.

But nothing stopped the onslaught of litigation. Keith's legal mercenaries were angling to have me indicted for bank fraud. Meanwhile, Kristin Keeffe filed suit against me, which led to another series of appeals, terminations, refilings, and so on to infinity.

Then my dog died. Jake, a very protective German shepherd, got sick after eating what I thought was a bad batch of dog food. I brought him to the vet, hysterical, but there was nothing that could be done. Years later, Kristin Keeffe intimated that a private detective staking out my house had poisoned my dog. "We couldn't get close to the house," she said. "The dog. The dog was always in the way."

Keith Raniere *killed my dog*.

Keith Raniere had taken my son's childhood, my career, my life savings, my parents' life savings, my brother's life savings, my mental health, my physical well-being, my beloved pet. That single sentence contains enough heartache and loss for multiple lifetimes. But it didn't end there. He'd poisoned every relationship I had since meeting him and ultimately destroyed my marriage to Scott Foley.

Scott and I took a much-needed and well-deserved vacation, renting a cabin on Canandaigua Lake. I had climbed out of the abyss and was working hard on myself, on my emotional recovery. For the first time in a long time, I felt optimistic. But I didn't get that vibe from Scott. Even on the drive there, he seemed off—distracted somehow. It was my birthday, August 12, so we went to dinner with some friends. When we got back to the cabin that night, there was an incredible thunderstorm. The bursts of lightning shone purple light on the mountain, and all of that majesty was reflected on the lake. "Come outside," I told Scott. "You can see God over the mountain."

"I'm good," he called from the back bedroom.

But it was too singularly beautiful to be missed. So I went inside to get him. Scott was sitting in bed, blanket over his knees, fiddling with his phone. His thumbs were moving at warp speed. He was so enthralled by whatever he was doing that he didn't see me come in. When he noticed me, he was startled, and dropped the phone. It wasn't his phone, I realized. It was a burner, the disposable kind that drug dealers use.

We both went for the phone. We grabbed it at the same time. But he was both stronger and taller, so he pulled it up over his head, and my grip wasn't tight enough to snatch it. So, I grabbed his scrotum instead.

"Let go of my balls!"

"Let go of the phone!"

"Let go of my balls!"

"Let go of the phone!"

At that moment, my beloved dog, Raymona, cried out and peed on the floor. Worried, I loosened my grip on his balls (if not for Raymona, I could have ripped them clean off). He broke the phone in half, went outside, and hurled it into the darkness. As it flew, a bolt of lightning crashed.

"I'm sorry," he said. "It's just—you're so distant, I barely know you anymore. Samantha makes me feel young, alive. Wanted."

"Samantha?" I spat the name at him. "Sa*man*tha?"

I packed up his things that night and sent him away. We were done. A few days later, I got an out-of-the-blue Facebook friend request from "Samantha Orr." She wanted me to know that she was the one who had been texting my husband. As soon as she relayed that message, she vanished. Her profile picture morphed into a faceless egg. Scott had never actually met her in person. He'd been catfished. "Samantha" was a honeypot, I realized, tasked with seducing my husband and ruining our marriage.

In the months that followed, Raymona—whom I loved more than I loved Scott, truth be told—developed a rare medical condition that caused her nails to painfully fall out.

Now even my *guard dog* had PTSD.

# CHAPTER 16:

# THE REVENGE PLAYBOOK

## Joseph O'Hara. Frank Parlato.

---

After the disastrous *Forbes* article, NXIVM began to invest heavily in public relations. The process would always play out the same way:

1/ A political insider with deep Albany connections would be hired to, basically, make the company, and Vanguard, look good.

2/ That insider would be generously compensated with Bronfman money.

3/ After a brief honeymoon period, the insider would realize that Keith Raniere was a spiteful, petty man who was engaged in legally suspicious activities.

4/ The insider would end the relationship.

5/ NXIVM would add him to its enemies list and go after the insider ruthlessly.

In 2004, NXIVM retained the services of the lobbyist Doug

Rutnik, a longtime Albany operative, paying him $100,000 over the course of four months to advance the interests of the company. He bailed when he discovered that Vanguard was bad news, and then they sued him to get the money back. At the time, his daughter, Kirsten Gillibrand, was in Senator Hillary Clinton's inner circle, and two years away from a successful run for the House. Gillibrand won that seat and would eventually replace Clinton as US senator. (Asked about her father's connection to NXIVM on the 2019 campaign trail, Gillibrand claimed never to have heard of the company until she read about Keith Raniere's sex cult in the news. That seemed unlikely, considering that her father was sued by the company and her father's wife was once a Nxian.)

Rutnik was able to escape Vanguard's clutches with "just" a six-figure hit on his bank account. His colleague was not as lucky.

On October 1, 2003, Nancy Salzman hired an attorney named Joseph O'Hara to consult on a variety of thorny issues, including "its pending lawsuit against Rick Ross and other parties; its generally unfavorable reputation with members of the local business communities; the potential negative impact of several articles concerning the company that had already been published by the media—and the potential negative impact of several other articles that were being prepared for publication," especially the *Forbes* piece, as O'Hara would explain in a complaint filed in 2012. At the time of his hire, he was unaware that NXIVM was shady, or that Keith Raniere was anything more than a quirky eccentric.

Over the next fifteen months, before he parted ways with the company in early 2005, O'Hara realized that NXIVM was, for all intents and purposes, a cult, and that, as he phrased it in his complaint, "the NXIVM/ESP-related business entities are part of a complex and conspiratorial scheme and agreement that involves a variety of tortious and/or illegal activities," which he listed as "bank fraud; bribery; business fraud and theft; charities fraud; conspiracy; corruption and/or attempted corruption of public officials; endangering the welfare of a child; filing false instruments; insurance fraud; violations of Federal and State campaign finance statutes and regulations; immigration fraud; labor fraud; mail fraud; money laundering; obstruction of justice; perjury; structuring; tax evasion; tax fraud; theft of services; and wire fraud." He determined that, while the various NXIVM companies were established to appear independent, they were all controlled, "in toto, by Raniere/Vanguard even though he has no acknowledged ownership interest in—and no formal position of authority in—any of those entities," and called for the "corporate veil" to be "pierced." He recognized NXIVM as an MLM that operated as a Ponzi scheme—exactly the sort of company that Keith Raniere, after the fall of Consumers' Buyline, was barred from ever again operating in the state of New York.

O'Hara alleged that the manner in which NXIVM treated the Bronfmans' $150 million investment may have circumvented tax law. He wrote "although much of this funding has been labeled as 'loans' for accounting and tax purposes, there is, in fact, no reasonable expectation that any of these funds will ever be repaid," and thus they should be treated as taxable income. Further, he argued that, because Vanguard and his minions were "financially dependent upon the Bronfman sisters for their existence," Clare and Sara Bronfman "should be held personally accountable and financially liable for all of the tortious and/or illegal activities" undertaken by anyone in the NXIVM outfit.

Along with the illegal activities, O'Hara also noted the relentless filing of lawsuits against Keith's enemies and the lobbying of various county district attorneys to bring trumped-up charges against a number of NXIVM detractors—charges that "were intended to silence [O'Hara] and other individuals who have been critical of—and/or who have important documents and/or information concerning—the company's operations and/or Raniere/Vanguard's debauched lifestyle." Among the targets of this terrorism by litigation: O'Hara; the New Jersey social worker and onetime ESP participant Stephanie Franco; the cult expert Rick Alan Ross; and me.

Around Thanksgiving of 2004, O'Hara received a status report from a private investigations firm called Interfor. Although his law firm had originally retained Interfor, he claimed he had little, if any, contact with Interfor and its staff—all of the correspondence had gone through Kristin Keeffe, the NXIVM legal liaison. Interfor was surveilling the cult deprogrammer Rick Alan Ross, against whom NXIVM had filed suit. Interfor's status report concerned this surveillance, and it contained information that O'Hara suspected could not have been legally obtained without a court order. When O'Hara brought this to the attention of NXIVM, he was told that the shady activity would cease. It did not. In the coming weeks, he received FedEx packages that contained what he believed were "items that had been retrieved from Ross' trash (e.g., coffee-stained receipts; crumpled credit card statements and phone bills; etc.). When he informed [Kristin] Keeffe about these packages, she instructed him not to open any more of them—and she appeared at his office later that day to retrieve all of the FedEx boxes that had already arrived."

Finally, O'Hara had enough. He met with Nancy and told her that, and tendered his resignation. She refused to take no for an answer. When O'Hara refused to reconsider, Prefect, sounding much like a female version of Keith, rattled off all of the unpleasantness that might befall him should he make good on his threat to leave: "he may be sued; he may get indicted; he may get disbarred," and so forth. It eerily echoed the veiled threats that had been made to me. When O'Hara ignored this, NXIVM sent another lobbyist, the Arkansas native Richard Mays, who was supposedly chummy with the Clintons, to talk him out of it. O'Hara was friends with Mays—indeed, it was O'Hara who originally introduced him to Keith and Nancy. Mays, however, failed to sway him. O'Hara left NXIVM for good in early January 2005.

In August of 2005, NXIVM sued O'Hara in the US Northern District Court, demanding a temporary restraining order and other "extraordinary relief" measures. Half an hour after those measures were rejected, NXIVM withdrew the suit and immediately refiled it with the New York State Supreme Court in Manhattan. In a complaint he later filed in the US Northern District Court on February 9, 2012, O'Hara explains:

> NXIVM/ESP's lawsuit against the Plaintiff included what has since become "standard litigation tactics" for almost all of the lawsuits that it—and other Defendants—file. These tactics include, but are not necessarily limited to, the following:
>     (a) Multiple causes-of-action;
>     (b) Onerous and duplicative demands for documents and records;
>     (c) Extensive motion practice;
>     (d) Complaints filed with licensing authorities;
>     (e) Attempts to have criminal charges brought against the opposing party;

(f) Refusal to produce documents and records;

(g) Refusal to produce witnesses;

(h) Perjured testimony;

(i) One or more requests for substitution of counsel;

(j) One or more requests for a change of venue;

(k) Witness intimidation; and

(l) Co-mingling of cases: e.g., using discovery in one case to obtain evidence and information for use in other cases.

It was the NXIVM revenge playbook in writing.

As all this was going on, and the various legal proceedings moved slowly through the court system, Kristin Keeffe, who spearheaded Vanguard's internal legal team, was hired as an unpaid legal intern at the Albany County District Attorney's office. Although she was used as a legal attack dog, Keeffe was not a law student. Keeffe did not even have an undergraduate degree. She was spectacularly unqualified.

Despite her obvious lack of credentials or experience, Kristin Keeffe was generally unsupervised, and as O'Hara notes in his complaint:

> was given privileges that normally would be limited to senior staff: e.g., she was assigned her own desk and workspace; she was given her own Xerox Key; etc. In addition, Keeffe was... allowed to undertake a variety of legal-related activities—including, but not limited to, the drafting of subpoenas for documents and records concerning the Plaintiff and the preparation of exhibits for the then-sitting Albany County Grand Jury.

Once embedded, she was able to keep abreast of the goings-on in the various cases, including the lawsuit against O'Hara.

Based upon information and belief, Keeffe copied some/all of the documents and records concerning [O'Hara] that were obtained via subpoenas that were issued by the Office of the Albany County District Attorney or the then-sitting Albany County Grand Jury.

Thereafter, Keeffe ... provided copies of some/all of those documents and records to one or more members of the Proskauer Rose law firm, which, at that time, was representing NXIVM/ESP in conjunction with its lawsuit against [O'Hara] ... Upon receiving copies of the documents and records that Keeffe had copied while she was working in the Office of the Albany County District Attorney, the Proskauer Rose law firm, based upon information and belief, immediately introduced some/all of them as exhibits in NXIVM's above-referenced lawsuit against [O'Hara]. This specifically included, but may not have been limited to, documents and records concerning one or more of the Plaintiffs then-existing bank accounts.

NXIVM spent considerable sums to wage a negative publicity campaign against him, going so far as to take out billboard advertisements to get their point across. The objective was to tarnish his reputation so badly that he would not be able to make a living in Albany ever again.

And they harassed him, just as they harassed me. Vanguard would not, could not, leave the man be, per O'Hara's 2012 complaint:

NXIVM/ESP...undertook a variety of activities that were intended to harass and/or intimidate [O'Hara]. These activities included, but were not necessarily limited to, the following:

(a) Filing fictitious change-of-address cards for him with the U.S. Post Office;

(b) Cutting the telephone line—and the cable television line—at [O'Hara's] former residences;

(c) Spray-painting the phrase "You will die in 7 days" at a construction site on [O'Hara's] property in New Baltimore, N.Y.;

(d) Filing a false complaint against [O'Hara] with the District of Columbia Bar;

(e) Attempting to have [O'Hara] indicted in several jurisdictions; and

(f) Filing Adversary Proceedings in [O'Hara's] bankruptcy case (Note: That bankruptcy case has been pending for more than forty-three (43) months—and has cost the Plaintiff more than $50,000 of legal fees and expenses).

These were the same tactics used against me, right down to the drawn-out bankruptcy proceeding.

To a certain degree, NXIVM's war against Joe O'Hara was successful. He did go bankrupt. He suffered from health problems related to the stress of the onslaught of actions taken against him. His legal career ended. But O'Hara never yielded to Vanguard. He was unafraid to tell the truth and was an early and important source for most of the first exposés written on Keith and his company. He would become my first true ally and the one person I knew I could always count on.

\*   \*   \*

If O'Hara initiated the lengthy process of convincing the federal government that NXIVM was a criminal enterprise, it was a subsequent PR hire who finished the deal. Frank Parlato Jr. was a real estate developer from Buffalo who also wrote for a number of upstate print publications. A good friend of the internationally notorious political operative Roger Stone and the locally notorious political operative Steve Pigeon—the former a Republican, the latter a Democrat—Parlato was active in local politics, where he had a reputation as a bulldog who was unafraid to roll up his sleeves and play rough. Like his friends, Parlato was a character: funny, charismatic, eccentric, volatile. It was through Stone and Pigeon, both of whom had done work for NXIVM, that Parlato made the acquaintance of Keith Raniere, who hired him in 2007. He was fifty-six years old—nine years older than his employer.

This was during Keith's "celibate monk" phase, when he told everyone he was a renunciate. "He would walk into meetings barefoot, in jeans and a t-shirt," Parlato recalled in an interview with Oxygen in 2018. "He would spout on the meaning of life, and the women would swoon." The groovy hippie crowd was not Parlato's scene, but Frank got on well with Keith. He knew "Vanguard" was more sizzle than steak—and ESP, BS—but that didn't much bother him. If lost souls felt compelled to fork over their hard-earned money to bask in the NXIVM glow, what did he care? As he told Oxygen: "Everyone seemed chipper about their life."

Unlike O'Hara, who almost immediately balked at being asked to do anything shady, Parlato had no ethical qualms about going after Keith's detractors. Like his friends Stone and Pigeon, he was something of a dirty trickster. The reason he was paid a whopping seventy-five grand a month was to do what more squeamish people would rather not. Besides, if Keith insisted that Toni Natalie had done this, that, and the other, why should Frank Parlato believe otherwise?

NXIVM provided Parlato with an enemies list, as well as a price list of what they'd be willing to pay if certain benchmarks were achieved. For example, disbarment was awarded a $20,000 bonus. Keith was willing to pay Bronfman money to compel the indictments of his three greatest enemies: Rick Ross, Joseph O'Hara, and me. The bounty on my head was $1 million. When Parlato refused to take the assignment, suggesting that Keith instead rehabilitate his name by generating positive news stories focusing on the core ESP business of human potential, Vanguard told him, according to Parlato, "Justice and ethics demand their indictments."

Over the course of the next year, it slowly dawned on Parlato that Vanguard was a fraud. That far from being a renunciate, he spent most of his waking hours engaged in sexual activities with a veritable harem of women. That despite not owning anything or reporting any actual income, Keith almost certainly had millions squirreled away in various hiding places. That NXIVM was a house of cards propped up by the massive wealth of the Bronfman sisters, whom Keith seemed to manipulate as if they were marionettes.

In 2008, Parlato learned that Keith had spent nearly $100 million of the heiresses' fortune—a staggering sum, even for Sara and Clare. The sisters had sunk $26 million into a Los Angeles development deal, Parlato said, and had nothing to show for it. They were millions of dollars overbudget, so they enlisted him to track down their investments and bring the project under control. In return, Parlato would receive a third of the profits. He was advanced $1 million.

Parlato asked Clare Bronfman about the tens of millions lost in commodities trades. He asked if she'd seen receipts.

Clare told him that Keith had used advanced metrics to develop a foolproof algorithm to predict the commodities market. The trades had failed not because of a miscalculation on Keith's part, but rather because her globalist father and his Illuminati cabalists had used their vast wealth to "thwart" Keith by artificially manipulating the commodities market, which caused his trades to fail. She said this with a straight face. The Jewish heiress bought into an anti-Semitic trope—because that's what Vanguard had told her.

Soon after, Keith Raniere fired Frank Parlato. By then, he was more than happy to bid adieu to NXIVM. But there were a million reasons to not let him get away so easily. Although Parlato had recovered quite a bit of their missing fortune, the Bronfmans demanded a refund of his $1 million payment. Parlato refused. That put Frank Parlato squarely on the enemies list, with Rick Ross, Joseph O'Hara, and me. The Bronfmans sued him. And in 2015—seven years later—the $1 million in escrow was a key component in a nineteen-count indictment against Parlato, alleging fraud. Reading the document, Parlato saw that Clare Bronfman had perjured herself—almost certainly at the behest of Vanguard.

"That's when I had an awakening," he recalled in a 2018 interview with *Vice News*. "I had no idea of the depths of their dishonesty...If they had done this to me, then all of these enemies that supposedly had cheated them were also probably similarly innocent." In an instant, he said, he realized that "this is more than a kooky group; this is a crazy group, a criminally insane group. And it's not just Raniere."

Frank Parlato regarded the indictment as an act of war. He was at war with NXIVM. And he would use every means at his disposal—his two Buffalo-area weeklies, *Artvoice* and the *Niagara Falls Reporter*; a new blog called *Frank Report*; his connections and money; his indomitable will; and, most of all, the knowledge that he was in the right—to prevail.

There were three things Keith Raniere did not anticipate: the Internet, a mother's love, and Frank Parlato. All three would contribute to his downfall.

# CHAPTER 17:

# TERMS OF ENGAGEMENT

## Rochester, New York, 2006–2009

---

**D**ee Dee Mitzen was a teacher at the Waldorf School of Saratoga Springs—the private school of choice for NXIVM members, who honeycombed the school's board of directors. (Keith Raniere attended Waldorf schools himself and convinced me to enroll Michael at Waldorf when we were living together.) Mitzen was a dyed-in-the-wool true believer. She was a friend and confidante of Nancy Salzman. In 2003, Mitzen was so enamored with NXIVM that she raved about it in a piece in the *Sunday Gazette*, which the anti-NXIVM blogger John Tighe quoted on his now-defunct blog, *Saratoga in Decline*:

> Dee Dee Mitzen found the program so vital that she became
> a trainer. She and her husband, Ed, who owns Palio
> Communications in Saratoga Springs, found the courses
> life-changing, she said. She discounts any talk that labels

ESP as a cult, or something that separates people from their families.

"I am the example of none of that being true. My husband and I are happily married, we have three kids and we're both successful in our jobs," said Mitzen...

She touts ESP as a "school of ethics and critical thinking," and says the program has helped her get the most out of her life.

Three years later, Mitzen had a change of heart. Her husband, Ed Mitzen, who owned a local communications company, woke up to the fact that NXIVM was a cult and Keith a fraud, and quit the organization. Rather than let him go quietly, Vanguard set out to destroy him. (By now, this should sound familiar!) He arranged a liaison between Ed and another woman—as he had done with Scott and "Samantha Orr"—and tried to blackmail him.

I found this out in May of 2006, when Dee Dee contacted me. She realized that, contrary to NXIVM's claims, I was not the devil, but I *was* Keith's oldest and most hated adversary, and therefore a potential ally in the fight against him.

She confirmed that Keith and Nancy were still actively working against me. This was not surprising at all, yet still shocking. There was no limit to what Vanguard and Prefect would do to hurt me.

But this was a watershed moment for me. For years, I had been fighting NXIVM alone. I thought I was the only one. Dee Dee confirmed my suspicions and validated my feelings. I wasn't crazy. I wasn't paranoid. They really *were* out to get me.

A month later, I received a fax from Joseph O'Hara, whom I

had not yet met. It was a six-page letter to O'Hara from Anna Moody, the executive vice president of the private investigations outfit Interfor. "Headquartered in New York," the boilerplate in the letter read, "Interfor offers comprehensive and confidential worldwide corporate intelligence services. These include litigation support, due diligence, asset search and recovery, and other fraud investigations."

The letter was dated January 14, 2005. The subject line said:

**TERMS OF ENGAGEMENT**

*Re: Toni Nathalie [sic]*

**Our Reference # Case 653B**

And was followed by this:

*We are pleased that The O'Hara Group & Associates, LLC has engaged Interfor Inc. ("Interfor") to perform research and investigative services in connection with Toni Nathalie [sic]...*

On the second page, there was a "Proposal":

*Interfor will conduct a discreet, confidential investigation on Toni Nathalie [sic]. Interfor will monitor the current activities of Ms. Nathalie [sic] at her house and certain other residences as discussed... Interfor will conduct an asset investigation of Toni Nathalie [sic] focusing on current holdings as well as possible fraudulent activity... Interfor will also look at the property owned by... Scott Foley and her parents (Joan and Alfred Schneier) to determine whether or not the subjects are misrepresenting the values of their properties.*

The proposed budget for the investigation was $10,000 plus

expenses—to the Bronfmans, the equivalent of the loose change found in a sofa.

The Interfor people were clearly not crack detectives. For one thing, they spelled my last name wrong. For another, they sent this confidential letter to an attorney who, by mid-January 2005, was an enemy of Vanguard.

The *Village Voice* was working on an exposé about the telegenic Juval Aviv, Interfor's president, who'd been a fixture on the cable TV news programs since 9/11, despite his laughably questionable qualifications; it would be published under the title "Secret Agent Schmuck," which gives you some idea of the *Voice*'s conclusions. It is wonderfully apt that a fraud security expert would be hired by the fraud founder of a fraud philosophical movement. The author, Chris Thompson, interviewed me for the story, after Kristin Keeffe sent him a dossier she had written about me. The *Voice* vetted the document and declined to publish a word of it. This is how it appeared in the story:

> Asked about Natalie's allegations, NXIVM spokesman Robertson says that Aviv was merely retained to investigate whether Natalie committed fraud when she filed for bankruptcy in 1999. "I couldn't tell you what Aviv did with this Natalie woman, except that he was certainly not authorized by us to do anything other than to find out if she's committing fraud," he says. As for her claims that Raniere and his associates stalked and terrorized her, Robertson replies that Natalie is a deranged felon who embezzled a fortune and defrauded numerous banks.
>
> "She is a habitual thief, and she's a criminal," Robertson says. (The *Voice*, however, could turn up no evidence that

Natalie has ever been charged with a crime.) "She's psycho-logically damaged. The woman is—she's a classic kind of person who likes to pretend fear where she's really the victimizer.... It's ridiculous to suggest, as Toni has, that she was harassed."

Then, after denying that Natalie had been the subject of harassment, Robertson e-mailed the *Voice* an obsessively detailed 25-page report on her compiled by NXIVM associate Kristin Keeffe...which was the result of an investigation into every aspect of her life—including her family, her husband, and the restaurant chain they operate—with 47 endnotes, including references to credit-card statements and lease invoices. Keeffe's report accuses Natalie of no fewer than 260 counts of bank fraud, racketeering, and money laundering. Somehow, Robertson expected that this report—almost frightening in its level of detail—would prove that Raniere has put his involvement with Natalie behind him.

Thompson also reported on NXIVM's relentless attempts to discredit, bankrupt, and perhaps even murder the cult expert Rick Ross—a story broken by the journalist Chet Hardin for *Metroland*. There was an elaborate scheme to lure him to a cruise ship, where he would meet with a woman who was allegedly trying to escape from a cult group. Once he was on the ship, Kristin Keeffe was to introduce herself as that woman. God knows what would have become of Rick Ross had he gone through with it.

This was all chilling, to be sure. But it again reinforced that I was not alone. Keith's vengeful ruthlessness was not limited to me, as I had once believed. *All* of his detractors were subjected to the same abuse: lawsuits, indictments, harassment, surveillance, sting operations…whatever demented shit he could dream up was imposed, not just on me, but on everyone: Rick Ross, Joe O'Hara, Ed Mitzen, and Frank Parlato; and, in time, Barbara Bouchey, a high-ranking Nxian and member of Keith's inner circle, Susan Dones, who owned the NXIVM center in Tacoma, and seven others collectively known as the NXIVM Nine, who defected in 2009; John Tighe, who ran the *Saratoga in Decline* blog; and journalists who wrote investigative pieces on Keith, including James Odato of the *Times Union*, Chet Hardin of *Metroland*, and Suzanna Andrews from *Vanity Fair*. There are, I'm sure, other targets of his vengeance that I don't know about.

After Joe O'Hara reached out to me, we compared notes. For the first time in ages, I felt validated. Keith Raniere was evil, and *I wasn't the only one who thought so.* Since leaving Keith, I had been playing defense. Once Joe opened my eyes to the breadth of the battlefield, I went on the offensive. I would do everything in my power to expose his true nature.

Chet Hardin was an ambitious young reporter writing for *Metroland*, an Albany weekly. In the summer of 2006, he contacted me. He proposed writing a piece about Keith and NXIVM, using me as the focal point. He wanted to tell my story.

By that time, I'd done a number of interviews with various journalists—anyone writing a feature about Keith sought me out as a source—but I'd never really bared my soul. The 2003 *Forbes* feature spends two paragraphs discussing my bankruptcy case, Keith's *Paradise Lost* letter and "Fall" timeline, and the hell he was putting me through, and includes a single quote: "I can't think.

I can't work. I can't pay my bills." But I'd never bared my soul. Hardin offered me the opportunity, and I seized it.

I told him how Keith had helped me quit smoking. I told him about Keith's "Smartest Man in the World" backstory. I told him about my experiences with Consumers' Buyline and how Pam Cafritz had been so excited to meet me. I told him about my brother John, Rusty and Michael, and my move to Clifton Park. I told him about the beginnings of ESP and how NXIVM taught its students that I was Lucifer. I told him how I broke up with Keith because he shrunk my wool sweater. I told him about my PTSD diagnosis. Chet used all of it, and more. The result was a long feature, "Stress in the Family," which ran right around my forty-eighth birthday, in August of 2006.

Chet supplemented my story with excellent reporting—so good, in fact, that NXIVM sued the owner of *Metroland* for $65 million; in the lawsuit, the company claims that Hardin conspired with "Syrian Jews" to destroy NXIVM. It was the first time the company filed suit against a newspaper.

One section of the piece was particularly illuminating:

> The pressure NXIVM places on its students to recruit others for Intensives is unremitting, says former Espian Maria (not her real name; she asked to remain anonymous for fear of retaliation). From a prominent Mexican family, she was 27 years old and studying for her master's degree in New York City when her brother recruited her...
>
> To understand The Fall, one must understand suppressives. When a person is a destructive force in the world, Maria says, such as a serial killer, a terrorist, or a critic of NXIVM, when they exhibit suppressive traits, when they destruct

value, they are referred to as suppressives. And just as Lucifer took a fall in Paradise Lost (an oft-referenced text in NXIVM circles), Espians are taught that suppressives are capable of taking The Fall. Once they have, it is taught that they have developed an anticonscience—good feels bad to them and bad feels good.

It was in the teachings about suppressives and The Fall that Maria began to feel that NXIVM was warning: You cannot leave, you cannot criticize or question the organization.

NXIVM has a strict hierarchy with Raniere (aka Vanguard) at the top...The higher in the hierarchy, the closer an Espian is to integration, akin to being enlightened, perfect: Thoughts flow together flawlessly, Maria says, "like a plate without any cracks." Salzman is close to integration, she says, and Raniere is completely integrated.

He is treated, she says, "like a Buddha or a Christ."

After being taught the module's material, the students break up into groups. Espians from every rank sit together and discuss the lesson. "When you are in the group," Maria says, "you will be asked questions like: 'Is suicide good? Is suicide bad?'"

A student might answer, "'I think it is bad, because you are being a coward.'" To which a coach might reply: "'I think suicide is not that bad. Because, if you are a bad person, if you are not constructing value, if you are destructing value, then you should not have a place in the world, and you should be happy to kill yourself.'" In this way, she says, a student's belief system is constantly undermined. Doubt is cast upon opinions, and beliefs are systematically torn down...

After training with NXIVM for six months, Maria suffered a

psychotic episode that she attributed to extreme stress. She began hallucinating and had to be taken to the hospital.

"It was in the moment before...I went into my psychotic break," she says. "I felt that I had to decide between my boyfriend and my life, and Keith. And that's when I broke. It's the devotion to him; you have to give your life to him. I didn't want to lose my boyfriend, and I didn't want to lose my life; he [Raniere] wants to have the control of your life."

Maria spent the next two years in treatment, taking antipsychotic and antidepressant medications. She still gets nervous talking about NXIVM and says that former Espians like herself are afraid to speak out because they know how suppressives are treated.

The meditations on suicide were especially alarming to me. I was intimately familiar with Prefect's techniques and how she seemed to get off on controlling people. What better way to measure how powerful you really are, how much control you really have, than by compelling your followers to kill themselves? This was the madness of Jim Jones, of Heaven's Gate, of the Order of the Solar Temple. Vanguard was planting the seed, so that if he one day wanted them to *literally* drink the Kool-Aid, they would guzzle it down. I thought about Gina Hutchinson, who was in contact with Keith before shooting herself. I thought about Kristin Snyder, who wrote that horrible suicide note before her disappearance.

And then, on March 12, 2009, I had the misfortune of revisiting Vanguard's warped views on suicide, when my brother John took his own life. Like my parents, he was suffering because of what Keith was doing to us. John was a wreck. He was seven years older and had regarded himself as the man of the house from a very young age. He felt responsible for me, responsible for my mother. He wanted to protect me from my tormentor, but there was only so much he could do.

John communicated sporadically with Keith for years, always trying to negotiate my freedom—as he'd done when I left back in 1999. But this was not a fight among equals. NXIVM had unlimited resources, while ours were tapped out. Keith was surrounded by a coven of brainwashed witches who would fly hither and yon at his command. My brother was desperate, exhausted, financially ruined, and mentally broken. He was taking strong medications to treat angina and hypertension. He was drinking too much. And he was in regular contact with Keith all through the winter. There were emails, phone calls, even a personal visit from Vanguard's fixer, Kristin Keeffe. The autopsy lists the cause of death as suicide by a lethal combination of metoprolol and diltiazem, John's heart medications. I thought about my brother, so damaged, so empathic, and wondered what fucked-up messages Keith had communicated to him in months days leading up to his death. In April 2009 I was diagnosed with fibromyalgia.

How many more lives would Vanguard claim before he was stopped?

# CHAPTER 18:

# "THE CULT SIDE"

Allison Mack. Bad Press. The NXIVM Nine.

---

L. Ron Hubbard, the founder of Scientology, recognized the value of recruiting high-profile celebrities to his religious movement. The Church of Scientology has always had a major presence in Hollywood. In Tom Cruise and John Travolta, Scientology produced the movie-star exemplars Hubbard had always dreamed of.

Keith Raniere had similar ambitions. Like Hubbard, he knew that the higher the profile of NXIVM's members, the higher the profile of NXIVM. Indeed, it was part of ESP's prime directive to recruit "people of influence." But Vanguard never made it in Hollywood. He never drew the big stars to his executive success company—perhaps because, if you're one of the most successful film actors of all time, why do you need executive success coaching? Keith had to settle for Vancouver, one of the two major Canadian film centers, and a gaggle of TV actresses most Americans couldn't pick out of a lineup.

*Smallville* is a cable TV show about the high school Clark Kent during the critical years when he realizes his enormous powers and evolves into Superman. In the pilot episode, we see the crash that brought the infant Kal-El to Kansas from planet Krypton. The baby is adopted by a kindly couple who have no children of their own; his father on the show is played by the ruggedly handsome John Schneider, of *Dukes of Hazzard* fame. Meanwhile, the fallout from the blast has given some of the locals weird superpowers. In the first season, each episode involves a villain who has gone mad with power as a result of overexposure to the crash site. It's campy and corny and fun and was popular with young audiences.

Clark's romantic interest on the show is the beautiful, popular, and friendly Lana Lang. His love for her remains unrequited, because despite his attraction, he gets physically ill every time he goes near her. This is not because of his social anxiety, as most of their peers assume, but because Lana Lang wears around her neck a shiny green gemstone that *we* know is Kryptonite—a tiny sliver of the exploded planet Krypton, exposure to which makes Superman lose his superpowers.

Lana Lang was played by a Canadian actress whose indeterminate ethnicity—in fact: half Dutch, half Chinese, with some Jamaican blood thrown in for good measure—made her especially attractive, and more exotic-looking in small-town Kansas than even the flying man from another planet. Her name was Kristin Kreuk.

Kreuk took her first NXIVM class in 2005, when she was twenty-three years old. She claims to have operated on the periphery of the organization; she took, and found value in, the training, she wrote on Twitter, but was unaware of the "illegal and nefarious activity" within the larger company. Three other Canadian actresses had already joined NXIVM by then: Nicki Clyne, the same age as Kreuk, and Allison Mack, who had a small role on *Smallville* but is best known for playing Callie on *Battlestar Galactica*; Grace Parks, star of the *Hawaii Five-O* reboot; and the first of the actresses to join, Sarah Edmondson, six years older than the others, who knew Kreuk from their days on the teen angst series *Edgemont*.

Lauren Salzman, the daughter of Prefect and by 2006 a high-ranking NXIVM member, was dispatched to British Columbia on a recruitment mission. She hit it off immediately with one of Kreuk's costars, the twenty-four-year-old Allison Mack. On the show, Mack played the spunky Chloe Sullivan, editor of the Smallville High newspaper, who was an aspiring investigative journalist and mapped out the various local weirdnesses on a bulletin board that would not have looked out of place in Keith's office. Chloe Sullivan would have been able to sniff out Vanguard as a charlatan; Allison Mack, sadly, did not possess that talent. And while Chloe Sullivan was a secondary character on *Smallville*, Allison Mack was to play a starring role in the NXIVM saga.

Keith immediately recognized the potential of the Vancouver NXIVM contingent, both for expanding the company's influence and for sating his own depraved desires. The actresses were all young, pretty, and thin, which he liked. They were also seekers, open to new ideas and experiences, and thus especially susceptible to his charms. Mack, a prototypical child actor, had been modeling and acting since she was a little kid. After earning critical praise for her portrayal of a troubled teen who took to cutting herself in 1998's *7th Heaven*, she scored her first series, *Opposite Sex*, two years later. *Smallville* debuted in 2001, when she was seventeen. The final episode aired ten years later, and while she enjoyed a decade of steady work, she had failed to make the leap from basic cable to something bigger. And Allison Mack desperately sought something bigger—not just professionally, but spiritually. At age twenty-four, as *Smallville* was on the wane, she was at a crossroads. This is when she met Vanguard, whom she believed could help revive her stalled acting career. She was dazzled by his brilliance. Keith, she was told, could coach anyone to do anything. He had coached a long-distance runner, an equestrian, a filmmaker, a tennis player, a scientist. Never mind that none of his charges benefited one iota from his "coaching" or that there was zero evidence to support Vanguard's technique. Mack was convinced that Keith could help her get over the hump from child actor to leading lady.

I'll say this about Allison Mack: she doesn't do anything halfway. She quickly became one of the most devoted of Vanguard's followers, as well as one of the most successful NXIVM recruiters. Her fervor approached the religious in temperament. Like some New Age missionary, she was forever on the hunt for new members. She was pushy; she was relentless; she was monomaniacal. She used social media to achieve these aims, clumsily attempting to entice the *Harry Potter* actress Emma Watson via tweet. Watson, like Mack, was a child actor who grew from girl to woman onscreen. Like Mack, she was concerned about humanitarian causes. Fortunately, Watson did not take the bait.

Interestingly, according to Lauren Salzman's testimony, Keith was not having sex with Allison Mack during her initial NXIVM period. As she was recruiting as many women as she could into the organization, Mack harbored the delusion that Vanguard was a renunciate. She would not know Keith sexually until years later, when she made the fateful decision to join the secret sorority known as Dominus Obsequious Sororium, or DOS.

After the *Metroland* story in 2006, no one could credibly claim to be in the dark about the true nature of NXIVM or its Vanguard. But Keith, Nancy, Clare Bronfman, Pam Cafritz, Barbara Bouchey, and the rest of the inner circle took great pains to deny the accuracy of the stories that slowly began to appear in the mainstream media. "The government is out to get me," Keith said. "They are suppressives, and they want to destroy the good work we're doing." It was the same sort of lie he'd told to the CBI employees all those years ago when Consumers' Buyline was being sued by all those state attorneys general. For the most part, the Nxians believed him. But as time went on, and the file of bad press clippings got heavier, some of the members began to doubt Vanguard's word—even though it was an ethical breach to do so.

The *New York Post*, never one to pass up a chance to smear the Clintons, ran a column by Charles Hurt and Jeane MacIntosh on October 1, 2007, under the headline "Hillary's $30,000 Fans Are Her 'Cult' Following." The opening paragraph is almost comical in its cherry-picking of the facts to make Bill and Hillary Clinton look as complicit as possible:

A purported pyramid-scheme operator who was run out of Arkansas when Bill Clinton was governor has reinvented himself as the head of an upstate group accused of being a "cult"—and his devotees have pumped thousands into Hillary Rodham Clinton's presidential run.

Whatever their motivation for writing the piece, the authors offer a wonderfully concise primer on Keith and NXIVM. They hit all the keywords: *Svengali, pyramid scheme, Bronfman, Cafritz* ("daughter of D.C. A-listers Bill and Buffy Cafritz"), *"It's a cult," defrauded, Kristin Snyder, suicide.* There's also this nugget: "The recent campaign contributions led one close observer of NXIVM to speculate that the group is trying to curry favor for its effort to expand training centers upstate." The Clinton connection likely drew their interest initially, but even so, they were able to cover a lot of ground—in 2007, *ten years* before the DOS story broke.

When Barbara Bouchey came to ESP in 2000, she was a successful financial planner. Her company managed almost $100 million in assets and showed annual gross revenue in the seven figures. She personally had $1.5 million in savings. Keith knew this and set about wooing her. He told her she was the only one for him and was destined to be his partner for life. They would have a baby together, he assured her—the Child Who Would Save the World. She fell in love with him.

"His mind created the curriculum and, because it's so powerful, you start to think differently of him," she told an audience of true crime fans at CrimeCon 2019. "I began to admire and respect what he created, the overall philosophy of wanting to better yourself, be a more peaceful, loving and compassionate person. As a woman that becomes very interesting and intriguing."

Keith told her he had a foolproof method for exponentially increasing her wealth. He had cracked the formula for making millions in the commodities market. Bouchey believed him, and gave him roughly $1.5 million, which Vanguard promptly lost. She continued to work at ESP, and then NXIVM, and was one of its main apologists in the media. Although at first she was brought into Keith's life under false pretenses, she, like many others, remained in his inner circle—mixing business with pleasure as one of his concubines, and a member of the NXIVM board. Barbara was also the financial planner for the Bronfman sisters, during the period when Keith pissed away $65 million of their money in commodities trades—losing their money the same way he'd lost hers.

By 2009, she'd had enough. She had serious concerns about the way NXIVM was being run, concerns shared by other company leaders, among them Susan Dones, who owned and operated the NXIVM center in Tacoma. Dones was a key player in what she calls "the training side" of NXIVM, as opposed to "the cult side," which she managed to steer clear of. Through the proper corporate channels, she, too, raised a series of concerns about how Vanguard and Prefect were running the company. When she flew to Albany in 2009 in advance of the Dalai Lama visit, Keith met with her and Barbara Bouchey in an arrogant attempt to assuage these concerns. He failed.

Keith being Keith, he allowed for these meetings to be videotaped, to preserve his singular genius for posterity (this is a habit that he would come to regret during the trial). There is a YouTube clip of part of the meeting. When Keith tries to dismiss Barbara Bouchey by saying, "You don't have the experience in running a company," she replies, "Well, in a way, neither do you," and brings up the CBI debacle. For a split second, Keith seems to get angry, but he quashes that emotion and changes the subject: "I've been shot at for my beliefs," he says. "I've had to make choices: should I have bodyguards? Should I have them armed or not? Um...I've had people *killed* because of my beliefs, and because of their beliefs, and because of things that I've said. And I'm mindful of that."

Ultimately, Bouchey, Dones, and the seven others who made up the so-called NXIVM Nine found Keith's arguments unconvincing, and left. Thus his greatest triumph, the Dalai Lama visit, was marred by the biggest mass defection in company history to that point.

Later, Dones would recall the concerns she had at the time, in a remarkable piece she published on the *Frank Report*:

1/ Raniere was having sex with multiple women at the same time—and lying that he was monogamous with each of them. It's a conflict of interest to sleep with most of the members of the Executive Board and unethical to sleep with your clients.

2/ Raniere was borrowing large amounts of money from "students" and losing that money in the commodities market and real estate ventures. Nancy Salzman, President of NXIVM, told me this fact. Not only did he "borrow" from the Bronfman sister but others. Some have never gotten their money back. Borrowing money from your clients is unethical. One shouldn't even ask.

3/ NXIVM brought large amounts of "cash" over the border from Mexico trainings and did not report it as income—which is money laundering and tax evasion. Nancy Salzman, the President of NXIVM, told me this herself.

4/ NXIVM does not pay their State or Federal taxes—which is something else that Nancy Salzman told me. Salzman even verbally abused me more than once for paying my state business and occupation taxes and federal taxes because she said that taxes were "unethical." I found out after leaving NXIVM that NXIVM had lied to the State of Washington, saying they've leased their coursework to me and that I was not a contractor to avoid paying taxes to the State of Washington. Another lie, I was a contractor, and they told the court in Washington when they sued me I was a contractor.

As soon as Dones left, Keith and Nancy responded in the usual Keith and Nancy way: by suing her and having her indicted for various fictitious "crimes." Susan Dones had invested considerable time and money in NXIVM. Not only was she forced to close her business and declare bankruptcy, but she then had to burn through all of her savings to defend herself. In the end, broke, she acted as her own attorney, and still managed to not only win her case, but flummox both Clare Bronfman and another high-level Nxian, Jim Del Negro, neither of whom could keep their stories straight under oath.

In 2010, two major magazines published features on NXIVM, focusing on the Bronfmans. The "cult" charge was revived in "The Heiresses and the Cult," a *Vanity Fair* investigative report by Suzanna Andrews. The leader of the "cult," Andrews explains, bled the heiresses dry:

Many [family friends] knew that Edgar Bronfman's daughters were involved in a secretive organization called NXIVM (pronounced "nexium"), a group that he himself had openly referred to as "a cult." But only a few were aware of what the court documents would reveal—the massive gutting by the Bronfman daughters of their family trust funds to help finance NXIVM and the alleged investment schemes of its leader, a 50-year-old man by the name of Keith Raniere. The amount— reportedly $100 million—was staggering and made for eye-popping headlines. But according to legal filings and public documents, in the last six years as much as $150 million was taken out of the Bronfmans' trusts and bank accounts, including $66 million allegedly used to cover Raniere's failed bets in the commodities market, $30 million to buy real estate in Los Angeles and around Albany, $11 million for a 22-seat, two-engine Canadair CL-600 jet, and millions more to support a barrage of lawsuits across the country against NXIVM's enemies. Much of it was spent, according to court filings, as Sara and Clare Bronfman allegedly worked to conceal the extent of their spending from their 81-year-old father and the Bronfman-family trustees.

The *Maclean's* piece, by Nicholas Köhler, is titled "How to Lose $100 Million." Both features include information from the deposition of Barbara Bouchey, a high-level Nxian—and Vanguard concubine—who had defected in 2009.

Both magazine features were, I would guess, met with a degree of schadenfreude among the reading public. Sara and Clare Bronfman are not exactly sympathetic figures. A smooth-talking charlatan demanded their money and insisted they call him a silly comic-book name, and they were gullible enough to fall for it. So what?

But it's one thing to grift a bunch of wealthy saps. It's quite another to rape underage girls—plural.

In 2012's "In Raniere's Shadows," a remarkably bold investigative feature in the *Albany Times Union* by James Odato and Jennifer Gish, Keith Raniere was exposed as a serial statutory rapist. Three different accusers came forward for that piece, which was unsparing in its details. Here is an excerpt about Gina Melita, one of the sources for the story, who was fifteen when Keith raped her:

> She and Raniere, then 24, went to arcades together, where he liked to play Pac-Man and a game called Vanguard, in which destroying enemies increases the fuel in the player's tank. He described himself as a genius and judo champion. She thought it was cool to be with an older, smart guy who might help her graduate from high school early. He took her virginity in a dark room, her T-shirt left flecked with blood. She told him it was painful, yet a short time later, he wanted more. During their four-month relationship, he hounded the 135-pound girl to lose weight and urged her to keep their relationship secret from her mother.
>
> After a while, she said she told Raniere she wanted to break off the relationship but he told her they should keep having sex. Even as a 15-year-old, she said, she realized Raniere didn't care about her.

The story dropped like a stone in Lake Ontario, leaving nary a ripple. Law enforcement sat on their collective hands, because, as the article bitterly notes, "the statute of limitations has long expired."

Nevertheless, word was getting out. Information was available. Nxians wrote it off as a media vendetta against Vanguard. The general public, meanwhile, didn't seem to care—and, more frustratingly, neither did state or federal prosecutors. What would it take to rouse the interest of the authorities? How much longer would the cult leader be allowed to walk free?

# CHAPTER 19:

# THE ERIN BROCKOVICH OF NXIVM

Rochester, New York, 2009–2013

---

The NXIVM contingent was familiar with Toni Natalie and had been for years. In their stupid modules, I was Lucifer, the apostate who dared to rise against their Vanguard/God. Women I'd never met, who were in grade school during my years with Keith, regarded me with abject horror, like *I* was the boogeyman. Outside that incestuous little bubble, however, I was just another person, anonymous.

When I began talking to the press, and especially after I told my own Keith Raniere story to Chet Hardin at *Metroland*, I started to gain some notoriety. My "digital footprint" expanded, and most of it was connected to NXIVM. A Google search of my name invariably linked me to Keith, and by the end of the first decade of the twenty-first century, Keith was regarded in the media as a cult leader. This had unforeseen consequences, both good and bad.

Because I was so steadfastly opposed to Keith Raniere, anyone defecting from NXIVM sought me out as an obvious ally and sympathetic ear. The enemy of my enemy is my friend.

Joe O'Hara and I were now in frequent contact, and I began to keep careful files on anything even tangentially related to Keith and NXIVM. Joe and I prepared a series of well-researched and documented emails detailing what we believed to be criminal activities NXIVM was engaged in. We sent these emails to Anita Barrett and Brian Whitehurst, the assistant attorneys general in the New York State Office of the Attorney General. They responded that we should stop sending materials, that they would get back to us. The emails were sent in October of 2011, and we have yet to receive a response.

I met Gina Melita, one of Keith's earliest victims. When Keith seduced her, she was fifteen years old. He was "24, and pudgy, short, and walked funny." They dated from August of 1984 until she broke up with him in December that same year. "He was so convincing, he would make up stories about having a terminal illness or about having important, dangerous things to do, just to make me need him, just to make me do what he wanted," she wrote. "I introduced him to some high school friends, I found out later he did the same to them, manipulating his way into their pants, all young and getting younger." One of these high school friends was Gina Hutchinson, who remained in Keith's clutches for years before committing suicide. "He's a dangerous, evil man," Melita wrote, "and I let him into my soul and he is rotten, and rotting others from within." She ended her email to me with this: "I am so grateful to finally tell my story, to have it be fully received and to feel the validation. Thanks, Toni." She emailed me in 2011; the following year, she would be a critical source in the *Albany Times Union*'s statutory rape piece about Keith.

I was contacted by John Tighe, who ran the blog *Saratoga in Decline*. He broke a number of critical stories about Vanguard and his inner circle. Like me, Tighe had been a target of NXIVM's helter-skelter tactics: his home was broken into and his possessions moved around; his car and his wife's car were broken into; he was sued and eventually indicted. His blog was taken down.

I met with Barbara Bouchey, Susan Dones, and other members of the NXIVM Nine in a rented house near Lake George, to avoid being tracked. I listened to the stories of their experiences and gave advice on how to handle the inevitable reprisals that would come from Vanguard, who was incapable of forgiveness.

I spoke with any reporter or journalist or TV producer who called. One of these was Frank Parlato, NXIVM publicist turned mortal enemy, who reached out after he launched his blog in 2015. He became a powerful ally.

One interview request didn't pan out. On February 22, 2012, I received an email from one Yuriria Sierra, who claimed to be a news anchor with Grupo Imagen in Mexico City. She wrote:

> *I am doing an investigative piece on several human development programs and organizations that have flourished in Mexico over the past few years. One of these organizations is NXIVM, which has been particularly successful in my country with its "Executive Success Programs." A few acquaintances of mine have even taken some of their programs. One thing that all these organizations*

*have in common is controversy. And it seems that NXIVM has had its fair share of it, although interestingly, not so in Mexico. As I've looked through the Internet to gather information, your name has surfaced many times in connection to NXIVM, and with its founder Keith Raniere... Being a former insider of NXIVM and having been personally involved with Mr. Raniere, I believe your input would be very valuable for this piece. Please let me know if this is something that would interest you.*

I responded that I would be happy to speak with her, but first I wanted to know about her credentials, as I believed that NXIVM had a stranglehold on the Mexican media. Then I asked if she was planning on traveling to the United States to conduct the interview, or if we could speak over the phone. She replied:

*I do apollogyse for this belated reply; these have been imposible days due to the tons of work i have been facing. Unfortunally, i am tollally unable to travel to the US (or anywhere else) these days, because as you probably know there is an electoral process in my country. So, as an news tv and radio show achor is quite impossible to skip my emissions until month of august. I was thinking, instead, that probably you'd be interested in traveling to Mexico City in order to have a talk with me. Does it appear possible to you?*

I knew about the Nxian attempt to lure Rick Ross to a boat, ostensibly to visit some harm upon him, so the whole exchange with "Yuriria" struck me as fishy. For one thing, she seemed to have lost her ability to write in English from her first to her second email. For another, despite being a prominent news anchor at one of the largest media companies in Mexico City, she was writing me from a Hotmail address. Prominent Mexican political and media families, I knew, were in the inner circle of NXIVM. The Mexican government was more corrupt than ours, and thus more susceptible to bribery. There was no way in hell I was going to Mexico, and I told her so, but nicely: I would only do the interview in New York. A month later, after she had magically reacquired the ability to write in proper English, she informed me that

> as a professional investigative reporter, I need well documented facts. The media coverage of this issue so far has been one-sided, poorly written, insufficiently documented, and of a gossip nature at best... The problem I am facing is this: In our country, Mr. Raniere is seen as having done many good things. The American media reports are seen as gossip because of questionable sources and presentation. This is made more difficult because the ESP/NXIVM sources appear reliable and straightforward, and the opposition appears evasive and seemingly dishonest... I had hoped to finally document thoroughly, from an investigative perspective, a true controversy. So far, the dissenting information I have is either hearsay from upset ex-lovers and employees, unverifiable, evasive, or outright false. If I cannot obtain good information for your side, I will not run a story.

> I have contacted a few other sources for this information and have only received one (1) reply. If you can, please give me something with which I can work.

I replied with a long email, referring to the excellent news articles in *Forbes, Vanity Fair, Metroland,* and the *Times Union* that had run about Keith, and asking her what specifically in those articles she did not believe. I ended with this:

> *I would like to repeat my offer to conduct an interview on Skype after answering my questions above. If not I have no reason to believe you to be sincere and not a plant for NXIVM at this point. If you're not willing to either fly to upstate New York or at the very least make contact through Skype and prove to me that you are who you say you are, then I guess all I have to say is waffles…*

"Waffles" was an inside joke between me and Keith. He had a gambling addiction and liked going to the casinos to play black-jack (with his 240 IQ, he claimed to be able to count cards). On one such trip, we started at a $5 table and wound up at a $500-a-hand table. Every hour or so, a voice over the loudspeaker would call out, "Waffles! Who wants waffles!" The word became our secret code—and it was indeed the last word here, as "Yuriria Sierra," or whoever it was who wrote those emails attempting to lure me to Mexico City, never replied.

There was no counterpart to the Bronfmans on our side. Keith had the liquor heiresses; we were all bankrupt. And Vanguard did everything in his considerable power to deplete our already scant financial resources. Sometimes, just being associated with him *at all* wound up costing me.

I'd found a job selling lingerie at an upscale boutique in Pittsford, an affluent suburb of Rochester. People tend to like me—the ones who aren't conditioned to believe that I'm Satan, that is—and my outgoing demeanor lent itself well to selling brassieres and bustiers. When I realized that the owners were withholding stock, immediately removing the previous year's merchandise and leaving it in storage in their attic, I suggested discounting the material and selling it. This strategy worked to such a profound degree that they made plans to open a second location and asked me to be the manager. Just before opening, however, they got wind of my past connection with Keith Raniere and fired me. Despite my many months of excellent customer service and increasing their bottom line, they were afraid of having a cult leader's ex-girlfriend as the face of their business. I was apparently too controversial a figure to sell women's intimates.

By this time, I had spent years already defending myself against Keith's legal onslaught. On July 7, 2010, I was subpoenaed in an advisory proceeding involving the Bronfmans' lawsuit against Joe O'Hara. This had nothing to do with me, but the Nxians hoped that by deposing me, they could get me to say something under oath that they might eventually take action on. A month later, an FBI agent named Michael G. Yerdon Jr., from the Buffalo/Rochester office, came to my place of business to inform me that I was under investigation.

On August 8, 2011, I was again subpoenaed by NXIVM, this time in a bankruptcy proceeding against Susan Dones. This had even less to do with me than the O'Hara lawsuit. They only wanted me on the stand to harass me or, better, to perjure myself somehow.

I did not have an attorney. As I'd done so many times before, I went to court with my mother. I asked the judge if I could read a statement. Pam Nichols, the high-priced NXIVM attorney in her $2,000 suit and Louboutin heels, protested. "No, no, no," she kept saying. But the judge allowed it. I stood at the podium, as I'd stood in front of so many audiences in my Awaken days, and read a statement I'd prepared, so I would not omit anything I wanted to say:

*The real reason why NXIVM wants to depose me has nothing to do with the bankruptcy cases of Ms. Dones…whom I had not even heard of before June 2009 and with whom I did not have any significant discussions until early 2010. In this regard, I believe that one of the primary reasons why NXIVM wants to depose me is to silence me from revealing things that I know about Raniere such as the fact that he is a compulsive gambler, a sex addict with bizarre desires and needs, and a con man that specializes in Ponzi schemes. In addition, I also think that NXIVM wants to depose me in order to make me reveal the names of the various women who have contacted me in order to discuss their involvement with Raniere, noting that at least one of which was well under the age of consent, their mental abuse by him and his followers, and the fact that they and members of their families were stalked by Raniere and his followers when they chose to leave him.*

I'd been sued so many times, but this time I was allowed to explain my side in court. It felt good, to finally get that opportunity. When I was done, the judge asked, "Would you like me to enter that into the docket?"

"Yes, Your Honor." And thus, my statement became part of the record.

On my way out, I pointed to Pam Nichols's designer handbag. "I hope you enjoy this," I told her, "because you bought it with blood money."

I was concerned that what I'd said would appear in the papers, so when I got home, I called Michael and told him to come over. He had never heard about the rapes. I didn't want him to know. I wanted to shield him from all of it. By now, he was twenty-three. He came, he listened to my statement, and he wept. It would've been easier for him to believe I left him with Rusty because I was a bad mother. Now he knew the truth.

On April 3, 2012, Keith Rainere, Nancy Salzman, Clare Bronfman, and five other Nxians filed a criminal complaint against me, Joe O'Hara, and John Tighe, on the preposterous charge of computer trespassing. During the course of the investigation, the NXIVM legal team made more than thirty visits to New York State Police Senior Investigator Rodger Kirsopp in an attempt to accelerate the process.

On September 2, 2013, the investigative reporter Chet Hardin, who by now was also a friend, forwarded me an email a colleague had passed along to him. It was from a woman we'll call Inez, who was involved in NXIVM in Mexico. She said she'd used Google to translate her note from Spanish to English, and apologized if it was hard to read. But what she had to say was easy enough to understand:

> *I am writing to you because of Keith Raniere...I have been involved with groups of Keith. I have began to think that I have make a mistake. So I have taken the decision to quit. I have to be careful how to handle this. Other people have tried get away. They were threatened. One woman died. They told me that it had been a suicide. Now I am afraid that it might not be true because of the things I have heard. If they know what I am doing I do not know what will happen to me and my family. But somebody needs to tell what is happening.*

> *I have come to understand that Keith is obsessed with sex and to get so much money from his followers. On the outside it may*

*seem that the messages of Keith and others, it is about spirituality and humanity. But once inside you knowing that it is sex and money.*

*I am ashamed to believed all this, and to becoming a part of it. I have spent more than one hundred thousands of dollars to Keith. This money will never return. Also I wish to leave is because of a thing named RAINBOW CULTURAL GARDEN. It is a program for the children. Keith says that he started this to help the children to learn.*

This was true. The philosophies Keith used to raise his own "adopted" son, Gaelen—the five nannies speaking five languages, and so on—he incorporated into this program, which was offered to children of Nxians. Inez continued:

*But I think that it is much worse than that. Some members have asked me if I want my children with Rainbow Cultural Garden. That put pressure on me. I ask many questions. They gave much talk about sexuality. Keith tell us that the main goals of the Rainbow Cultural Garden is to teach children that sex is beautiful. He say it should be practiced open. At first I thought I do not understand the translation in English. But I became frightened when I knew it is true. It was then when I realized I must do something to protect myself and my children. And to tell the world what this man and his people is doing.*

*Sex is one of the major philosophies of Jness also.*

Jness was a "women's empowerment" program trumpeted by the NXIVM TV actresses. Allison Mack had tried to recruit Emma Watson into Jness.

*Those of us that women are told we are as equal to all men. Nancy Salzman is the boss of Jness. She is a partner with Keith for many years. She had sex with Keith many times. There have many other sexual partners. Keith and Nancy tells us practice sex open and without fear. It is encourage to women members of Jness to have sex with men, especially with Keith. They say that having sex with many people teaches us to be more human and to have compassion. I have resist these things. I think that some of the members have reject me because I never wanted anything like this.*

*If adults want to do such things I cannot see why it is bad. But I begun to see things similar between Jness and Rainbow Cultural Garden. That was when I got scared. It seems that Keith, Nancy and others are creating a club to teach the young girls to become sexual partners. They believe that sex may release the children and to help them to be stronger. I heard of stories about Keith having sex with young girls. It seems that everyone think this is a good thing. Keith says many times that young people should have sex with adults. He says that it helps them to grow and to learn to be humans.*

*Some people talk about bringing children to the branches Mexico or Guatemala. They want to hide the children from other people who might try to stop the Rainbow Cultural Garden. The groups are very secret. The people that speak outside of the groups are punished. They ask me to help because I live here. But I do not want to help. But they put more pressure on me and I have to be careful on how to respond to them.*

*There are many other people that participate with these plans. The people have much money. Some of the people are famous…*

*These people have a great amount of power with other people. They put a lot of money on projects of Keith. I don't know how much involved some of the people are...Many of them are sexual inside the group.*

*Allison Mack is a star of television. She has a relationship that is sexual with Keith. Allison is very deep with the groups of Keith, especially Jness. She has tell some people that she would want to have a child with Keith. Or perhaps adopt a child. Sometimes she say that they are a couple. Other times say that they are good friends only. But they have sexual relationships with many couples. Some of the girls I have seen with Keith are teenagers. Perhaps even more young...*

*I think that Keith wants to create children that only is raised by Rainbow Cultural Garden. They have adopted a child with this order already, and I think that they want to have more. Keith wants children have his genes.*

*Many are the stories that appeared in the news these days some criminals kidnapping young people and forcing them to the sex and prostitution. If you can imagine when I have begun to learn about these things, I was concerned about this. Especially when I heard the idea about moving children to Mexico and Guatemala. This is very serious for me.*

*The community can never learn that I did this emails. This risk I take is large. I have learn how to hide myself on the internet to send the emails. There is no way to communicate for us after this. As I have said I must to protect myself and my family. I know that you may not be able to use my story...*

*I am to write to as many people as I can find. Especially to the families of the children who may be in danger of kidnap or sex abuse. I also try to send this to the police. But I do not know who is the contact person in the United States or in Mexico. And I have no hope that they will listen to. I hope I am wrong. I want to warn as many people as I am able to before that this leads to something much worse.*

*That I would be so relieved if the group was exposed and I was able to get to know my family will be safe. But also I could not live if I knew that a child was injured and I said nothing.*

I forwarded the email to Rodger Kirsopp of the New York State Police. He later claimed he never received it.

We received Inez's email in 2013—five years before Keith was finally arrested. I didn't think it was a hoax at the time, and now I know that every word that poor woman wrote was true.

# CHAPTER 20:
# THE HUMAN PIÑATA

## Rochester, New York, 2014–2017

I don't recognize the number, so I let the call go to voicemail. Usually a telemarketer won't leave a message, or the message will be short—a few seconds of silence while they lazily end the call. This message is more than two minutes in length.

"Toni, it's me," comes a familiar voice, like a ghost come back from the dead, "it's Krissy. You have to help me. I don't know who else to call. They're after me. Keith and Pam, they're after me. They have a gun. They're going to kill me and take Gaelen away from me. They want him back, and they don't care about me anymore. I'm expendable. You know how they are. I'm staying at a women's shelter, but he'll find me soon if I don't keep moving. I need you to take Gaelen for me. Take him and keep him safe, so I can run. It's too hard, when he's with me. Please, Toni. I know I've been...I know what I've done, and I know you must hate me, but I can't let them take my son. I can't let them. You know Keith. You know he won't stop. Please. Please."

Mentally, I tick off all the shit Kristin Keeffe has put me through since my own defection: The crazy, angry letters. The days spent in front of A Place of Creations Café, raving about me being the Chosen One. The clumsy attempt to buy a position in my mother's debt, to prevent her bankruptcy from going through. The relentless paralegal work, to ensure that the last fifteen years of my life were spent in court, that all of my money was wasted on legal fees. The "internship" in the district attorney's office, where she had access to documents and people she should never have had access to. And now, in her hour of need, she has the audacity to ask *me* for help?

On the other hand, where else could she go? Keith knows where her mother lives, where her brother and sister live. And Kristin knows better than anyone how he operates. Probably there are already Nxians in parked cars staking out all of those places. It was smart to go to the shelter. It was smart to call me. Keith probably would not anticipate that move.

And, for all the bad blood between us, I still had a soft spot in my heart for Kristin Keeffe. She helped me when I needed it, when I first moved to Clifton Park. She spent hours watching Michael, and he adored her. Parents never forget when people are kind to their children. Also, she was the same age I was when I ran away from Keith—and Gaelen the same age as Michael was. Besides, is Kristin really evil, or just one of the longest-suffering of Vanguard's victims?

I call Rodger Kirsopp, the head of investigations for the New York State Police in Clifton Park, and explain the situation. He promises to help her and instructs me to bring my phone to the barracks in Farmington, so they can capture the voicemail message. Then I call Kristin at the shelter.

"What made you leave?"

"There's no big conspiracy here," she says. "You of all people know why I left. I couldn't stand the abuse anymore; I had to protect my son."

I tell her the plan: contact Kirsopp, who has been apprised of the situation and is waiting for her call.

"Are you sure we can trust him?"

"You know better than I do."

"Yeah. Oh, Toni?"

"Yes?"

"Stay out of Mexico, okay? Keith has a lot more pull down there than he does here. If you cross the border, you'll never come back."

I flash on the email exchange with "Yuriria Sierra," the supposed news anchor writing me from a Hotmail account. She was so eager to interview me in Mexico City.

"I don't have a passport," I tell her. "And I have no desire to go there."

"Good." There is an email account, she explains—a Gmail account named PEACEMEXICO that Keith uses to communicate with Emiliano Salinas, inner-circle Nxian and son of a former president of Mexico. "They will write an email and save it in drafts, so there's no trace of it. This way they can communicate secretly. Keith writes the notes, and Emiliano translates them into Spanish." Their scheme, she explains, is to bring false charges against me and other enemies, so we can be thrown into some godforsaken Mexican prison, raped and tortured, and then killed.

"They've already bribed a judge to do this. The charges are already filed. Seriously—stay the *fuck* away from Mexico."

I end the call. None of this is surprising, not really, but it still freaks me out.

Kirsopp proves up to the task. He collects Kristin and Gaelen from the shelter and whisks them away to safety. I don't know where he takes them—and more important, neither does Keith Raniere.

I was dating a man named Chris. I'd already been divorced several times, not counting the eternal breakup from Keith, and I was wary of having my heart broken yet again. We took it slow. But it was a good match. Chris was divorced and had three kids, including a son, Curtis, who had special needs. I loved that boy to pieces, and he loved me, too. "You really seem to understand him," Chris said. "He really lights up when he sees you."

Then Chris's ex-wife googled me. She formed the false impression I was some ex–cult member weirdo, and she prohibited the kids from seeing me. Curtis didn't understand any of this. It was upsetting to him.

"Can't you fight this? Tell her to screw off."

"She said if I continue to let them see you, she'll go to court and demand full custody. You know how the courts are. They tend to favor the mother."

His refusal to stand up to his ex-wife irked me, and I wasn't shy about making my feelings known. "It's my past," I said. "It's not my present, and it's certainly not my future. If you're not man enough to stand up to your ex-wife and let me answer any questions your children may have, we're done."

On the other hand, it was just as well Curtis was not with us on October 23, 2013, the day after my ultimatum.

It was a Wednesday. Chris had spent the night. We had fallen asleep pissed at each other, and lay back to back. At six in the morning, an hour before dawn, we were awakened by the doorbell and the loud knocking at the door. "Open up! Police! Open the door!"

I grabbed Raymona—who was on alert—put her leash on, and headed to the door. She was trained to protect me, and my fear was that she would be hurt by the police. She was growling and barking as I opened the door. A team of indistinguishable officers stood there, all leathery faces and closed-cropped hair. One of them put his hand on his gun. "Do something about that dog," he said, "or I will."

Immediately I put her in her kennel, pleading, "Please, *please* don't shoot my dog."

They weren't there to arrest me, thank God. They were there to search the premises. One of them explained this to me as he brandished some sort of warrant. I wasn't listening.

As they rifled through my things, I grabbed my phone and sounded the alarm. I called everyone I knew. *They're here, they're at the house.* I wasn't the only Keith detractor raided that morning: Joe O'Hara and John Tighe also had their houses raided that morning, equipment seized and files confiscated—all at the same time, as if we were al-Qaeda.

The cops took boxes of files that they claimed, ludicrously, were the property of NXIVM. They seized both of my computers. As I used my laptop to work—I was doing media sales for a start-up company—I was effectively put out of business. (I believed I would be successful today if I didn't have a Bronfman-financed psychopath deliberately sabotaging every business venture I engaged in.)

"You're here because of Keith Raniere," I told the cop with the warrant. "He sent you, because he has rich and powerful friends who made this happen. You think I'm the bad guy, but you're wrong—he is."

Chris was in the kitchen muttering, "What if my kids were here? What if my kids were here?" He had a point.

A short time later, we broke up.

May 26, 2014, was the lowest point of my life—a life that was not without more than its fair share of low points. My mother had not been feeling well. She never got sick and never complained about anything. She was a force of nature. Her doctor sent her over to the hospital. She called to let me know she was fine: the doctor said she was dehydrated and needed some fluids. I told her I would be right over. "No," she said, "I'm fine, you need to stay at work. They are just going to give me some fluids and send me home." I stopped home quickly before heading to the hospital. I called to let her know I would be there in about twenty minutes. My mother said, "No rush. They just finished giving me a test. They're bringing me back to my room now." Five minutes later she called back. "I have very bad news," she said. "I have cancer. I'm going to die, and they're going to do everything they can to keep me comfortable." My life from that point on would never be the same. The thought of going to jail didn't scare me anymore; cancer did. Losing my mom, my best friend: that scared me.

For fifteen years, Keith had tried everything he could think of to hurt me. I suffered because of him, but the most pain he ever inflicted on me was when he involved my family. My mother stood by me throughout that ordeal. She dutifully documented every infraction that Keith and his minions subjected me to. She kept timelines of events. She appealed to judges. And when I needed financial help, she went broke helping me. The prospect of continuing the fight without my mother at my side was too much to bear.

Then the phone rang.

It was Rodger Kirsopp of the New York State Police. He wanted to know where I was. After searching my computers, they had decided to charge me with computer trespassing. He wanted me to make arrangements for him to come and pick me up. I asked him, "Rodger, are you calling to arrest me?" I told him where I was and what had happened. "I'm with my mother, and if you want me, you're going to have to come arrest me at the hospital. I'm not going anywhere."

I walked back into the hospital room, and I should have won an Oscar for this performance. My mom, sensing something was amiss, asked if everything was okay. "Yes, Mom. They were just giving me an update on when I'll get my computers back."

The future looked bleak. My father, a disabled World War II veteran, required a part-time caregiver, a role my mother filled. I was her only living child, and if I had to go to prison, I would not be able to care for them. If I served any time, I might never see them again.

I didn't tell them right away. I couldn't bear it. I knew the news would crush her. But I had no choice, and ultimately, they needed to know. "I thought the worst thing I would ever hear was that I had cancer," my mother said, "but that's not true. *This* is the worst thing. Why won't he leave us alone? Why will no one stop him?"

Joan Schneier passed away on October 17, 2014, just five months after the diagnosis. I still remember her last words to me: "You're not crazy, Toni. Don't let them make you think that you are." My father, Al, heartbroken, died less than a month later.

I was alone.

On February 27, 2015, I was indicted on four felony counts of computer trespassing.

In September of 2015, Kristin calls me again. She is very afraid and needs a safe place for her and Gaelen. She is out of cash, has no ID, and is several states away, but I find a way to get them to my house. I have an extra bedroom, and I'm curious to see her and meet her son. Although the NXIVM people still surveil my home, it's unlikely that Keith would think of looking for her here.

It's a strange visit. She and Gaelen stay in Rochester for twenty-two very long days. On the one hand, she was once a close friend who knew my son when he was little. We have a lot of history, and not all of it is bad. On the other, she has spent the last sixteen years making my life miserable. As Keith's legal attack dog, she is dangerous. But I cannot in good conscience turn my back on her and her son.

Gaelen is the spitting image of Keith. He's very sweet, but I can sense his fear. I can't imagine what it's been like for them, to be on the run for more than a year. He's very bright, which is no surprise; Kristin herself is smart and great with children. One night, we watch the presidential debate. Not only is he able to follow it, but he asks very insightful questions. Kristin patiently answers all of them. It's like watching a PBS commercial. She's amazing with him. It's nice to see.

Unable to go outside, he spends hours in his room playing

*Minecraft*. He has a habit of grinding his right big toe into the carpet. He does that almost constantly, for twenty-two days, as if he's digging for gold. The indentation in my carpet is still there.

Kristin is a mess, figuratively and literally. Her state of mind is precarious, as if she can't quite hold it all together, and she drinks a lot. Keith is the sort of abstemious teetotaler who hates *anyone*, let alone the mother of his child, to drink *anywhere*, so Kristin had not had much occasion to get wasted in her NXIVM days. Her taking to the bottle is perhaps a way of acting out—one last ethical breach against Vanguard. I do my best to encourage her to go to the feds with her NXIVM information. Yes, she's also complicit, but if she cooperated, maybe she could avoid charges.

One night after a few too many glasses of wine, Kristin tells me about the visits she had with my brother, at Keith's request. Back then, she was Keith's most fearsome lieutenant, a brilliant and vindictive cutthroat. She would have done anything for her Vanguard—she was the one who'd tried to lure Rick Ross to a boat—and John was just another assignment. She talks about how my brother would shake as he popped a Xanax. "He was a nervous wreck," she says, drunkenly laughing at the visions of John in her head.

I realize the boogeyman that had been chasing me all these years is sleeping down the hall. Twenty-two days was long enough. It was time for them to go.

For the next two and a half years, I was basically a human piñata that Keith's high-priced attorneys took turns having a whack at. There was the computer trespassing case, in which the Albany district attorney somehow decided to go after three of the people trying to expose NXIVM's crimes, rather than NXIVM itself. There was the civil complaint filed against me, Joe O'Hara, John Tighe, the reporters Suzanna Andrews, who wrote the *Vanity Fair* Bronfman piece, and James Odato, who published a number of excellent exposes on NXIVM and Keith for the *Times Union*, and a whopping *fifty-nine* John and Jane Does. According to the complaint, we had accessed confidential and proprietary information contained on a password-protected website. NXIVM sought millions of dollars in damages. There was the quixotic suit Keith filed in Washington State against Microsoft and AT&T, asserting that those blue-chip companies had infringed upon five of his patents involving the technology for conference systems. I got dragged into that one because I allegedly owned the patents through my ownership of a dissolved company called GTI. Meanwhile, he used all the means at his disposal to keep my confiscated computers away from me and to wipe them clean before they were returned, in violation of a court order.

All of this stuff was fantasy dreamed up by Keith or his attorneys and put into action by the might of the Bronfman family's wealth and influence over feckless politicians. None of it stuck. But the point wasn't to make any of it stick. The point was to divert all of my resources—financial, intellectual, emotional— into the courtroom and away from anything else. The point was to break me: terrorism by litigation.

The civil case was thrown out on September 17, 2015— ironically, during the three-week period when Kristin Keeffe was living with me. The judge, Lawrence E. Kahn, dismissed the case because of Clare Bronfman's perjured testimony (although, needless to say, perjury charges were not filed against the liquor heiress).

The following February, the computer trespassing case was

resolved. After wasting thousands of dollars on legal fees, I agreed to what's called an ACOD—adjournment in contemplation of dismissal. Basically, the court agreed to dismiss the charges if I declined to participate in further computer trespass attempts. As I am not a hacker, this was not a problem.

Still, Keith kept at it. Another process server looking for me; now what? Keith sued Microsoft and AT&T. He knew something even I didn't know: I somehow owned the patents he was claiming belonged solely to him (a first for Keith, claiming something in his own name). He waited until he had me tied up in a criminal and civil suit before he filed his lawsuit. Blue-chip corporations had just as much money to spend on lawyers as he did, and he lost, big-time. He was liable for the defendants' legal fees, to the tune of tens of thousands of dollars.

In any event, the strategy backfired when the suit in Texas was thrown out. He then sued me in Washington State, where the company that owned the patents were registered. The patent lawsuits are ongoing, but by 2017, Keith had more pressing legal matters to tend to.[3]

On June 19, 2017, Frank Parlato, writing on the *Frank Report* blog, reported on the existence of a secret group within NXIVM:

---

3   Keith filed a lawsuit against me in the state of Washington, claiming I was just holding the patents for him, back in the early nineties. He thought he would just simply win by summary judgment. Then came a call from the attorney Michael Grygiel: "Toni, I would not be able to put my head on my pillow at night to sleep if you have to go one more round with this guy without proper representation. Our firm is going to take your case pro bono." This was unheard of for the law firm of Greenberg Traurig. The judge overseeing the case did not believe our response; she ordered my deposition to be held on March 12, 2018, nine years to the day my brother died. But with that, we would have our chance to depose Keith. Grygiel was more than ready for him...or would have been. Keith was scheduled to be deposed on April 2, 2018. By then, he was in federal custody.

Dominus Obsequious Sororium, or DOS. This sorority, Parlato explained, was a select group of emaciated women who served as the slaves, sexual and otherwise, of Keith Raniere. As if that wasn't lurid enough, there was an aspect of DOS that got everyone's attention: "the hallmark of the plan," Parlato wrote, "was branding women."

Each of the slaves had Keith's initials branded on her skin with a cautery pen.

I had to read it three times before it sunk in.

A charge like that, levied by a vocal enemy of Vanguard on his own subjective blog, was easy enough for NXIVM to refute. Who could believe such a thing? When the *New York Times* subsequently confirmed the *Frank Report*'s report—on October 17, 2017, three years to the day of my mother's passing—the truth became harder to deny.

The company certainly tried. "A media outlet unfoundedly, and incorrectly, linked NXIVM corporation, its founder, and its related companies, with a social group," read the official statement on the NXIVM website. "The allegations relayed in the story are built upon sources, some of which [*sic*] are under criminal investigation or already indicted, who act as a coordinated group. This story might be a criminal product of criminal minds who, in the end, are also hurting the victims of the story . . . NXIVM was not able to participate in this story because it painfully held true to the due process of our free world justice system."

Taken together, the remarkable level of detail in the *Frank Report*, the confirmation by the paper of record, and the oddly worded nondenial by NXIVM could only mean that the story was true. At long last, the world knew what I'd known for years: Keith Raniere was a monster.

# III:

# PRISONER NO.
# 57005-177

# CHAPTER 21:

# COLLATERAL DAMAGE

## The Death of Pam Cafritz. DOS.

---

**B**y the time I met Keith Raniere, in the early 1990s, he was already Vanguard, in everything but name. His lifestyle was exactly what it would be twenty-seven years later, when he was finally arrested by the FBI. The only thing that changed was the scale of the operation. He grew bolder, and lazier, and more debauched, until he was taken down by his own audacity.

The complaint and affidavit in support of the arrest warrant of Keith Raniere, "also known as 'Vanguard,'" filed under seal on February 14, 2018, in the Eastern District of New York by FBI Special Agent Michael Lever, helps prove this point:

NXIVM maintains features of a multilevel marketing scheme, commonly known as a pyramid scheme, in which members are recruited via a promise of payments or services for enrolling others into the scheme.

In 1991, Keith also owned an MLM that was exposed as a pyramid scheme: CBI.

> Based on information obtained during the course of this investigation, since ESP's founding, RANIERE has maintained a rotating group of fifteen to twenty women with whom he maintains sexual relationships. These women are not permitted to have sexual relationships with anyone but RANIERE or to discuss with others their relationships with RANIERE.

In the nineties, Vanguard already had his coven of doting handmaidens. When he was my boyfriend, Keith didn't have quite as many women who were exclusive to him sexually, but those he did possess constituted a harem: Karen, Pam, Kristin, and Barb Jeske. And—although I had no idea at the time that the relationship was not monogamous—me.

Dominus Obsequious Sororium was already a thing. It just wasn't as formal, or as depraved.

As Charles Manson groomed his Squeaky Frommes and Susan Atkinses and Leslie Van Houtens, so Keith Raniere knew exactly which women he could target to break down and control. For his inner circle, he looked for pretty, overachieving seekers who were also insecure and damaged in some fundamental way. He used that damage and insecurity to manipulate them to do his bidding.

Keith used these women for sexual gratification, first and foremost. But his concubines had other functions as well. After the various state governments came after him about CBI, he determined that it was better if his considerable assets were not in his name—easier to cheat the tax man that way. The journalist Michael Freedman hints at this in the *Forbes* piece:

> Raniere says by the end of 1993 he had sold $1 billion in goods and services, employed 80 people and had a quarter-million believers paying him $19 a month to hawk his goods. He claims he was worth $50 million. Yet he appeared to carry no money...In 1993 the New York attorney general filed a civil suit alleging Consumers' Buyline was a pyramid scheme. Without admitting wrongdoing, Raniere settled for $40,000, of which he has paid only $9,000. He says he can't pay the rest, though he also says his ample finances let him live on savings.

Keith's inner circle of women became, essentially, human shell corporations, masking the identity of the true owner. Nancy Salzman, Prefect, often served this role. I'd done it for him too.

If Keith needed his "girls" to conceal his assets, he also needed them to underwrite his activities. Long before the slave branding, when Allison Mack was still a child actor on a cable network superhero show, the NXIVM saga was the source of some fascination in certain media circles because of the involvement of the liquor heiresses. One might conclude that, without that enviable revenue stream, NXIVM would never have achieved the power it did. There's some truth to that. But the fact is, Keith always had well-financed backers. Sara and Clare Bronfman were not the first wealthy society heiresses to fall under Vanguard's spell; they were merely the richest. The earliest iteration of the Bronfman sisters was already in Keith's thrall in 1992, when I met him. *Even then*, Keith had access to money—and not nouveau riche money, either.

The Pale of Settlement is the name given to territory acquired by the Russian Empire from 1791—a region that includes present-day Lithuania, Belarus, Moldova, and most of Ukraine. Until the revolution in 1917, Jews were legally permitted to live in the Pale of Settlement, but not within the traditional borders of Russia. When the reformist tsar Alexander II was assassinated in 1881, false rumors circulated that the Jews were somehow responsible. Pogroms escalated. To avoid persecution, many Jewish families fled to North America in the last two decades of the nineteenth century.

Samuel Bronfman was born in the Pale of Settlement in 1889. His was one of the Russian Jewish families that immigrated— first to Saskatchewan, then to Manitoba. Once in Canada, he made a vast fortune in the liquor business. Among his many grandchildren were Sara and Clare Bronfman.

Morris Cafritz was born a few months before Samuel Bronfman, also in the Pale of Settlement. He moved to the United States when he was ten, about the same age as Bronfman when he made his move, and went into business with his father in the District of Columbia. Cafritz owned a grocery store, a saloon, and eventually, a chain of bowling alleys. He was a successful businessman.

But it was in real estate that Cafritz amassed his fortune. He constructed developments in Petworth, in Northwest DC; in the Greenwich Forest neighborhood of the tony Maryland suburb of Bethesda; in Arboretum, also in Northeast DC; the luxury

Westchester apartments; and commercial office buildings along K Street. When he died in 1968, he left behind the largest estate ever probated in the District of Columbia, worth a whopping $66 million—half a billion bucks in today's dollars. His great-niece, the daughter of the socialites Bill and Buffy, was none other than Pam Cafritz.

My erstwhile friend had been at Keith's side since the beginning. They met at a ski resort in the late eighties. They boarded the ski lift as strangers, and by the time the contraption delivered them to the top of the mountain, she was his. I don't know what year it was that they first had sex—1987 or 1988, I believe—but I know the day: February 14. Each year, they celebrated their "anniversary" on Valentine's Day.

Pam lived in the town house at 3 Flintlock. Pam recruited Kristin Keeffe, whom she found selling T-shirts on one of the quads at SUNY Albany. Pam was one of the founders of, and the principal investor in, Consumers' Buyline. Pam welcomed me into the fold, befriending me from the get-go; she served a similar function with all of Keith's new "girls," including Marianna Flores, his favorite concubine and the mother of his second child. Pam hired the middle schooler to walk her dog, as an excuse to get the girl to Flintlock, where Keith could more discreetly rape her. Pam chauffeured him around to many of his illicit rendezvous. Pam reached out to any of Keith's "girls" who dared to defect and was very good at "re-enrollment." Pam was one of only two holders of the Purple Sash, the highest possible NXIVM rank. Pam zealously participated in group sex with Keith and other women, which many of his lovers, notably Kristin Keeffe and Ivy Nevares, did not go for. Pam was not as bright as the others, and Keith tended to treat her like a patient father did a dim child. But what she lacked in intelligence she made up for in ardor and loyalty. No one—not Karen Unterreiner, not Kristin Keeffe, not even Nancy Salzman—was as useful to Keith Raniere as Pam Cafritz.

In 2015, Pam was diagnosed with cancer. She declined rapidly and died a year later. The other holder of the Purple Sash, Barb Jeske, had died in 2013. Kristin Keeffe defected in 2014. Of the old guard, only Karen Unterreiner remained, and by that point, her influence was negligible.

By all accounts, Pam's death had a profound effect on Keith. And I'm not talking about grief—Keith is a psychopath, and that sort of human emotion does not exist for him. Pam Cafritz was the last bond tying him to humanity. With Pam terminally ill and effectively out of the picture in 2015, Keith transformed completely into a demon—or, to use the Nxian patois, he became "fully integrated" into evil.

It is no coincidence that DOS was founded in the wake of Pam's exit from Keith's life.

By 2015, Keith's inner circle had turned over. Newer, younger recruits from prominent Mexican families now held sway, and the likes of Rosa Laura Junco, Daniela Padilla, Monica Duran, and Loreta Garza were unable to temper his more prurient impulses, as Pam or Kristin might have done. His chosen concubine, Marianna Flores, a former party girl and amateur tennis player, was spoiled and selfish and regarded as a sort of tyrant by the other women. The actresses Allison Mack and Nicki Clyne, meanwhile, almost worshipped him. In 2017, Mack conducted a ninety-minute interview of Keith Raniere that was posted to YouTube. The idea, I think, was to show the world what a scintillating genius the Smartest Man in the World really was. But there is something off about the video. Mack appears fresh, bubbly, thoughtful, and she gazes upon him with an unnatural expression—like he is the risen Christ, returning from heaven to judge the living and the dead. It's awe, mixed with excitement, mixed with nervousness, mixed with fear. At one point, she asks him something about creativity—a favorite topic for her—and his response, although completely banal to the objective viewer, is so moving to her that she actually tears up. She hasn't just drunk the Kool-Aid; she's swum in a giant pool of it. Mack looks like she's been completely brainwashed. Watching the clip, it's obvious that Allison Mack would sooner jump off a bridge than defy Vanguard. All of the new girls, I'm sure, held him in the same regard. None of them could replace Pam Cafritz, who, despite her disgraceful complicity, may have managed to keep his most depraved ambitions in check.

The year 2015 was also when the movie adaptation of *Fifty Shades of Grey* was released. The kinky novel, an overwrought romance between the ridiculously named Anastasia Steele and the eponymous Christian Grey, had been a publishing sensation for three years, selling a whopping 125 million copies by the time the movie came out. I have no idea if Keith saw the movie or read the novel, or plumbed through its more literary, and more erotic, antecedents—*The Story of O, Venus in Furs, Justine, The 120 Days of Sodom*, and so forth—the works of Sade and Masoch that give sadism and masochism their names. But *Fifty Shades* seems to have informed his activities going forward. If nothing else, the book helped normalize BDSM and thus make what Vanguard demanded more palatable to his recruits.

While Keith always sought as much control as possible, he

did not have an overt interest in BDSM when I was with him. At least, he never tried any S and M activities with me. None of his other lovers who have talked to me about their experiences with him have mentioned it, either—although I was aware of a rumor that he once went to a Buffalo sex club with the then obscure tattoo artist Kat von D. Revealing naked photographs? Absolutely. Polyamory? Most definitely. Whips and chains? No. It was only after *Fifty Shades* that Keith began to weave the BDSM concept of "total power exchange," or TPE, into his sexual relationships. I don't think TPE turned him on as much as it gave him a more formal means to exercise control over his women. By eroticizing a 24/7 Master/slave relationship, he could win more recruits to Dominus Obsequious Sororium.

DOS was a secret society within the larger secret society of NXIVM proper. A number of prominent Nxians were not recruited into, and were likely not aware of the existence of, DOS until the story broke in the papers. Nancy Salzman was not asked to join and knew nothing about it. Marianna Flores, the chosen concubine, was left out even though her younger sister Camila was in the group. None of the high-ranking Nxian men—Mark Vicente and Emiliano Salinas and Alejandro Betancourt—had so much as heard of DOS. Even DOS itself was secretive. For some time, the eight first-line slaves were not aware of the identities of the other slaves. Poor Nicki Clyne believed she was the *only* slave Vanguard owned, that she was Anastasia Steele to Keith's Christian Grey. She was reportedly devastated when she found out that her friend Allison Mack was a slave too.

Revealing anything about DOS, even confirming its existence, was an ethical breach against Vanguard. The first rule of DOS was: don't talk about DOS.

The second-line slaves—that is, the women recruited by the first-line slaves—joined under the false pretense that DOS was an exclusively female organization. They had no idea that the sorority was not actually about extreme women's empowerment, but rather the fulfillment of Keith Raniere's warped fantasies. He wanted sex slaves, yes, but more than that, he wanted *actual* slaves—attractive automatons who would do his bidding, no questions asked. He wanted an army of badass women willing to do *anything* he desired: deny themselves sexual pleasure, starve, lie, cheat, steal, kill, even die. Is suicide honorable? Keith taught that laying down one's life for one's Master was the ultimate sacrifice.

The DOS slaves were not brought in off the street. They were cultivated from the ranks of NXIVM and its subsidiaries, like Jness, the "women's empowerment" group. The ESP modules were supposed to open the mind, free the spirit, allow greatness to be achieved. In fact, the opposite was true. Everyone in NXIVM was conditioned, from the very first class, to honor Vanguard, to regard him as superior to everyone else. He was "fully integrated," and only he could help you become integrated yourself. In short, the female members of the NXIVM community were all predisposed to wanting to bow to Vanguard. Any woman put off by that concept would have left after the first couple of classes. As fancy New England boarding schools feed students to Ivy League universities, so NXIVM was a feeder system for DOS.

The Society of Protectors, NXIVM's society for men, preached many of the tenets of the "red pill" or "men's rights" movement: that women were naturally submissive to men; that males should strive to be "alpha" at all times, especially in the confines of their own marriages and romantic relationships; that men should protect their women, just as women should serve their men. Jness, meanwhile, the alleged "women's empowerment" group, taught that women should be faithful to one man, while men should be polygamous. As Lauren Salzman would later testify, "through the curriculum it legitimized the lifestyle that I think Keith wanted to live, and had a whole community of people who could understand that and support it or even defend and protect it against criticism." The DOS recruits had been brainwashed for years before joining the group, conditioned to believe in the supremacy of Vanguard.

A potential slave was approached by one of the first-line slaves, all of whom were perceived in the larger NXIVM community as being close to Vanguard, and thus enjoying higher status. "There is a sorority," the pitch went. "A secret society of women, for women, dedicated to the empowerment of women. Would you be interested in joining?" Coming from an Allison Mack, a Nicki Clyne, a Rosa Laura Junco, a Lauren Salzman, this was an exciting prospect. *Of course* they were interested.

"In order to maintain absolute secrecy, we have to insist on collateral." As a bank forecloses on a house when the mortgage is not paid, so DOS would release the "collateral" if secrecy was not maintained. It was a formality, but an important one. The submission of collateral denoted seriousness. Collateral was what the *National Enquirer* calls *dirt*. It could be anything that might cause damage if released. Maybe a crime would be confessed to. Maybe there would be a letter written to a parent, disclosing something terrible. But always, the collateral involved nude photos and/or sexual videos. The recruits were resistant, but when it was explained that Allison Mack had done so—what would that do to her acting career!—or Rosa Laura Junco, the Mexican publisher's daughter, with her conservative Catholic background, they complied. NXIVM routinely demanded its members sign a dizzying array of nondisclosure agreements, so, again, they were conditioned to trust in Vanguard.

After the first collateral was acquired, the recruit was apprised of the expectations. They were to be slaves to the Master— Mack or Clyne or Junco or whoever recruited them. As such, they would have to obey, no matter what. The Master would become the focal point of their existence, and her wishes would take priority over anything else. They would have to practice self-denial and perform "acts of care" for their Master. They would have to participate in "readiness drills"—responding to texts within sixty seconds, no matter the hour. In time, as the secret society grew, they would have slaves of their own, just as the first-line Masters were slaves in turn to a higher-ranking Master. They would have to wear a collar, such as a necklace or similar piece of jewelry denoting ownership, that could not be removed. And they would receive a brand—a mark of the secret society, a symbol of the permanence of the commitment to the group. If they consented to all of this—and almost all of them did; it was unthinkable not to—they would have to submit more collateral, every month, if not more frequently.

There was an erotic aspect to all of this. Meetings of the slave groups began with members removing their clothes and posing for a "family photo." The photographs, with their stark emphasis on the vagina, were pornographic in nature. Bad behavior was punished by whacks with a paddle acquired at an online sex shop.

Much has already been written about the branding itself. The slave was splayed naked on a table, pinned down by her sisters.

After a short ceremony, Danielle Roberts, a physician who was also a DOS slave, fired up the cautery pen and executed the brand. The symbol itself, a clumsy rendering of *KAR*, was ugly. So were the scars. The pain was off the charts. And not the sort of pain associated with the BDSM community—an eroticized flogging or spanking that produces endorphins, that stimulates the libido. This was a third-degree burn, carried out slowly and methodically over the course of half an hour, on one of the more sensitive parts of the body. The pain did not abate when the ordeal was over. It lasted for days afterward, until the wound healed into a permanent and hideous reminder of the torment.

What the slaves were *not* told was that the Master of their Master was Vanguard, the only man in the sorority: Keith Raniere. He was the one who demanded that the slaves limit their daily intake of calories, so they were anorexically thin—he liked his girls that way. He did not approve of waxing or grooming the pubic hair, so that, too, was forbidden. He insisted upon total celibacy. His slaves were not allowed to masturbate, to relieve their pent-up carnal desires. He wanted them sexually frustrated, as that made them easier to control and more likely to acquiesce when they were given an assignment by their Master: seduce Vanguard. None of the women realized that this command originated with Keith.

The response to the seduction mission was always the same: shock, discomfort, disgust. While Nxians all held Vanguard in the highest esteem, he was, at the time, supposed to be a renunciate. They were not used to thinking of him in a sexual way—and they didn't want to do so. Keith Raniere was almost sixty years old. Short. Pudgy. Creepy. One of the slaves, Sylvie, was so stumped as to how to carry out the "seduction" that she texted him that his glasses were sexy. After a mental inventory of his physical features, that was the best she could come up with. He replied, "You have to do better than that."

Keith had sex with some of the slaves. He performed oral sex on others and liked to play voyeur as one slave went down on another. When Keith and I were together, he was good in bed. If the court testimony is any indication, he seems to have lost this ability with time. Erectile dysfunction was a recurring problem for him. Since he couldn't keep them sexually satisfied, he had to resort to other means to keep them in line: fear, coercion, peer pressure, blackmail. The "collateral" that the slaves willingly supplied to their individual Masters was passed along to Keith. Digital images were kept in a Dropbox folder, maintained by Loreta Garza, one of the first-line slaves.

If the *Frank Report* is to be believed, "collateral" is baked into the very name of the company. NXIVM, he theorizes, derives from the Latin *nexum*, a contract of bondage common in the Roman Republic, dating from the fourth century BCE, in which debtors put up themselves as collateral. The Roman scholar Varro held that the term *nexum* was a contraction of *nec suum*, meaning "not one's own." NXIVM, of course, is a homonym of *nec suum*—and being *nec suum* was the point of NXIVM. It is likely that the Smartest Man in the World was aware of this.

When I read about the "collateral," about the nude images of the DOS slaves, I recalled the Polaroids of a naked Pam Cafritz.

And then it hit me. Those pictures of Pam were the very first collateral.

# CHAPTER 22:

# BRAND AWARENESS

## DOS Revealed

---

Among the first-line DOS slaves, the lone holdover from the old days was Lauren Salzman, Prefect's daughter. I first met Lauren and her younger sister, Michelle, in the late nineties. She was in college then, bright and capable, full of promise, a world of possibility ahead of her. Her father was a doctor, her mother, flawed though she was, unmistakably brilliant. Lauren's was one of the many lives that Keith Raniere completely and ruthlessly destroyed.

In 2002, while ascending the ESP hierarchy, Lauren was teaching classes in Monterrey. During that period, she met and befriended many of the Mexican nationals who would be so important to NXIVM in the years to come: Rosa Laura Junco, who would help recruit her into DOS. Loreta Garza, the keeper of the DOS collateral. Emiliano Salinas, son of the Mexican president Carlos Salinas de Gortari, an economist whose mismanagement caused the worst economic crisis in the country's history. And the Flores family, especially the three sisters Marianna, Daniela, and Camila, who would prove pivotal to the events that ultimately took down Vanguard.

Lauren Salzman was in love with Keith Raniere. She wanted to be with him forever; she wanted to be worthy of him; she wanted to have the honor of being the mother to his children. Keith knew this and exploited it. "I will give you a child," he told her, "when you are sufficiently integrated." The way to become sufficiently integrated was to simply do whatever he commanded, no questions asked. When he wanted to sleep with her, she did that. When he wanted to stop sleeping with her, she consented to that. When he asked her to remain celibate but also faithful to him while he continued to sleep around, she agreed to that, too. Whenever she marshaled the strength to leave, he would say, "We will have a child soon," and she would agree to wait. If she dared to entertain the flirtations of other men, he would upbraid her for not being "integrated" or for an "ethical breach." She would blame herself, beat herself up, promise to work harder, to be better, to make him proud. Keith nicknamed her "Forlorn," a pun on her name, because, as she later testified, "I was sad and suffering."

Lauren was the best recruiter of the first-line DOS slaves. As a high-level Nxian, she knew exactly which of her students to tap. She was the most convincing in her pitches, the most creative in her torments, the most efficient in organizing her charges. Keith didn't seem to notice or care. When she found out that he was having a baby with Marianna, whom she considered spoiled and very much *not* integrated, she lashed out, only to be chastised for having a "tantrum" and not owning her shit.

Lazy as ever, Keith put Lauren to work on a sort of DOS tome, a guidebook that set forth the various rules and expectations of membership in the secret sorority. This seems to have been especially inspired by the *Fifty Shades of Grey* novels. The Master's will must be done—that was the primary rule. He should be at all times the highest priority in the slave's life. Every action the slave took should be undertaken with the Master in mind, to better his station and confer honor upon him. Vanguard should be more important than a slave's children or a slave's husband. If he commanded the slave to have sex with someone, she had to do it, even if she was married.

On June 5, 2017, Frank Parlato revealed the existence of DOS on the *Frank Report*. The news sent shock waves through the NXIVM community. Keith hemmed and hawed, denying that he had knowledge of the society at all. It was his most devoted concubines who started it and ran it, and what was he supposed to do about it? Some Nxians believed him. Crucially, many others did not. Within the top-down framework of NXIVM, it was simply not possible that Vanguard could have been unaware of DOS. It was far more likely that the whole sordid affair was his idea.

With the exception of Allison Mack and Nicki Clyne, who married each other to allow Clyne, a Canadian national, to stay in the United States, the first-line DOS slaves were single. Some of the second-line slaves, however, had husbands. Sarah Edmondson, the actress, was Lauren Salzman's slave in DOS. She was also, in real life, married—to a committed Nxian named Anthony "Nippy" Ames, a handsome former college quarterback turned actor. After hearing about DOS, he discovered that his wife had been branded... because she was his wife, and she suddenly had Keith's initials burned into the skin near her vagina. How could she have kept that a secret? At a Coach Summit in May of 2017, Nippy was furious, demanding answers.

Nxians defected in droves. Edmondson and Ames left. The filmmaker Mark Vicente left, following his wife, the actress Bonnie Piesse. Emiliano Salinas publicly denounced NXIVM.[4] Other DOS slaves left too, once they realized that they had been lied to, that the "women's group" wasn't a women's group at all, but a formalized harem. One of Lauren's slaves, Rachel,[5] threatened to file a lawsuit to get back her collateral. Yes, Rachel had made a vow of obedience and voluntarily turned over the collateral, but because she had done so under false pretenses—she did not know Keith was involved and did not want him to be—she claimed the contract was null and void. Rachel left NXIVM. So did Sylvie, the former equestrian and runner who worked for Clare Bronfman; in DOS, she had been Monica Duran's slave.

Nancy Salzman was not appalled at the news that Vanguard owned well over a hundred female slaves, many of them said to be branded. She did not blame *him* at all. Instead, she was mad at her daughter for allowing the secret to come out—and, according to Lauren, for allowing DOS to happen in the first place. Sarah Edmondson had been Lauren's slave, and thus Lauren's responsibility. Lauren, then, was to blame for the mass defections and the negative publicity. "This is going to ruin the company," she hollered. "My company, my life's work. You've ruined it."

---

4  Salinas denounced NXIVM to try to distance himself from Keith, but as of this writing, NXIVM-related businesses, formally known as Rainbow Cultural Gardens and now called MulticultirED in Mexico City and Sunshine in Guatemala, are still up and running.

5  Rachel's name has been changed to protect her identity.

The media was suddenly interested in the lurid tale of branded slaves in the sex cult. The NXIVM grotesqueries cut across various news beats. Because of Allison Mack, entertainment outfits were interested, while business media were interested because of the Bronfmans. Sarah Edmondson and Catherine Oxenberg, the actress whose daughter India was a branded DOS slave, talked to anyone who would listen about the creepy Vanguard and his deranged operation. After the initial Barry Meier *New York Times* piece, the story was reported by CBC News, Canada's largest news outfit; by A&E, on a program about cults; by *Rolling Stone*; by ABC News. On November 24, 2017, I appeared on the *Dr. Oz* show, the first major media outlet to give me a platform. The newsmagazine *20/20* did a segment on Keith and NXIVM on December 15, 2017, in which I am interviewed. *Vice News* did a profile of Frank Parlato, where he appears in all his eccentric glory.

The DOS genie was out of the bottle.

The remaining NXIVM brass conferred, figuring out strategy. Should they deny the story? Impugn the defectors? Should they release the collateral on everyone who left, as they said they would do? It was the *ethical* thing to do. Ultimately, Keith decided not to do that as he believed it would present NXIVM as vindictive and make a bad situation worse. Instead, they opted to invite a journalist to do a story on the group—someone chosen by them, given access to them, and thus more likely to paint them in a positive light.

Vanessa Grigoriadis, the journalist who wrote *Blurred Lines: Rethinking Sex, Power, and Consent on Campus*, wound up writing the subsequent feature for *The New York Times Magazine*. "Inside NXIVM, the 'Sex Cult' That Preached Empowerment" is a balanced piece of journalism, and Grigoriadis goes out of her way to explain the group's appeal:

> Many members and ex-members of NXIVM that I spoke with—most of them fans of science and math, funny and strikingly perceptive—agreed on one thing: The "technology" worked. Raniere could program you. He had solved the equation of how to be a joyful human. Decide on your ethics and make them the guiding force in your life; do not make decisions that are not in line with those ethics. Look to create strength and character through discipline. Look to create love. Do not reject your family (unless your family rejects NXIVM, in which case some other steps may be necessary). Do not be a slave to your fears and attachments. Pain creates conscience; do not be afraid of pain.

But if the objective was to make NXIVM appear like something other than a crazy cult, the mission was a miserable failure. Nancy Salzman, Clare Bronfman, and Allison Mack are described as bright, friendly, courteous—and that makes them seem all the crazier, for going along with such an obviously unconventional program.

> Anything in the group about skinniness, about punishment, about self-denial was simply to help members evolve. "If something's uncomfortable for us emotionally, we choose to smoke, we choose to drink, we choose to eat, we choose to dissociate," Bronfman told me. "We have so many strategies." The purpose of NXIVM was to "feel those things so that you can work them through and then they're not uncomfortable anymore."

At first blush, that sounds logical. Who doesn't want to evolve? Keith Raniere used one of his strategies to help me quit smoking—and it worked. But helping a binge eater overcome binge eating is not the same thing as actively starving an otherwise healthy woman. The DOS diet is not about health or well-being. It's about a man exercising control over a woman's body, based on nothing more than his aesthetic preference.

All the talent and might of the NXIVM PR team could not spin DOS in a positive light. How could any objective individual read these three paragraphs and think, *Wow, that sounds like a great sisterhood. I want to join!*:

Michele, a 31-year-old member...recalled that a member asked her to lunch. "This was someone I really admired from afar. I was superexcited and flattered that she wanted to talk to me." She told me, "I knew if she was involved, there were probably other badass women involved, and I want to be a badass woman—I'm struggling to do that." Michele said she found her experience of giving collateral "growthful."

To this day, dedicated DOS members insist that they began the secret group themselves when one of them was deeply upset and others decided to help her by pledging ultimate commitment. Over time, the group morphed into a military-style boot camp that was simply trying to address the place of women in the world, to make them realize that they were not victims...

Promising to seduce Raniere—which was apparently the way he preferred to be approached sexually, rather than putting himself on the line—was also one of the ways some women later said they were told to show commitment to the sisterhood. It was a test of faith in DOS, a proof of ultimate commitment, of loyalty. And if you didn't have faith, DOS wouldn't work for you, and you would lose all your sisters and your chance at badassness.

Allison Mack, the DOS alpha slave, was a professional actress. She has a lovely speaking voice and is flirtishly charming. She comes across as painfully sincere. If she couldn't sell a friendly journalist on the wonders of Keith Raniere, no one could. In the piece, she sounds like a lunatic:

> In her apartment, I was surprised to hear Mack take full responsibility for coming up with the DOS cauterized brand. She told me, "I was like: 'Y'all, a tattoo? People get drunk and tattooed on their ankle 'BFF,' or a tramp stamp. I have two tattoos and they mean nothing.'" She wanted to do something more meaningful, something that took guts.
>
> To be honest, I was surprised that she was sitting there at all.

That was a lie, of course. It was not Allison's idea to brand the slaves. It was not Allison's idea to give each slave the task of seducing Vanguard. It was not Allison's idea to starve them half to death, or to deny them masturbatory pleasure. But it *was* Allison's idea to *claim responsibility* for the branding. She wasn't supposed to have done that. It was ad-libbed when the reporter started asking questions.

These women had been indoctrinated for years. They would take a bullet for Vanguard. And if they were willing to die for him, they were certainly willing to lie for him.

But it was all in vain. Vanessa Grigoriadis piece ran on May 30, 2018.

By then, Keith Raniere was already in federal custody.

Vanguard's defense boiled down to this: DOS was a group of consenting adults. There was video of each branded slave *asking* to be branded. BDSM was not unlawful. Further, the sorority was a social group, and while its members were all Nxians, DOS itself was completely separate from NXIVM. To impugn the company because of the unorthodox but entirely legal behavior of some of its members amounted to kink shaming. It was an attack on freedom! It was an attack on the American way of life!

And if it had been Jeff Bezos at the center of a bizarre sex cult, if Jamie Dimon's initials were being branded near the vaginas of a coven of emaciated women young enough to be his daughters, perhaps the story would have gone away. But NXIVM was not Amazon or JPMorgan Chase. Since its inception, NXIVM operated in the shadows, shaded by insular employees and the best legal team that liquor money could buy. The depraved DOS story effectively shined a bevy of spotlights on the company. Maybe consensual branding was lawful, but the other shady stuff the company was doing was certainly not. This was not some blue-chip Fortune 500 corporation that added value to society. NXIVM was a sham.

As I always knew, the charges levied against NXIVM by Joe O'Hara in his 2012 lawsuit were not unfounded. The company really was a pyramid scheme, artificially bolstered by the Bronfman fortune, and should not have been able to legally conduct business in the state of New York. Keith Raniere was opposed to paying taxes and did everything in his power to evade them.

How could he own everything but also own nothing? What was the provenance of the half million dollars in cash the feds found stashed in Nancy Salzman's basement? The operation really was a criminal enterprise.

For whatever reason, NXIVM had been more successful recruiting Mexicans and Canadians than Americans. This led to a host of problems with immigration laws, which the company took great pains to circumvent. The Canadian national Nicki Clyne, who is not a lesbian, married the American citizen Allison Mack, also not a lesbian, so that the former could live near Keith in Clifton Park. The Flores family were all Mexican nationals. When her visa expired, Daniela Flores was smuggled into the country by Kathy Russell, made to do intellectual labor for Keith Raniere and housework for other Nxians without due compensation, and held in a room in Knox Woods for almost two years. Her older sister Marianna, Keith's favorite concubine, lived with Vanguard for years, as did her younger sister Camila, who was a DOS slave, and her brother Adrian, or "Fluffy," who resided with the filmmaker Mark Vicente. Sylvie, the equestrian DOS slave, was British. Lack of American citizenship helped Vanguard impose more control.

By the end of 2017, Keith could read the writing on the wall. His hand was caught in the cookie jar, and he knew it. He called for DOS to disband until things settled down. He and Marianna and their infant son—the Chosen One, who was born that August—ran off to Mexico in October of 2017. He came back briefly a few weeks later, to tie up loose ends. He cleared cash he'd accumulated for years from one of his minions, Dawn Morrison, out of various safes; he collected letters and other writings; he forwarded a bunch of the naked pictures to an email address he could access remotely; he left behind his cell phone and purchased a few burners. Then he fled for good: he flew to Mexico, where he holed up in a gated community in Punta Mita, on the Pacific coast, near the resort town of Puerto Vallarta. He left no forwarding address. Very few people knew his whereabouts.

There would be one last DOS hurrah, a "recommitment ceremony" planned for the last week of March 2018. Even now, in the face of fire, his girls remained loyal to him. Five first-line slaves traveled to the remote fishing village of Chacala, ninety miles outside of Puerto Vallarta: Loreta Garza, Daniela Padilla, Nicki Clyne, Allison Mack, and Lauren Salzman. The "ceremony" would involve all five of the slaves performing oral sex on Vanguard, in tandem, while kneeling before him, naked.

Much to the relief of at least one of the slaves—Lauren Salzman—the group sex act never took place. Instead, on March 26, 2018, the police raided the house, machine guns at the ready. Nicki, Allison, and Daniela Padilla had been outdoors when they came and were detained there. Loreta opened the door and was immediately whisked away. The only DOS slave who remained with Keith was Lauren Salzman, who ran to the bedroom where Keith had been napping, to protect him. She could see the police outside the window, with their bulletproof vests and masks. Allison and Nicki and Daniela were out there too. She was alone with Vanguard when the police banged on the bedroom door.

"What should I do?" she asked her Master.

"See if they have a warrant," was his idiotic reply. Then the Grandmaster of slaves, the alpha male who preached that men should strive always to protect their women, the great and wonderful Vanguard, the Smartest Man in the World, hid in the closet, leaving Lauren to handle the *federales*. She wound up on the floor, four officers training machine guns at her head. She held out for a few minutes, wondering if she should lay down her life for him, before calling out his name—before giving him up.

He's been in custody ever since.

Keith Raniere, prisoner number 57005-177.

# CHAPTER 23:

# THE FALL OF NXIVM

Rochester and Brooklyn, New York,

2018–2019

---

I was at a doctor's appointment when the text came: Keith had been arrested in Mexico and charged with sex trafficking, among other crimes. I was stunned. I never lost faith that this day would come, but I was still shocked when it happened.

The text came from my friend Dennis Yusko—a sign from the universe. Dennis wrote some of the first NXIVM stories for the *Albany Times Union*. He'd almost been fired in 2003, after covering multiple stories about NXIVM for the paper, because of pressure from Vanguard's minions, who told his editor that he had a vendetta against them. On October 13, 2003, he walked into a meeting with his editor, Clare Bronfman, Nancy Salzman, and Barbara Bouchey and tossed the hot-off-the-press *Forbes* magazine on the table, with Keith's creepy face on the cover. Like me, Dennis knew the truth about NXIVM.

Keith was apprised of the charges in Fort Worth and then

transported by bus to Brooklyn, city of his birth, where he was arraigned. He was denied bail on three separate occasions. One bail motion proposed a bond of $10 million, with home detention in Brooklyn, to be supervised by a private team of twenty-four-hour armed guards. The court denied the motion, finding that Raniere posed a substantial flight risk, and that if he were released, he may "unlawfully exploit women or obstruct justice." He spent the winter in the horrible prison in Brooklyn, notorious for its defective heating. He froze his ass off, as the other inmates tormented him, wiping shit on his mattress, stuffing shit in his shoes. Men in prison tend not to look kindly on male prisoners who abuse women—especially underage girls.

The others were arrested and charged in the weeks that followed: Allison Mack, Nancy Salzman, Lauren Salzman, and Kathy Russell. If Pam Cafritz were still alive, she almost certainly would have joined them; same with Barb Jeske.

Clare Bronfman was indicted on July 26, 2018. I was on a plane to New York for a hearing scheduled for the following day. On the runway, I received word that Clare would be appearing in the Eastern District Court in Brooklyn at 3:30. I made it with only minutes to spare. There she was, the heiress to the Seagram fortune, who'd fecklessly funded the destruction of my life and the lives of so many other innocent people. I was shocked at how small she was—how someone that small could cause so much pain. She was dressed as if she'd just pulled her clothes out of a laundry hamper: rumpled pink T-shirt, baggy sweatpants, and flip-flops. Her attorney at the time, Susan Necheles, was a hot mess: frustrated, interrupting the judge. She released a ridiculous statement: "Clare Bronfman did nothing wrong... [Charges] against Clare are the result of government overreaching and charging an individual with crimes just because the government disagrees with some beliefs taught by NXIVM and held by Clare." After the hearing, Necheles was unable to find her car, leaving Clare to wander the streets while photographers snapped her picture.

Karen Unterreiner—once Keith's college girlfriend and thus one of the first of his enablers, the keeper of all of his secrets for more than thirty years—somehow managed to avoid arrest, as did numerous members of NXIVM's inner circle: Jack Levy, Alejandro Betancourt, Emiliano Salinas, Jim Del Negro, Dawn Morrison, and Sara Bronfman, as well as most of the first-line DOS slaves: Rosa Laura Junco, Nicki Clyne, Daniela Padilla, Monica Duran, Loreta Garza, and Camila Flores. Maybe they would face the music later, maybe not. Maybe it was enough that they had all been victims of Keith Raniere, had lived under his tyrannical reign for years. Their world had collapsed around them, and now they had to somehow try to start over, to make a new life outside the NXIVM cult.

Kristin Keeffe was not charged, probably because she had been cooperating with the authorities since her defection from the group. For decades, she was Keith's legal attack dog. She knew exactly who to ask, and exactly what to proffer for immunity. Did she deserve to pay for her crimes? Yes. But when I last saw her, she was already broken—and she obviously did what she could to help take down Vanguard.

NXIVM suspended operations in June of 2018. Its website doesn't work. Its social media pages are vacant. The accounts of the upper-level Nxians are all active but abandoned. The last tweet on the Jness Twitter feed is a quote from Sylvie, the aspiring equestrian turned DOS slave. "Jness allows women to come together, work together, and discover how to bring their best selves to the world."

The first time I saw the quote, I misread it as "bring their best *slaves* to the world."

One by one the codefendants turned on their Vanguard.

Prefect was first, on March 26, 2019. "I am pleading guilty," Nancy Salzman said, "because I am, in fact, guilty. It has taken me some time and some soul searching to come to this place. When I began working with NXIVM I believed that we would be helping people. I still believe that some of what we did was good. The problem began when I compromised my principles and did things which I knew or should have known were wrong. I justified them to myself by saying that what we were doing was for the greater good. Now, having had time to step back from the community I was immersed in for nearly 20 years, I accept that some of the things I did were not just wrong but criminal...By my plea of guilty I hope to at least begin atoning for my actions and to start the next part of my life." She described NXIVM as "an enterprise comprised of people close to Keith Raniere" that engaged in "racketeering activity," and expressed remorse. Nancy, cold as ever, knew a superseding indictment was coming, and she was going to be the first one on the bus—leaving her daughter Lauren, whom she long ago sacrificed to Vanguard, to fend for herself. As she left the courthouse that day, Nancy was smiling. Was it because she was finally free of her partner in crime? Or because of how much she managed to get away with? To me, she is as guilty as Keith, if not more so. Nancy, Prefect, was the one who gave him permission to be Vanguard.

Lauren Salzman defected a few days later, agreeing to testify for the prosecution. She would be one of the star witnesses. In her riveting testimony a few months later, she told the court that her perception of Keith Raniere changed forever on the day of his arrest—when she stood up to the police, with their machine guns and gas masks, while he cowered, putting them all at risk. She explained that "everything he taught us was this: Society of Protectors—this is what men are, this is what men do; this is what is noble; this is what women don't do, this is what women can't do. And then he didn't do it, and I did it." She concluded, "I could not make sense of how that could even be in any universe where he was who I believed he was."

On April 8, it was Allison Mack's turn. "I am prepared to take responsibility for acts in which I was involved, some of which I now recognize were wrong," she told the court. "I joined NXIVM first to find purpose. I was lost and I wanted to find a place, a community in which I would feel comfortable. Over time, I truly believed that I had found a group of individuals who believed, as I did, and who were interested in trying to become better people and in doing so make those around them better... Through it all, I believed that Keith Raniere's intentions were to help people, and that my adherence to his system of beliefs would help empower others and help them. I was wrong." She confessed to supporting a "criminal enterprise" engaging in "criminal conduct," and she laid out her overseeing of DOS, particularly her collection of "collateral." As she spoke, she looked terrified, and her apology sounded more heartfelt than Nancy's.

Kathy Russell, the bookkeeper, came next, on April 19. She confessed to violating immigration law by presenting false documents to the US consulate in Mexico so that Loreta Garza, a DOS slave, could stay in the United States for a longer period of time. "I know what I did was wrong, and I'm very sorry for the trouble I have caused. I compromised my own principles and I will have to live with that for the rest of my life."

Last but not least was the liquor heiress and latter-day Patty Hearst, Clare Bronfman. "Your Honor," she told the judge, "I was afforded a great gift by my grandfather and my father. With the gift comes immense privilege, and more importantly, tremendous responsibility. It does not come with the ability to break the law; it comes with a great responsibility to uphold the law. I failed to uphold the following laws set forth by this country, and for that I'm truly remorseful . . . I am truly sorry. I endeavored to do good in the world and to help people, however, I have made mistakes. This experience has taught me the gravity of my responsibility, and I will take these lessons forward in every future decision. Thank you."

To me, that apology and confession rang hollow. It did not scratch the surface of Clare's complicity in the criminal enterprise that was NXIVM. Without her money, the company would have collapsed years ago, and none of the lawsuits against me, against Rick Ross and Stephanie Franco, against Joe O'Hara and John Tighe and Frank Parlato, against Barbara Bouchey and Susan Dones, against *Metroland* and James Odato, would have been filed. Clare deserves more than a slap on her emaciated wrist.

Some justice is better than none at all.

Rochester is five hours away by car, but I have dutifully attended most of the NXIVM court proceedings. If Keith Raniere appears in a courtroom, so do I. When in town, I stay in the Brooklyn Heights apartment of my always supportive and generous friend

Stanley Zareff—my shining light in some very dark days; I don't know how I would have done this without him.

On trial days, I rise at five in the morning, and by six, I'm waiting in line outside the courthouse. In the winter, it was dark at that hour, and bitterly cold, the tall buildings creating a wind tunnel. Now winter has given way to spring, and spring to summer. Now the sun shines on me in the line outside the big stone fortress.

I am a fixture in that courtroom. At times I was joined by ally and friend (and my bookend) Catherine Oxenberg. Without her prestigious reputation with the media and her diligent fight to free her daughter India from Vanguard's evil clutches, we would not be here today. The journalist Chet Hardin has worked with me since 2006 to expose, document, research, and file NXIVM materials. He has flown in from St. Louis to witness the proceedings. Most of the time, I sit alone—to watch Keith.

At first, the judge must have wondered, "Who *is* this woman?" By now, I believe he knows and understands. His name is Nicholas Garaufis. He's seventy years old and has been on the bench at the United States Eastern District for almost twenty years. During my decades of legal trouble instigated by Keith Raniere and his lackeys, I have come to know a number of judges. Garaufis is as solid as they come: smart, objective, compassionate, patient, and, most important, not swayed by the Bronfman money.

I have marveled at Moira Kim Penza, the lead prosecutor, as she powers around the courtroom in her four-inch stiletto heels. This is by design. As she weaves her argument and makes her case, she is communicating a message to Keith: *This is what you like, and you can't have it, and you'll never be able to have anything like it ever again.* She and her team have been masterful in general, but especially adroit at subtly reminding the court of Vanguard's erectile dysfunction problems.

I have watched as the court security officers, hearing that the defendant was the Grandmaster of a gaggle of more than a hundred sex slaves, have glanced at the short, unkempt guy in the courtroom, as if to say, *Really? Him?*

In the rare instance I can't be there, I am the first to receive updates. My dear friend Stanley Zareff was my eyes and ears at the eighth Curcio hearing—seven more than are usually necessary—when the court tried to determine if there were any conflicts of interest in the case. The NXIVM legal team was rife with potential conflicts of interest. Mark Geragos, the celebrity attorney whose high-profile clients included Michael Jackson, Winona Ryder, Scott Peterson, and Chris Brown, was retained by Clare Bronfman. Teny Geragos, Mark's daughter, was already one of Keith's attorneys. "It's good to have families in the room," the judge quipped. The real conflict was that the Bronfman family fortune was underwriting the legal fees of all seven NXIVM defendants. But even that unorthodox arrangement was given the green light. The purpose of the eighth Curcio hearing was even more strange.

"Please tell us the attorneys you have retained," the judge said to the liquor heiress. This was before she pleaded guilty.

Clare's voice was soft and reedy. She was putting it on a bit, exaggerating her physical weakness. She looked terrible: flat, lifeless hair pulled back to accentuate the avian features of her spinsterish face; pale, almost jaundiced skin; casual clothes draped over skin and bones. She listed the names of her lawyers. She skipped the one the judge was interested in.

"Did she retain Mr. Avenatti to represent her in this case," the exasperated judge asked Clare's attorneys, "yes or no?"

A law partner of Mark Geragos, Michael Avenatti had become famous as the attorney of adult film actress Stormy Daniels,[6] and, later, as a foil to President Donald Trump. Now it appeared that Avenatti had met with prosecutors on Clare Bronfman's behalf, apparently attempting to swap dirt on Nike for leniency for the liquor heiress. This was thorny to begin with, because Clare was not a known client of Avenatti. The fact that Avenatti was indicted for extortion a few days later raised all kinds of alarm bells. Clare had likely given her consent for Avenatti to parlay with the feds, without bothering to tell any of the other defendants. And now the whole thing had blown up in her face, like an exploding cigar in an old cartoon.

"Yes or no?"

The liquor heiress was standing to address the judge. Her eyeballs rolled up, only the whites showing behind her glasses. She swooned from side to side like a reed, gasped, and then collapsed. If the attorney had not caught her, she would have fallen onto the cold courthouse floor. Paramedics were called. The fire department came for some reason. To his obvious annoyance, the judge was forced to delay the hearing. It may have been the most eventful Curcio hearing in the history of New York.

I smiled as, one by one, Keith's codefendants turned on him.

I pumped my fist as Mark Vicente, the filmmaker whose name will forever be associated with NXIVM, unleashed on Keith, calling him "evil." I'd reached out to Mark in 2010, after watching him

---

6   There is an Internet rumor that Stormy Daniels was involved in DOS and bore a slave brand. This rumor is completely false.

extol Keith Raniere in a TED Talk on bravery. I wrote in part, "For me bravery is still standing after 12 years of your mentor, Raniere, trying to silence and destroy my family, my friends and so many others like me...Hasn't it ever occurred to you to ask 'Why' when Keith (and his ever loyal 'inner circle' of women) describes me as a suppressive? It would take bravery for you to voice the thoughts and questions about Raniere and NXIVM that you have suppressed for so long. It would take bravery for you to save others from becoming involved with an organization whose core is rotten and based on lies, lies that Keith will stop at nothing to cover up. DO YOU HAVE THAT KIND OF BRAVERY?" It took eight more long and arduous years, but in the end, Mark did demonstrate the bravery I spoke of.

I was disgusted when the owner of a company called Extreme Restraints, which sells sex toys to the bondage community, rattled off a list of items purchased by Daniela Padilla, one of the branded first-line slaves, for use in their DOS dungeon.

I was aghast as Sylvie described her torment at the hands of Clare Bronfman, Monica Duran, and Keith Raniere. My heart broke as Daniela Flores—so bright, so strong—recalled her twenty-month imprisonment at Keith's command. I noted how both women described a similar initiation into the sexual relationship with Keith: he went down on them, and although they were revolted, they didn't feel like they could say no.

Even knowing what I know, I was blown away by the amount of time and energy he and his inner circle put into destroying the women—the girls—around him who dared to say no or tried to walk away. Without the enabling help of his inner circle, who knew the deplorable truth, he never would have been able to get away with all of this for as long as he did.

And I wept as Lauren Salzman testified against Vanguard. All the poor girl wanted was to be loved—or even noticed—by her heartless mother. She was unquestionably responsible for inflicting significant emotional damage on many, many individuals, at Keith's behest. On the other hand, I don't know that any one person suffered more, or lost more, than Prefect's daughter, who is looking at twenty years in prison on each of the two charges against her. Forlorn, indeed.

Keith Raniere could have pleaded guilty at any point during the trial. There was no doubt in my mind that this would ever happen. He would never admit wrongdoing, ever. So I laughed to myself when Keith's high-powered defense attorney tried to claim that everything Keith did had been the work of Kristin Keeffe— that the almighty Vanguard, the Smartest Man in the World, had been coerced.

# EPILOGUE:

# THE VERDICT

## Brooklyn, New York, June 19, 2019

---

I wake up knowing today will be the day. The prosecutors have rested their case. The defense offered one of the most creative justifications for NXIVM ever devised—it was all consensual—but I know, in my heart, that it will not be enough. Today is the day Keith Raniere will go down.

*COUNT ONE: Racketeering Conspiracy*

From my usual seat in the back of the courtroom, I sit, listen, and carefully watch as the judge and his clerks charge the jury. Reading all 140 pages of instructions to the jury regarding the counts against Keith Raniere takes more than five hours. For most of that time, I am the only nonworking person in the courtroom. I am alone with the judge, the jurors, the prosecution and defense, and of course Vanguard. He slumps at the defense table, nonplussed, as a few sketch artists take the opportunity to draw his picture.

*COUNT TWO: Racketeering*

Drawing on what I learned all those years ago in "Irresistible Communications," I observe the faces of the jurors as each count is read. The expressions do not require a certificate in neuro-linguistic programming to analyze. Some of them nod as the letter of the law is explained on each count, as if to say, *Yes, yes, guilty, for sure guilty on that count.*

*COUNT THREE: Forced Labor Conspiracy*

Keith sees me, of course. He knows I'm there. We give each other dirty looks all day long, as we have done throughout the trial. He uses his stubby middle finger to push up his glasses as they slide down his nose, glowering at me while doing so. I respond in kind to this middle school gesture, using my own middle finger to brush back my bangs. In NLP, they call this "matching and mirroring."

*COUNT FOUR: Wire Fraud Conspiracy*

As the jury files out to deliberate, I say a little prayer. I think about my mother, my father, my brother, how happy they would have been today.

*COUNT FIVE: Sex Trafficking Conspiracy*

The tension in the room is palpable when the first note from the jury comes in, like on the court procedural shows. "Need materials," it reads. Shortly after that comes a second note. A decision has to be made—both sides have to argue their positions, so the monster is led back into the room. Moira gives me a smile, and Big Mike, the FBI agent, winks. I know it's going to be okay.

*COUNT SIX: Sex Trafficking of Nicole*

*This may be the last time I'm ever going to see you,* I think to myself. *These are your last moments of freedom. You won't be able to hurt anyone any longer.* It all starts to happen quickly now. FBI agents who have been working the case for almost two years lock eyes with one another. The room is suddenly filled with reporters and government officials, as well as survivors of the NXIVM cult and its criminal enterprise. The return of a verdict this quickly has to be bad news for Vanguard. Court security officers try to keep order in the room as Moira Kim Penza and her team—Tanya Hajjar, Mark Lesko, Kevin Trowel, and Karin Orenstein—file into the chamber, followed by FBI agents Michael Weniger and Michael Lever, and Investigator Charles Fontanelli of the New York State Police. We all hold our breath as the judge and jury enter the courtroom.

*COUNT SEVEN: Attempted Sex Trafficking of Jay*

For six weeks, Keith Raniere had feverishly scrawled on Post-it note after Post-it note, pink, blue, yellow, passing them to each of his attorneys as he tried vainly to control his inevitable situation. At each break, Marc Agnifilo, his lead attorney, would sharpen pencils to keep him occupied during the trial. It was clear that Keith was not the Grandmaster in the room—the judge was—and he was not the one who had the final say: the jury was.

He stands to await the verdict, his face devoid of expression. The first charge is read, and the judge asks, "How does the jury rule?" The foreman, a stocky, bald white man, utters the word we've all been longing to hear: "Guilty."

This is repeated six more times, and the verdict is the same each time. *Guilty. Guilty. Guilty. Guilty. Guilty. Guilty.* Guilty on all seven counts.

With each guilty verdict, a tear streams down Moira's pretty face. Members of the jury catch my eye and nod. Keith, meanwhile, looks stunned. Did he really think he was getting off? That the jury would somehow be swayed? As the realization washes over him, his expression changes to one I have not seen before: disbelief.

Keith is in disbelief.

A minute later, it's all over. The cuffs are slapped on him and he is led out of the courtroom, forever to be known by his prison number: 57005-177.

*The next time I see you, you'll be dead or in jail.*

For decades, Keith Raniere harassed me, he stalked me, he chased me through courtroom after courtroom, attacking me in an onslaught of bogus litigation. Because of him I lost more than I can say. He took it all and was never satisfied. He had to either possess me completely, or destroy me completely.

He did neither. And for that, I am grateful. Gratitude, in fact, is what I feel the most right now.

To my superheroes of the United States Eastern District of New York: Moira, Tanya, Mark, Big Mike, Mike, Charlie, Megan, Megan, Delise, and Laura, and to all the court security officers, with special thanks to Lou, Sean, Rich, Jack, and Kevin: words cannot express how grateful I am to all of you, for all of your hard work, for believing in people who for decades no one would listen to.

To the jury, whom I spent so much time watching…

Juror #5: Your inability at times to hide your tears, disgust, and disdain, you were my favorite. Frowning so hard I worried your forehead was going to get stuck that way.

Juror #6: When you rolled your eyes and your nostrils flared at the things you were hearing when Daniela and others were on the stand, truth brought justice.

Juror #12: Your strength showed every day as you stared at Keith in disbelief as each witness shared their story.

Juror #11: How many notebooks did you use? I loved watching you meticulously detail all of the evidence presented.

Juror #10: You made me nervous. You were always looking at me, probably wondering who the hell I was. I wondered that sometimes myself.

Juror #4: I loved your hair! I watched your face as Nicole testified. Her innocence showed through as she apologized to the judge when she said "bullshit" while testifying. She broke our hearts with her story.

To the Muslim jurors who had to listen to all of this horror during Ramadan, I am forever grateful.

Juror #1: Our foreman, you were blocked from my view, so I only saw you as you entered the courtroom each day. I had no doubt that you and all the other jurors would see him for exactly what he was: a monster.

To each and every one of you, thank you. You have saved more lives than you will ever know.

And last, but not least, to our judge, the Honorable Nicholas Garaufis: thank you, Your Honor. You made me believe in justice again.

After my brother died in 2009—the year the Dalai Lama came to Albany, the year the NXIVM Nine defected—I got a tattoo of a favorite expression of John's, a spin on Aeschylus. I think of that quote, and of my brother, as I leave the courtroom for the last time: *"In war, truth is the first casualty... but not this time."*

# ACKNOWLEDGMENTS

With grace and gratitude, I acknowledge the following, for their strength, courage, and support. Without each and every one of your voices, we would not be here today. Although at times bruised and battled from the war, we won.

To Yfat Reiss Gendell at Foundry Literary + Media, "the best agent in the world," who said, "I will walk into hell with you to get your story told." Thank you for believing in me from day one. Never have I experienced such support, guidance and strength. I will be forever grateful.

To Greg Olear, we cannot thank you enough. Without your support and guidance, this would have never been possible. Thank your wife and children for sharing your precious time—may the sage keep the vultures away from your home forever.

To our editor, Maddie Caldwell at Grand Central Publishing, you had me the minute you proposed the story tagline: "Mother, Father, Felon." Thank you for your unwavering support in helping to bring this book to life.

Chet and I are ever grateful to our larger visionary team at Grand Central Publishing, who bravely connected with this project at first blush (telling our agent, Yfat: "It's not *if* we want to publish this, it's how soon can we do it") and who championed my unusual path to trade publishing through many twists and turns—this story could not be told in this way without your dedication to shepherding the voices of women and journalists. A special thank-you for Jarrod Taylor and Albert Lee's cover design; Kristen Lemire, Carolyn Kurek, and Marie Mundaca's understanding and flexible production process; Eileen G. Ghetti's dedicated copyediting; the ongoing guidance of Linda Duggins on publicity; the essential collaboration of Tiffany Sanchez on the marketing of this project; and of course the support of Grand Central Publishing and Hachette Book Group's leadership.

Thank you to the greater team at Foundry Literary + Media for supporting this project on the long road to publication, with a special thank-you to Jessica Felleman for her editorial and contracts support, Klara Scholtz and Sasha Welm for their on-going support, to controller Sara DeNobrega and assistant to the controller Sarah Lewis, a big thank-you to foreign rights director Michael Nardullo and team members Claire Harris and Yona Levin, along with Foundry's foreign coagent team at The Riff Agency, Abner Stein, Andrew Nurnberg, La Nouvelle Agence, Mohrbooks, Read n' Right, Deborah Harris Agency, Italian Literary Agency, Tuttle Mori, KCC, Graal, MB Agencia, and Ackali Copyright. A thank-you to director of filmed entertainment Richie Kern, along with very, very special appreciation for the hard work of contracts director Deirdre Smerillo and team members Melissa Moorehead, Hayley Burdett and Gary Smerillo.

Many people helped us uncover and begin sharing this story along the way:

We are grateful that Toni found Rick Ross when she did. He

was a valuable resource for her as she struggled to understand the abusive gaslighting techniques of a cult. His early work with Morris and Rochelle Sutton made him NXIVM's Enemy Number One—an honor Rick never failed to live up to.

The events underlying this harrowing story of comeuppance would never have taken place if not for brave members of the press, and we want to thank them for everything they did and sacrificed, noteable among them:

*From Toni*:

Chet Hardin and *Metroland* gave me my first voice and always believed me, and believed *in* me—something I will forever be thankful for. We needed an ending to this story and we got one.

Michael Freedman brought an early story to the cover of *Forbes* magazine, the first true exposé into Keith Raniere and Executive Success Programs known then as ESP. This groundbreaking article set the precedent for all that was to follow.

Dennis Yusko also took an early stand against the evil behind NXIVM—fighting so hard that he almost lost his job with the *Albany Times Union*.

Jeane MacIntosh's tenacious work to bring Keith Raniere's crimes to the *New York Post*'s wider audience time and time again.

Suzanna Andrews's remarkable *Vanity Fair* investigation into the Bronfman sisters put her straight into the crosshairs of NXIVM's legal retaliation as one of my co-defendants.

Barry Meier wrote and *The New York Times* published the story that finally forced people in power to pay attention.

Toni also had the honor of working closely with James Odato and Jennifer Gish of the *Albany Times Union* as they dug deeply into decades of Raniere's crimes. After two years of hard work, they produced a brilliant, award-winning four-part series that stands as a singular resource to understanding the depth of Raniere's depravity. They stood behind their work when NXIVM struck back with frivolous lawsuits.

John Tighe's bold, in-your-face reporting on his blog, *Saratoga in Decline*, was for years the sharp end of the spear for ESP and NXIVM. Few people fought as hard, or as bravely, as John did— and few sacrificed more.

To Dr. Mehmet Oz, Jessica Yankelunas, and the *Dr. Oz* show. Thank you for your unconditional support.

Toni has always said that there were three things that Keith Raniere never anticipated: the Internet, a mother's love, and Frank Parlato. With his upstate media empire, Frank Parlato achieved more than any single outlet could have in the fight to bring Keith Raniere to justice. It is not hyperbole to say Keith wouldn't have seen his day in court without the *Frank Report*.

A true army of attorneys fought and continue to fight against the darkness that fuels Keith Raniere. We extend tremendous gratitude for your guidance and belief in what is right to Chris Dribusch at The Dribusch Law Firm; William Dreyer at Dreyer, Boyajian, LaMarche, Safranko, Attorneys at Law; Eugene Z. Grenz; David Gonzalez; Michael Grygiel at Greenberg Traurig, LLP; Bruce E. H. Johnson, Davis Wright Tremaine, LLP; Peter Skolnik, LLC; Luke Lieberman at Rosenfeld, Meyer & Susman, LLP; Chris Nolan; Neil L. Glazer and Zahra R. Dean at Kohn, Swift & Graf, P.C.

And to those who help the attorneys do what they do best, directly and indirectly:

## ACKNOWLEDGMENTS

Joe Wolodkecich of Intelligent Technology Solutions, the daring IT professional who helped prove I wasn't a hacker.

Special love and thanks to: Dr. and Mrs. Bernard Plansky, MD; Marianna Schwab, LCSW; Dr. Jahn Forth-Finegan L. PhD, LMHC, NCC, CASAC.

And then, to the superheroes of the United States Attorney's Office for the Eastern District of New York: Moira Kim Penza, Tanya Hajjar, Mark Lesko, Kevin Trowel, and Karin Orenstein; the New York Field Office of the Federal Bureau of Investigation: Michael Weniger, Michael Lever, Megan Buckley, Delise Williams, and Megan Rees; FBI Victim Services: Laura Riso; New York State Police Investigator: Charles Fontanelli; and The United States Department of Homeland Security, Chris Munster.

With special thanks to: Chief Security Officers Lou, Sean, Rich and Jack...

With never-ending gratitude to the Honorable Nicholas Garaufis.

Wars won by brilliant battle strategists cannot succeed without whole armies in the trenches, among them we wish to gratefully acknowledge:

The Warriors: Joe O'Hara, John Tighe, Gina Melita, "my person," Heidi Clifford, Lori Ann Christina, Chitra Selvaraj, Heidi Hutchinson, Christine Marie Katas, "L," Natalia and Yuri Plyam, Becca Ann Friedman; The NXIVM 9—Susan Dones, Barbara Bouchey, Kim Woolhouse, Angela Ucci, Ellen Gibson, Nina Cowell, Jan Heim, Sheila Cote and Kathy Cote-Ethier; Kristi Lahusen, Kristin Keeffe, Mark Vicente, Bonnie Piesse, Sarah Edmondson, Anthony Ames, Maayan Tuati Saraga, Toni Zarattini, Rhiannon, Souki, Jenn, Sylvie, Daniela, Nicole, Jay,

India. And to those of you who prefer to remain anonymous—warriors, friends, and acquaintances—thank you from the bottom of our hearts.

*From Chet:*

Michele Wright, thank you for your sanity and love over so many years. My ship came in when I met you. And to Annyong for running in so many circles. Noel, Dorothy, and Jill Hardin, you are always a welcome sight, and Larry and Sharon Wright, thank you for lending a hand. Toni Natalie, thank you for trusting me, believing in me, stressing me out, and proving to me that the good guys can win. My friends Kate Holton, Bill Forman, Shawn Krider, Christy LeLait, David King, Kirk Woundy, George Fero, Mike Feurstein, Marc Finley, Goodship, Mary Coleman, Alicia Solsman, and Linda and Bruce Brookoff. Russ Cichon and my brothers and sisters, wu sao up. Springs Wing Chun, you owe me one million punches.

*From Toni:*

Additional thanks to my soul sisters—who held me up when at times I was unable. Lisa LoPresti, Carla Piccarreto, Christine Bailey-Clar, Mandy Chase Raville, Marion Romig, Mindy Topel Walsh, Wendy VanSickle, Kimberly Eichorn and Kim Vogan Leonard, one more time!

To my angel, Ron Von, who prefers to remain anonymous, Aunt Patty Peckam, who provided Raymona with the love and care she needed so I could do what I needed to do in bringing Raniere to justice, and a special thank-you to Eric Bell with licks from Raymona and love from both of us.

To Rusty DeCook, Buddy Bob Blake, Scott Foley, Tom Foley-Captain, Susan Ciminelli, Chris Arvay, Tony Natalie, Heather Hill-Natalie, Kimberly Natalie, Linda Pastorelle, Jill

Purpura, Lori Bogan, Patti Giunta Nadiak, Stacey Wren Tesch, Celeste McGovern Kidd, Nick Francesco, Pamela Morgan-Vidal, Tammy L. Fallon, Nate Rider, Angie Cooney Calaci, Elizabeth Davis, Christin Cleere-Martin, Seana Wurth Sartori, Barbara and David Rose, Joanne Bailey, Debbie Renna-Hynes, Georgia Trianrafilou Beebe, Jim Wood, Joan E. Lincoln—*Panache*, Alain Benhamou, William Dovidio, Princess Elizabeth Karageorgevic, Elizabeth Matthews Richardson, Andrew Dallow, Mike Green, Mike Denero, Dano Mastrodonato, Tim Rice, Joey Brucato, Jimmy Paulino, David Lopresti, Sherrod Hamlin-smeenk, Mary Jo Leonardo Vella, Neil Jacobs, Colleen Vogan, Don Vogan—"ping," Bob Broomfield, George Weiss, James Piccarreto, Istvan Olah (aka Delicious), Tina (Tita) Prande, Michele Sica, Karen Holgersen, Mary Ann, Shannon Lamendola, and my sisters at Burn Boot Camp, Pittsford, New York, and to my cirque family at ROC City Circus, who help me believe I can fly!

To Stanley Zareff: God sent me such a gift when he put you in my life; you kept me safe and laughing even through the tears, making my darkest moments bright with your gracious heart.

To Catherine Oxenberg, my bookend—I thought I was waiting for a White Knight when I was actually waiting for a princess riding in on a dragon. Thank you for your determination.

To my best friend in the whole world, Kim Vogan Leonard, "The General," who almost died in the making of this book—Raymona and I would be so lost without you. Your genuine love and support mean more to me than I can ever express in words. And to Raymona, my wonder dog and constant companion, our love is unconditional.

To my late father, Al, thank you for being my dad—love is what bonds us, not blood.

To my beautiful, brilliant son, Michael DeCook. You taught me what being resilient really means. You truly are my heart and my soul.

It took a village of love and support to keep me alive and strong enough to keep fighting for the truth over the last twenty years, and I have lived by this quote, given to me in 2001 by a friend:

The world is a dangerous place, not because of those who do evil... But because of those who look on and do nothing.

I will be forever grateful to all of you.

# RESOURCES

This book deals with serious and often distressing incidents. If you feel at any time you need support in relation to similar situations, here are some suggestions for resources and confidential support.

## BOOKS

*Cults Inside Out: How People Get In and Can Get Out*
    Rick Alan Ross
*Cults in Our Midst: The Hidden Menace in Our Everyday Lives*
    Margaret Thaler Singer and Janja Lalich
*CAPTIVE: A Mother's Crusade to Save Her Daughter from a Terrifying Cult*
    Catherine Oxenberg
*Take Back Your Life*
    Janja Lalich and Madeleine Tobias
*Freedom of Mind*
    Steven Hassan
*Recovery from Cults: Help for Victims of Psychological and Spiritual Abuse*
    Michael D. Langone
*Traumatic Narcissism: Relational Systems of Subjugation*
    Daniel Shaw, LCSW
*Shoes of a Servant: My Unconditional Devotion to a Lie*
    Diane Benscoter
*Coercive Control: How Men Entrap Women in Personal Life*
    Evan Stark

## OTHER RESOURCES

TheFallofNXIVM.com

## ONLINE SUPPORT

Cult Education Institute: https://www.culteducation.com
International Cultic Studies Association (ICSA): http://www.icsahome.com/elibrary/faqs
Open Minds Foundation: https://www.openmindsfoundation.org
Cult Experts: http://www.cultexperts.org
Families Against Cult Teachings: https://familiesagainstcultteachings.org
Freedom of Mind: https://freedomofmind.com/resource-links
reFOCUS: http://www.refocus.org
Catherine Oxenberg Foundation 501-c-3 EIN# 82-1511988
   The Catherine Oxenberg Foundation is a human rights organization dedicated to reclaiming female sexuality from the cultural shadow.